YEAR OF DISCOVERY

YEAR OF DISCOVERY

from the editors of

ARCHAEOLOGY
M A G A Z I N E

An Official Publication of the Archaeological Institute of America

HATHERLEIGH PRESS
New York • London

The Year of Discovery
A Hatherleigh Press Book

The articles in this book were previously published in ARCHAEOLOGY MAGAZINE

Published by Hatherleigh Press
An affiliate of W.W. Norton and Company, Inc.
5-22 46th Avenue, Suite 200
Long Island City, NY 11101
Toll Free 1-800-528-2550
Visit our website, www.hatherleighpress.com

Hatherleigh Press books are available for bulk purchase, special promotions and premiums. For more information on reselling and special purchase opportunities, please call us at 1-800-528-2550 and ask for the Special Sales Manager.

Library of Congress Cataloging-in-Publication Data

Year of discovery 2002 / from the editors of Archaeology magazine.

p. cm.

Articles originally published in Archaeology, a publication of the Archaeological Institute of America.

Includes index.

ISBN 1-57826-111-2 (cloth: alk. paper) -- ISBN 1-57826-112-0 (paper: alk. paper)

1. Archaeology. 2. Antiquities. 3. Civilization, Ancient. 4. Excavations (Archaeology)

I. Archaeological Institute of America. II. Archaeology.

Printed in Canada
Interior design and layout by Corin Hirsch

10 9 8 7 6 5 4 3 2 1
Printed on acid-free paper.

ABOUT THE ARCHAEOLOGICAL INSTITUTE OF AMERICA

THE ARCHAEOLOGICAL INSTITUTE OF AMERICA (AIA), publisher of ARCHAEOLOGY Magazine, is North America's oldest and largest organization devoted to the world of archaeology. The Institute is a nonprofit group founded in 1879 and chartered by the United States Congress in 1906. Today, the AIA has nearly 10,000 members belonging to 103 local societies in the United States, Canada, and overseas. The organization is particularly unique because it counts among its members professional archaeologists, students, and many others from all walks of life. This diverse group is united by a shared passion for archaeology and its role in furthering human knowledge.

Contents

Preface. 3
A Bounteous Subject
By Peter A. Young

Part I:
NEWS BRIEFS 2001

January/February 7
March/April 11
May/June 18
July/August 21
September/October 23
November/December 26

Part II:
AFRICA

1. Ancient Ancestors 33
Kenyan fossils complicate the picture of early hominid evolution.

2. Faking African Art 36
A five-year investigation reveals that most West African terra-cotta sculptures are fakes that have fooled specialists, sold for hundreds of thousands of dollars, and ended up in some of the world's most prestigious museums.

Part III:
EGYPT

3. Sacred Sands 47
Exploring the tombs and temples of ancient Abydos.

4. Quest for Weni the Elder . . . 53
An Old Kingdom cemetery yields the tomb of a "True Governor of Upper Egypt."

5. New Life for thc Dead. 56
Atlanta's Emory University unveils a unique collection of Egyptian mummies and decorated coffins.

6. Case of the Dummy Mummy 62
Psst!... Hey buddy, wanna buy a falcon?

7. A Thoroughly Modern Mummy 65
Experimental archaeology—step by gruesome step, the Egyptian way.

Part IV:
ASIA & THE MIDDLE EAST

9. Saga of the Persian Princess. . 77
In a dangerous corner of the world, uneasy neighbors clamor for the gilded remains of a mummified noblewoman. Trouble is, she's a fraud.

10. Biblical Iconoclast. 81
Israel Finkelstein tilts with colleagues over the history of Early Iron Age Palestine.

11. Letter from Israel. 87
A fight over sacred turf: Who controls Jerusalem's holiest shrine?

12. Cultural Terrorism. 93
The world deplores the Taliban's destructive rampage.

13. Afghan Museum Under Siege 96
Attacked and looted by warring factions, Afghanistan's National Museum has now been stripped of 70 percent of its collections.

14. Roots of Tibetan Buddhism .105
A U.S.-Chinese team hopes to clarify early Buddhist history in the high plateau of western Tibet.

Part V:
EUROPE

15. Land of the Golden Fleece . 112
Legendary Colchis lives on in the Republic of Georgia.

16. Celebrating Midas. 124
Contents of a great Phrygian king's tomb reveal a lavish funerary banquet.

17. Bacchic Mysteries 130
Spiritual life in antiquity.

18. When Gluttony Ruled! . . . 134
Bones recovered from a Roman villa attest to an age of culinary hedonism.

19. Savoring the Grape 139
For Romans, wine was the elixir of life, from cradle to grave.

20. Rome 2000 142
The Eternal City celebrates the jubilee in grand imperial fashion.

21. Roman Life on the Danube 147
A legionary town becomes an archaeological park.

22. Gallic Blood Rites 151
Excavations of sanctuaries in northern France support ancient literary accounts of violent Gallic rituals.

23. Scotland's Irish Origins . . . 155
Tracking the migration of Gaelic speakers who crossed the Irish Sea 1,700 years ago and became the Scots.

Part IV:
SOUTH & CENTRAL AMERICA

24. Parlours to Pyramids. 164
Fleeing the "gilded cage of English civilization," artist and adventurer Adela Breton became a skilled copier of Maya murals and reliefs in the early 1900s.

25. On the Healer's Path. 170
A journey through the Maya rain forest.

Part VII:
NORTH AMERICA

26. Flight of the Anasazi 178
Where did they go after abandoning Mesa Verde? A site in southern New Mexico provides intriguing clues.

27. Closing the Ignorance Gap 183
Florida's once neglected history and prehistory now get top billing in K–12 textbooks statewide.

28. Remembering Africa Under the Eaves 186
A forgotten room in a Brooklyn farmhouse bears witness to the spiritual lives of slaves.

29. Birthplace of American Booze 192
Celebrating Washington's own whiskey distillery.

30. Fire Fight at Hembrillo Basin 195
Buffalo Soldiers hold their ground in a nighttime skirmish with the Apache.

31. Ham Hocks on Your Cornflakes. 202
Examining the role of food in African-American identity.

32. Diving on the *Titanic*. 207
An archaeologist explores the famous wreck.

33. Titanic in the Courts 212

About the Authors. 217

Index 221

PREFACE

A BOUNTEOUS SUBJECT

Highlights from ARCHAEOLOGY'S 2001 editorial year.

by PETER A. YOUNG

ARCHAEOLOGY'S STORIES, AS THIS VOLUME WELL attests, take many forms. Some focus on breaking news, the discovery of ancient ruins or the human remains and artifacts of distant civilizations. Others are angled to capture the spirit and vision of a noteworthy professional; the work of an artist inspired by the past; the adventure of digging in remote places; the illicit trade in antiquities; the powerful connections between past and present.

Our 2001 editorial season began by taking readers behind the scenes with master forgers. Our man in Mali, Belgian journalist Michel Brent, reported on his five-year investigation of "export quality" terra-cotta fakes emanating from Dary, a hamlet on the Niger River. The forgeries are so sophisticated, he wrote, that dealers themselves cannot always distinguish authentic from counterfeit. Brent's experience was echoed in Kenneth Lapatin's companion piece on forgers who ran circles around Sir Arthur Evans, famed excavator of Knossos, in the early 1900s. Fooled along with Evans were members of the archaeological establishment and a number of European and American museums. To this day, Lapatin wrote, the fake Minoan art that abounds in textbooks and encyclopedias plays "a crucial role in fashioning modern conceptions of Aegean prehistory."

Gathering story material in a remote part of the world struggling to recover from civil war and prolonged economic chaos can be a difficult experience. No one knows this better than our managing editor, Kristin Romey, who spent a month combing the countryside of the Republic of Georgia for insights on legendary Colchis, the land where Jason and his Argonauts searched for the Golden Fleece. Her adaptability to the political terrain and sensitive eye for the archaeological landscape served her well, as our March/April cover story made clear. "It's no wonder," she wrote, "that Georgia remains an endless source of fascination and admiration for historians and archaeologists. The Greeks were among the first outsiders to experience the allure of this tiny country. In the capital of Tbilisi, I found myself drinking Argo beer with a guy named Irakli (the Georgian form of Hercules) while watching a television channel named after the Colchian king Aeetes. For an archaeologist, life doesn't get much better than that."

Archaeology is about the sum of human experience.

It is hard to imagine enslaved Africans living in a four-foot-high space under the eaves of a lean-to attached to a Brooklyn farmhouse. Yet in the late eighteenth century, when New York was the home of the largest number of slaves of any colonial English settlement except Charleston, South Carolina, what went on at the Lott farm may have been common practice. Archaeology has supported the notion that slavery was a Southern phenomenon, in that it rarely uncovers undisturbed archaeological deposits in Northern urban centers from before the turn of the nineteenth century. Urbanization, reported H. Arthur Bankoff, Christopher Ricciardi, and Alyssa Loorya, "has obliterated evidence of slave life, whereas on large plantations in the rural South, slaves were typically housed in separate quarters whose archaeological remains still exist today." Archaeology is finally giving voice to those Africans huddled in the eaves of the Lott House and others like them across the North.

Many of our editors have crisscrossed the globe in search of important and compelling stories about archaeological discovery. Angela Schuster is one, having sailed aboard a replica Viking warship along the Norwegian coast, rappelled down cliffs in Mali to explore ancient burial caves, and encountered scorpions in Egyptian tombs. For her story on Maya medicine in our May/June issue, Angela journeyed to the rain forest of Belize, where she followed traditional Maya healers into the world's first ethno-biomedical forest reserve in search of natural remedies for all manner of human affliction, from snake bites, to cancer, to AIDS. "Hiking through the rain forest is a magical experience," she wrote, "full of distinct sounds and smells—howler monkeys and trees soaring up through a forest canopy of tangled vines and lush bromeliads. Given our proximity to some of the greatest Maya cities, I could not help wonder if the shamans of antiquity had harvested their potions from the very tract of forest through which we were trekking."

Ancient Egyptians mummified in the hope of joining body and soul in the afterlife would have been horrified at the treatment of their remains by dealers, collectors, and museums and even by fellow Egyptians who, according to Mark Twain's apocryphal tale in *Innocents Abroad*, fueled steam engines with mummies purchased by the lot. Neglected mummies from curiosity shops and sideshows are now entering museum laboratories. A case in point was our September/October cover story about a collection of mummies recently acquired by Atlanta's Michael C. Carlos Museum. Scholars there have identified a temple chantress, a lady-in-waiting to Nubian princesses, and the unwrapped body of a male that could turn out to be Ramesses I, the founder of the 19th Dynasty. All were unstudied showpieces in a now-defunct Canadian museum. It is a measure of the care that scientists now lavish on such remains that so much is being learned from them. A tooth can tell you about diet, a piece of stomach tissue can reveal what parasites plagued the ancient Egyptians. "Mummies are little encyclopedias," says Egyptologist Bob Brier, "You just have to know how to read them."

We closed out the year with a report on man's inhumanity to man. Until late August, our offices had been in Lower Manhattan in the shadow of the World Trade Center. For 15 years we had produced this magazine a mere three blocks from the large and luminous Twin Towers. We brainstormed with writers and lunched with advertising clients at the 107th floor Windows on the World, and treated our children to sky-high views of New York Harbor and the Statue of Liberty. We shopped in the center's bookstores, snacked in its subterranean fast food outlets, and commuted to and from home through stations many levels below ground. In the aftermath of that fateful day in September, archaeologists volunteered to comb rubble from the Trade Center for physical and material remains, evidence of America's staggering loss. This was archaeology at its best, in the service of a greater understanding of a tragic event.

Archaeology is about the sum of human experience. In his 1946 annual report, Sterling Dow, president of the Archaeological Institute of America, our parent organization, wrote:

"Archaeology is a bounteous, indeed an inexhaustible, subject...there is an abundance for everyone-providing it is attractively packaged, agreeable to peruse, and valid."

We honor that mandate.

PETER A. YOUNG *is the Editor-in-Chief of Archaeology.*

PART I:

NEWS BRIEFS

January/February

"God's Hands" Did the Devil's Work

KAMITAKAMORI—Prominent Japanese archaeologist Shinichi Fujimura has been caught red-handed burying artifacts at a site, prompting demands for a review of the nation's Palaeolithic record. Nicknamed "God's Hands" by colleagues who marveled at his luck in locating ancient sites, Fujimura was senior director at the Tohoku Paleolithic Institute. His discovery of stoneware dated to the early Palaeolithic period (600,000–120,000 years ago) at the Kamitakamori ruins in Miyagi Prefecture in 1994 established the site as Japan's oldest. Fujimura's team recently made headlines again following discovery of postholes that provided evidence for early Palaeolithic dwellings at Kamitakamori.

Fujimura's hoax, occurring less than a month after his team's headline-making posthole discovery, was exposed by Japan's *Mainichi Shimbun* newspaper, which published three photographs on its front page of him deliberately burying 61 artifacts on the Kamitakamori site. The artifacts were taken by Fujimura from earlier excavations. He has also confessed to deliberately burying artifacts at the Palaeolithic site of Soshinfudozaka, but insists his other discoveries were authentic. "I did something that I shouldn't have done," Fujimura said at an emotional press conference. "I had wanted to find more ruins that include stone artifacts."

Fujimura first won acclaim with his discovery of 40,000-year-old stoneware in 1981. The self-taught archaeologist has investigated more than 150 archaeological sites in Japan, including most of the country's Palaeolithic sites. In light of his confession, Fujimura's involvement in several important discoveries at these sites has brought many fundamental ideas about Japan's Palaeolithic—and the content of many textbooks—into question. The Japanese Archaeological Association is debating whether to reinvestigate sites he excavated. The Tokyo National Museum has removed more than 20 artifacts discovered by Fujimura from display; other museums are following suit.

Many archaeologists privately questioned Fujimura's discoveries, but he was rarely publicly challenged. Chairman of the Japanese Archaeological Association Ken Amaksu conceded that Japan's academic environment may have played a role in the ongoing ruse. "We need to examine... whether enough information was disclosed and enough theories were exchanged among researchers with differing opinions concerning the new discoveries."

Fujimura has been expelled from both the Tohoku Institute and the Japanese Archaeological Association. The incident has also irreparably damaged the reputation of the Tohoku Institute. "There's nothing more you can say," said its former chairman Toshiaki Kamata, who resigned in the aftermath of the scandal. "With this media coverage, all our work over the years is as good as ruined."

—Kristin M. Romey

Mimbres Court Evidence

NEW MEXICO—Three men have been arrested for digging up potsherds at the East Fork site, a Mimbres settlement in New Mexico's Gila National Forest. The looters, Aaron Sera and brothers James and Michael Quarrell, were convicted and may face up to two years' imprisonment and fines of $20,000 or more; sentences are pending.

Officers of the Forest Service Law Enforcement Agency had earlier found evidence of digging and had placed a seismic sensor in the area to monitor human

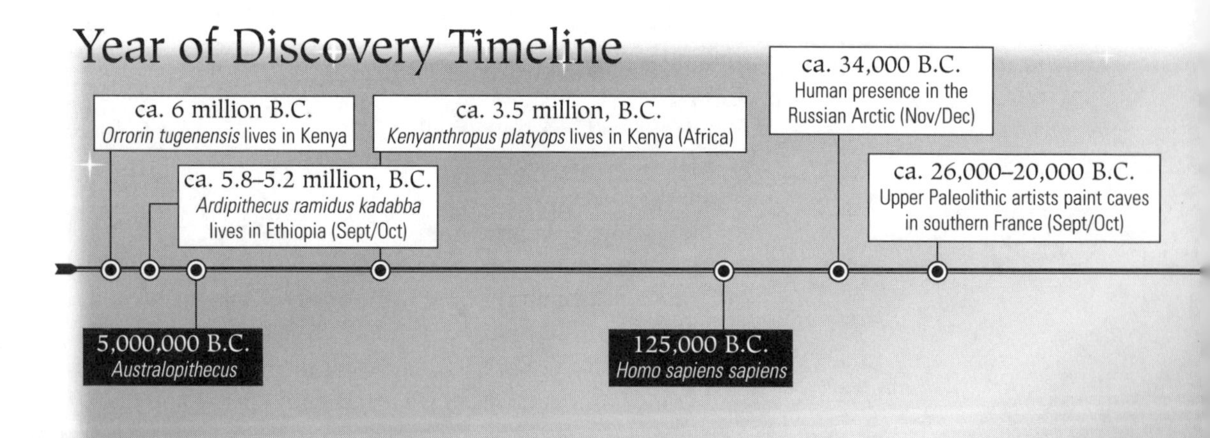

activity. One month later, the sensor was activated and officers caught the men looting the site. Upon questioning, Michael Quarrell admitted their intention to sell the pottery they found.

The Mimbres, who lived in southwestern New Mexico and a small section of northern Mexico from A.D. 900 to 1200, produced pottery famous for its black-and-white geometric patterns and depictions of animals and humans. The vessels, often associated with burials, were likely placed on the head of the deceased, whose soul escaped through a hole punched in the bottom.

The 1979 Archaeological Resources Protection Act prohibits excavation without a permit and removal or damaging of archaeological materials and human remains located on public land. The act also prohibits the trafficking of artifacts wrongfully removed from sites.

—CAROLYN SWAN

Slaves' Graves?

GEORGIA—In the scenic former mill town of Newnan, Georgia, plans to lay walking trails on a forgotten piece of city-owned land were halted when Newnan native Bobby Olmstead informed officials of a legend that the site was an old cemetery. "It's been called a slave cemetery since I was a boy," notes Newnan's landscape architect, Mike Furbish. A solitary child's headstone marked "1869" survives above ground.

A 1928 copy of a missing 1828 map designates the spot "negro graveyard." Contract archaeologist Steve Webb was called in, and probe analysis revealed 243 burials oriented roughly east to west, traditional of Christian burial, and grouped in clusters, perhaps reflecting family ties. Ellen Ehrenhard, director of the local historical society, speculates that the burial ground was long out of use by 1895, when it became pasture land.

Was it really a slave cemetery? "We haven't gotten far enough, in my mind, to say," notes Webb. The map is not an ideal source, being redrawn from a lost one made 100 years earlier. Oral history may prove to be the best source, and interviews with elders in the African-American community are planned. "What's so puzzling is that no one has come forward, but they will," says Ehrenhard.

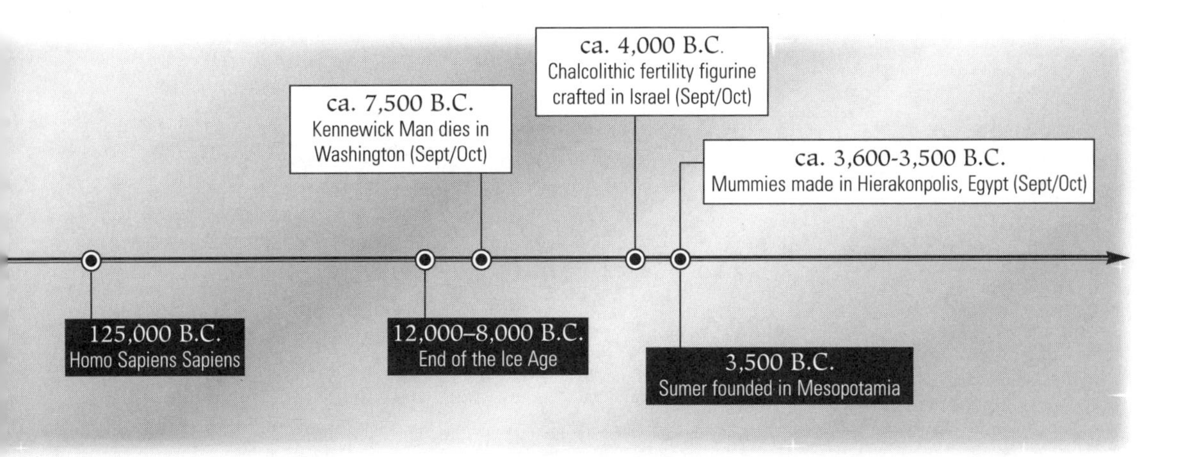

"People don't talk about slavery in this community; it's still a sore spot."

—ELIZABETH J. HIMELFARB

Γινεσθωι! Sayeth Cleopatra

BERLIN—A single Greek word, γινεσθωι (*ginesthoi*), or "make it so," written at the bottom of a Ptolemaic papyrus may have been written by the Egyptian queen Cleopatra VII herself, says Dutch papyrologist Peter van Minnen of the University of Groningen. Received in Alexandria on Mecheir 26 (February 23, 33 B.C.), the papyrus text, recycled for use in the construction of a cartonnage mummy case found by a German expedition at Abusir in 1904, appears to be a royal ordinance granting tax exemption to one Publius Canidius, an associate of Mark Antony's who would command his land army during the Battle of Actium in 31 B.C. The text reads as follows:

We have granted to Publius Canidius and his heirs the annual exportation of 10,000 artabas [300 tons] *of wheat and the annual importation of 5,000 Coan amphoras* [ca. 34,500 gallons] *of wine without anyone exacting anything in taxes from him or any other expense whatsoever. We have also granted tax exemption on all the land he owns in Egypt on the understanding that he shall not pay any taxes, either to the state account or to the account of me and my children, in any way in perpetuity. We have also granted that all his tenants are exempt from personal liabilities and from taxes without anyone exacting anything from them, not even contributing to the occasional assessments in the nomes or paying for expenses for soldiers or officers. We have also granted that the animals used for plowing and sowing as well as the beasts of burden and the ships used for the transportation [down the Nile] of the wheat are likewise exempt from 'personal' liabilities and from taxes and cannot be commandeered [by the army]. Let it be written to those to whom it may concern, so that knowing it they can act accordingly.*

Make it so!

"Written in an upright hand by a court scribe, the document was meant to be an internal note from Cleopatra to a high official charged with notifying other high officials in Alexandria," says van Minnen. "The personal nature of the communication is evident in the lack of any formal introduction of Cleopatra herself (she is not even

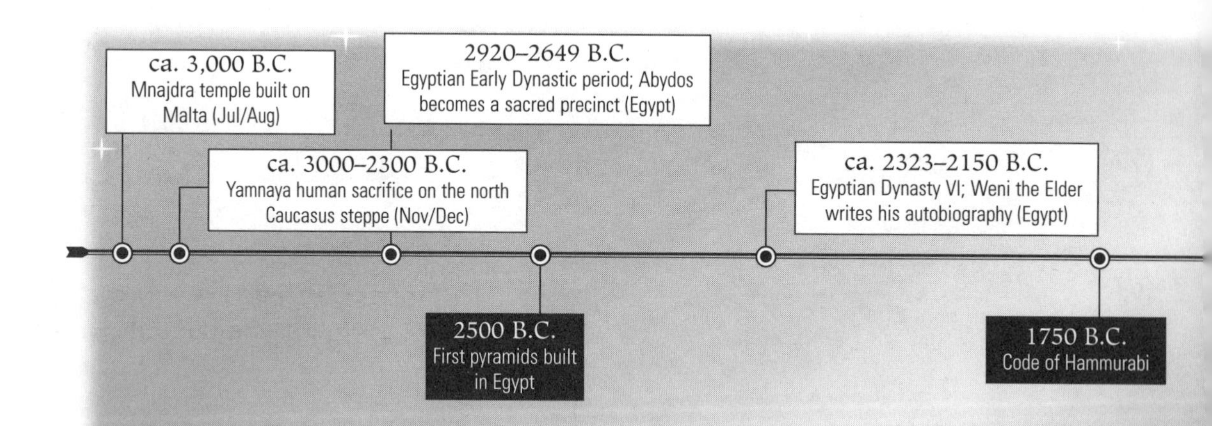

mentioned by name) and the absence of a title after the name of the official to whom it was addressed (the name cannot be read)." The manuscript is not one of the copies received by the other officials, as there is no forwarding note attached to it and because it was executed in multiple hands. The text of the ordinance was written first, Cleopatra's written approval second, and the date of the document's receipt in Alexandria third. As for the "make it so" subscription, there are only two parallels from antiquity, says van Minnen, citing one of Ptolemy X Alexander I, who signed a document "take care" in Greek in 99 B.C. and another such closing penned in Latin by the fifth-century Roman emperor Theodosius II in a petition to Appion, the bishop of Syene.

According to Lorelei Corcoran of the University of Memphis, such documents would have been both written and signed by a court scribe; however, given the nature of this particular papyrus, Cleopatra herself would have been the only one who would have had the authority to approve such edicts. The document, known as Berlin P 25 239, is on display at the Ägyptisches Museum und Papyrussammlung in Berlin.

—ANGELA M. H. SCHUSTER

March/April

Legacy of War

FLANDERS—A considerable number of towns in northwestern Belgium may be sitting atop a "time bomb," according to scientists who believe World War I tunnels may be responsible for the structural failure of buildings in Nieuwpoort, Flanders, that led to the evacuation of some families.

According to University of Greenwich geoscientist Peter Doyle, who has been researching the problem along with geological engineers from Nottingham Trent University and members of the Association for Battlefield Archaeology (ABA) in Flanders, systems of tunnels built by the Allies in 1917 to protect their troops from shelling and poison gas threaten large areas within the town and surrounding areas with collapse. Tunnels and chambers were hollowed out of the coastal sand 12 to 35 feet beneath the

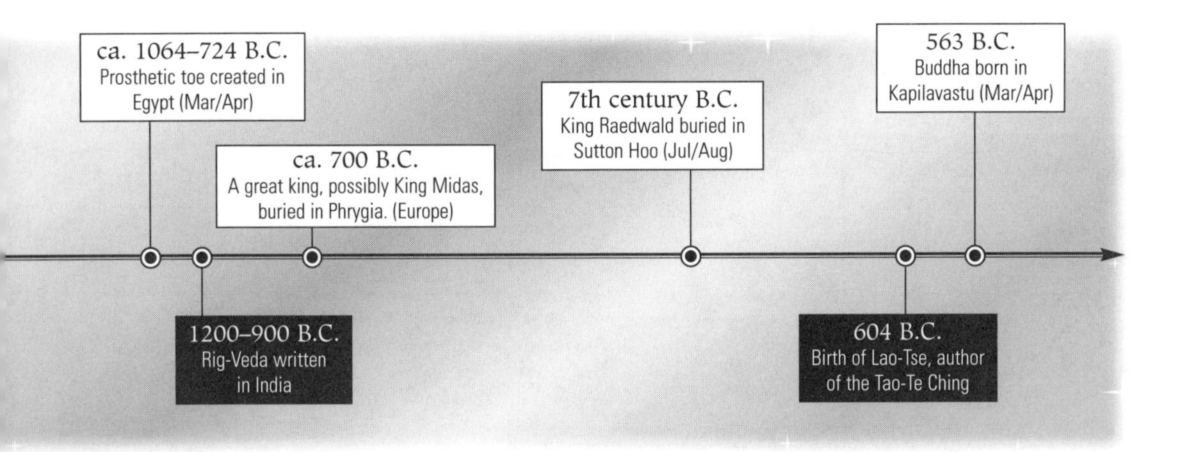

town and were accessed by hundreds of staircases and thousands of shafts. Some of the chambers housed staff offices while others were large enough to shelter more than 1,000 men.

The tunnels were buried under up to ten feet of rubble when Nieuwpoort was leveled and rebuilt after the war. They were not filled in because nobody was aware of them at the time, according to the ABA's Peter Barton.

Timbers that shored up the walls of the system have been decaying and are now beginning to give way, leading to the collapse of buildings built above them. A more complete survey with ground-penetrating radar will determine the full extent of the problem. One remedy, albeit extremely expensive, may be to fill in the tunnels.

The researchers believe that the problem affects towns along much of the former Western Front. Mike Rosenbaum of the Geohazards Research Group at Nottingham Trent University is less than optimistic. "It may be that we are seeing the start of a major problem: the tip of an iceberg."

—KRISTIN M. ROMEY

Taíno Cave Art Under Siege

SAN CRISTOBAL—Blasts from limestone mining operations near the Pomier Caves in San Cristobal, Dominican Republic, continue to threaten 2,000-year-old rock art painted by the Taíno, Carib, and Igneri peoples. Discovered in 1851 by Sir Robert Schonburgk, then British consul to the Dominican Republic, the 54 caves contain some 6,000 images of birds, fish, reptiles, and humans. The largest of the caves contains some 590 drawings, considered by scholars to be among the finest Precolumbian rupestral works in the Caribbean.

Mining to obtain limestone for the manufacturing of concrete and antacids is not new to the area, nor is its damaging effect on the rock art. The nearby Borbón Caves Anthropological Reserve was extended in 1996 to include and thereby protect 12 of the Pomier Caves from limestone quarrying. The rest lie outside the protected zone; five of these have suffered severe damage.

—ANGELA M. H. SCHUSTER

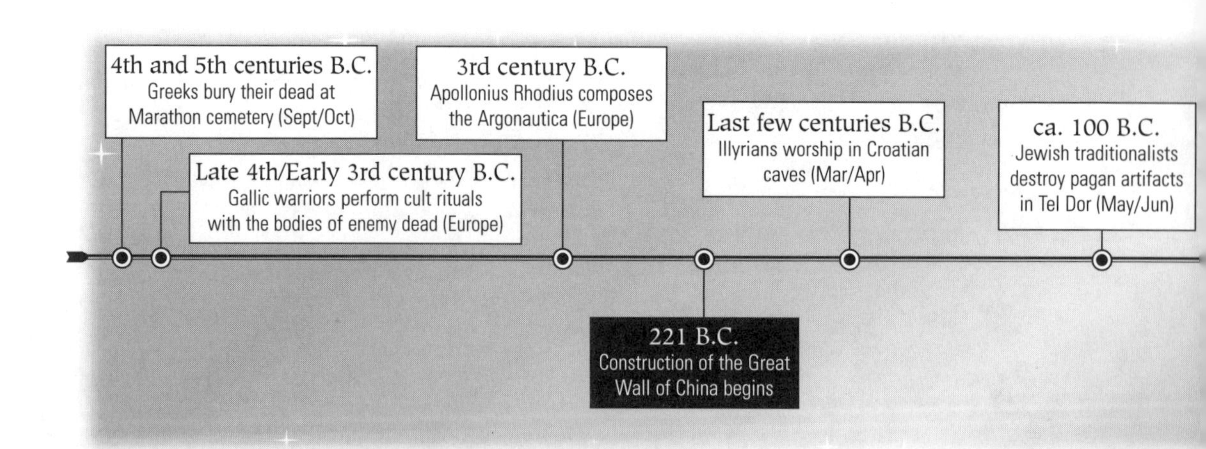

Egyptian Toe Job

MUNICH—While evidence of surgery and amputation has been found in ancient Egyptian human remains, medical researchers from the Ludwig-Maximilians University in Munich have discovered what they believe to be the first known case of a prosthesis made for use during a person's lifetime. Discovered on a mummy found in the New Kingdom necropolis at Thebes, the prosthesis, a big toe, had been fashioned out of three pieces of wood for a woman thought to have lived during Dynasty XXI or XXIII (1064–724 B.C.). She was 50 to 55 years old at the time of her death.

Examination of her right foot revealed that the amputated big toe had healed over; in its place was a delicately carved wooden prosthesis complete with a toenail. The wooden toe had been attached to the woman's forefoot with a fine linen lace. It is clear from wear on the bottom of the prosthesis, says Andreas G. Nerlich, leader of the research team, that the wooden toe was worn during the woman's lifetime rather than added by embalmers during preparation of the body for burial, a common practice in the New Kingdom. A mummy in England's Manchester Museum had been given wooden legs before being wrapped in linen to appear whole in the afterlife.

—ANGELA M. H. SCHUSTER

Bad, Bad Boudicca

COLCHESTER—The brutal tactics of Queen Boudicca, who led her Iceni tribesmen in a revolt against Britain's Roman rulers in A.D. 60/61, are being revealed by salvage excavations on the future site of a multiplex cinema in Colchester, England. The destruction of Colchester, ancient Camulodunum, the de facto capital of Roman Britain, by Boudicca's forces was methodical and thorough. Excavation director Philip Crummy notes that the Romans' clay-and-timber buildings were burnt to the ground. "It would have been quite hard work, because the buildings were largely of clay and not easy to set alight," he said. The destruction layer is characterized by the red-and-black remains of burnt clay walls.

Queen Boudicca launched the revolt after

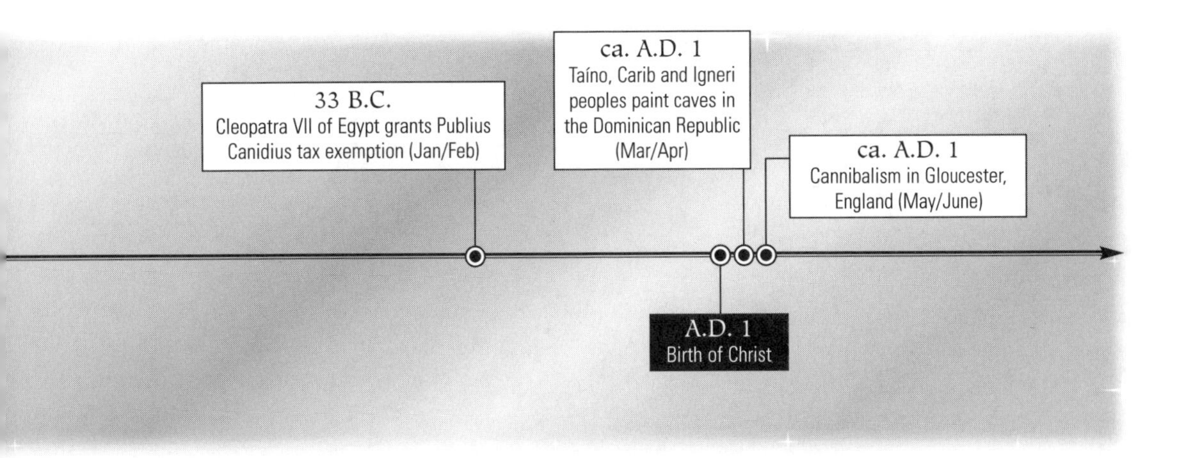

Roman troops annexed Iceni territory following the death of her husband. Roman historians say over 70,000 people died in the revolt. Following the destruction of Camulodunum, Boudicca went on to level Verulamium (modern St. Albans) and Londinium (London), where the queen is said to have poisoned herself rather than fall into Roman hands.

—KRISTIN M. ROMEY

Last Minute Monuments

WASHINGTON D.C.,—Will President Clinton's eleventh-hour use of the 1906 American Antiquities Act lead to a backlash against this venerable legislation? The act, prompted by destruction of archaeological sites in the Southwest, authorizes the president "to declare by public proclamation historic landmarks, historic and prehistoric structures...situated upon lands owned or controlled by the Government of the United States to be national monuments...." Theodore Roosevelt used it to create 18 National Monuments, including Chaco Canyon and Gila Cliff Dwellings. Since then, presidents have invoked it to protect sites from Aztec Ruin, to Mound City, to Russell Cave.

As of November 9, 2000, Clinton had created 11 new monuments, including several of archaeological importance: Agua Fria, Canyons of the Ancients, Grand Canyon-Parashant, Grand Staircase-Escalante, and Vermillion Cliffs. On January 17, just days before leaving office, he created seven more, including Pompey's Pillar and the Upper Missouri River Breaks, which preserve important Lewis and Clark expedition landscapes.

Reacting to the latest National Monument designations, a Bush-Cheney transition team spokesman said, "We are reviewing all eleventh-hour executive orders, rules, and regulations by the Clinton administration...." Monument designations can only be modified or rejected by act of Congress, something that may be difficult to do given the close split between Republicans and Democrats. Insight on the new administration's intentions may be gleaned from testimony by Gale Norton, Bush's nominee for Secretary of the Interior. Asked by Senator Jeff Bingaman, D-New Mexico, if she would

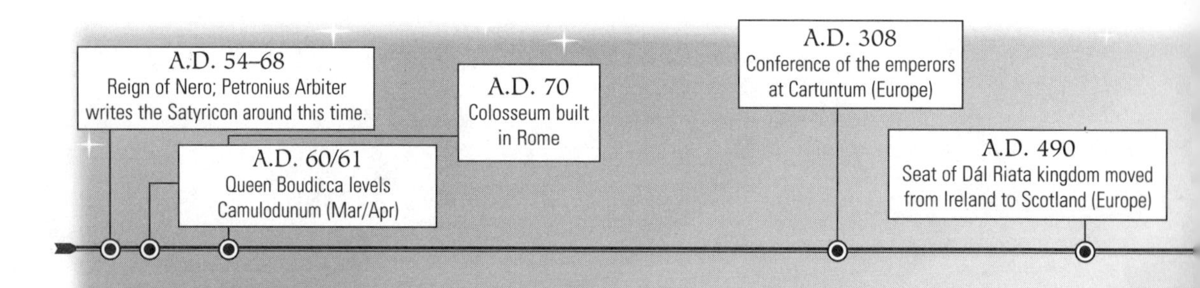

advocate change or repeal of the Antiquities Act, she said, "I would like to see a process of involvement of the people most affected by decisions. ... Whether that would require changes in that statute for the long term is a decision that I have not made...."

Concern that overuse might lead to calls for revision or repeal of the Antiquities Act may have been behind the president's January 10 decision not to use it to further protect the Arctic National Wildlife Refuge in Alaska, despite an appeal from former president Jimmy Carter. Another last-minute request, from New York senators Charles Schumer and Hillary Rodham Clinton, asked the president to use the act to protect two historic forts on Governor's Island in New York Harbor. On his last day in office, President Clinton proclaimed 20 acres on the island, including the forts, to be a National Monument.

—Mark Rose

Shakespeare Slept Here

SUSSEX—Bad news for the picturesque tourist attraction believed for the past two centuries to be Shakespeare's mum's childhood home. Tree-ring dating and an ancient lease found in a Sussex archive prove that a modest brick-clad farm near Stratford-upon-Avon—not the half-timbered vision of Olde England bought by the Shakespeare Birthplace Trust in 1930—was home to Mary Arden.

Arden's real home, which she inhabited until 1557, when she married John Shakespeare and moved to Stratford, turns out to have been the next farm over from the touristic hot-spot. A 1587 rental agreement identifies Glebe Farm as the home of Agnes Arden, Mary's stepmother. The discovery was made by Nat Alcock, a Warwickshire buildings historian.

Glebe Farm itself, although refaced with Victorian red brick, has proved to be an almost intact late medieval farmhouse. Tree-ring dating shows it was built in the summer of 1514 or shortly thereafter and consisted of a hall, buttery, and living chamber; a stone-walled kitchen wing was added a few years later. Although it was modernized around 1650, there was very little alteration until Victorian times.

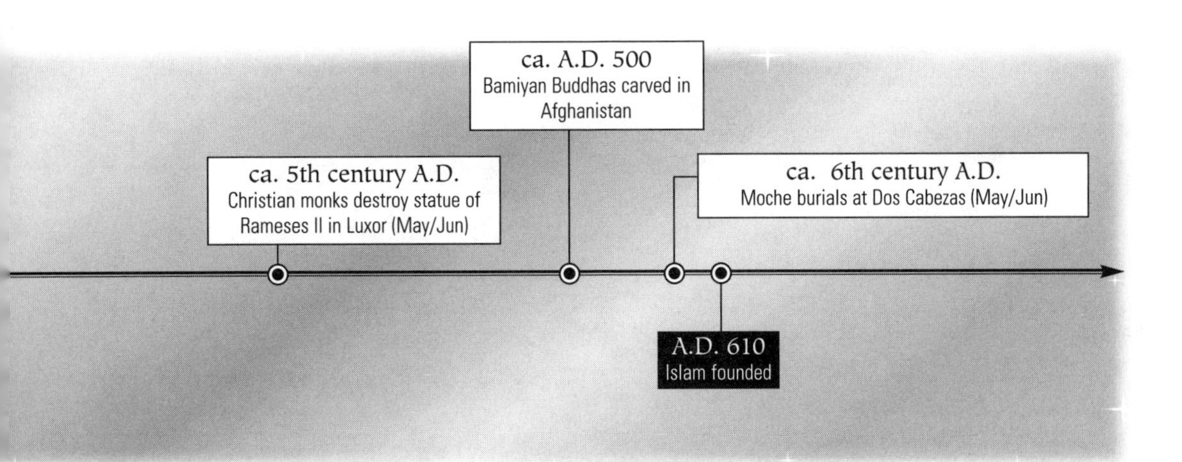

"Shakespeare would probably have played there as a child when visiting his maternal relatives," says Jean Wilson, author of *The Archaeology of Shakespeare.* "He would almost certainly have known the house."

Alcock's parallel study of what until now has been called Mary Arden's House shows that it was built far too late to have been her childhood home. The earliest part of the house is a parlor wing of around 1569, when Shakespeare himself was already a child.

—NORMAN HAMMOND

Corinth Loot Returned

CORINTH—The FBI has handed over to Greek officials nearly 300 artifacts stolen from the Archaeology Museum in Corinth in April 1990 (see ARCHAEOLOGY, July/August 1990, p. 22). Valued at over $2 million, the objects were recovered in 1999 when the FBI, acting on a tip that the artifacts had been consigned to Christie's for auction, found them hidden in crates of fresh fish in Miami (see ARCHAEOLOGY, November/December 1999, p. 16). Two men are now on trial in Greece for the theft. Two others, thought to be in Venezuela, are being tried in absentia.

—MARK ROSE

Competing Claims on Buddha's Hometown

TILAURAKOT—Excavations at Tilaurakot in southern Nepal have reopened a long-standing debate about the true hometown of the Buddha. Nepali and British archaeologists have uncovered evidence the site was occupied during the Buddha's lifetime, sometime between the seventh and fifth centuries B.C.

Tilaurakot was first identified as the possible site of Kapilavastu, the Buddha's childhood home, at the end of the nineteenth century when archaeologists attempted to link Buddhist remains and topographical features with the descriptions of Chinese pilgrims.

In 1962, however, new excavations at Tilaurakot concluded that the town could not be ancient Kapilavastu, as the earliest settlement began centuries after the Buddha's

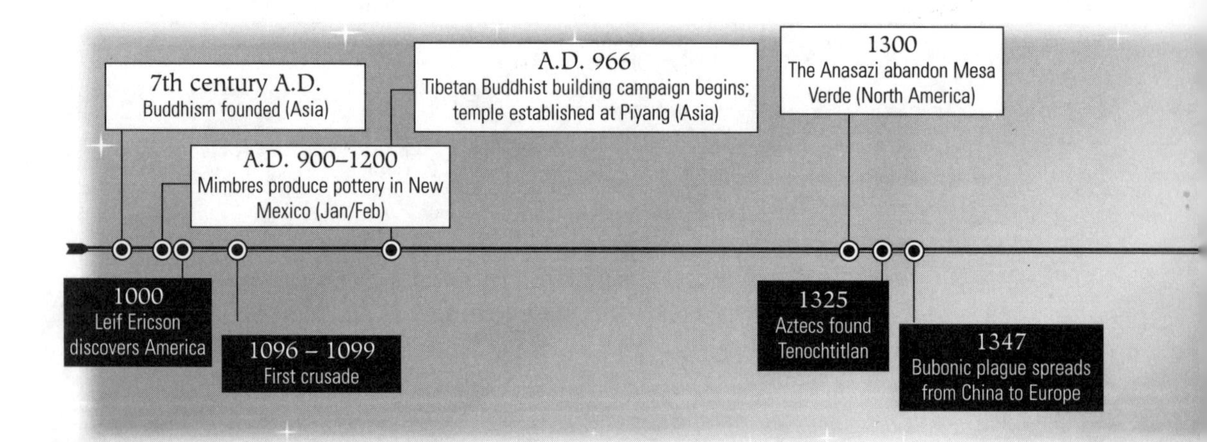

death. Indian archaeologists subsequently identified the Indian town of Piprahwa, ten miles south of the Indo-Nepali border, where the earliest remains date to the third-century B.C., as the Buddha's hometown.

Now the focus has turned back to the Nepali site. The latest excavations at Tilaurakot have uncovered artifacts dated to the Iron Age of the Ganges Plain, between the beginning of the early first millennium B.C. and the sixth or seventh century B.C. According to excavation co-director Robin Coningham, "there is little reason to continue to doubt the original nineteenth-century identification of the site of Tilaurakot as the childhood home of the Buddha, ancient Kapilavastu."

—Chris Hellier

Phallic Cult

CROATIA—Hundreds of fine ceramic vessels used in Illyrian drinking, feasting, and fertility rites—possibly of an orgiastic nature—have been discovered along with a phallus-shaped stalagmite in a cave near the abandoned village of Nakovana, on the southern tip of Dalmatia, the region of Croatia bordering the Adriatic Sea. Archaeologists hope the finds will clarify previously hazy theories about the religious beliefs of the Illyrians, warriors and neighbors of the Greeks, who lived in the area during the last few centuries B.C.

For ten years, the Royal Ontario Museum's Tim Kaiser and Staso Forenbaher of the Institute of Anthropology in Zagreb have directed a team studying the region's Illyrian and earlier occupants. In 1999, they discovered a central, phallus-shaped stalagmite in the second of the cave's three connected chambers. Surrounding the stalagmite was a large number of artifacts, including shards of high-quality Hellenistic Greek and Illyrian pottery. Among these were broken votive offerings, with dedications to Dionysos and Aphrodite scratched in Greek on some of them. Returning last summer, they noticed the absence of a corresponding stalactite, which led them to conclude that the Illyrians had deliberately moved the stalagmite to the chamber's center, where it could be illuminated by sunlight. The Illyrians additionally reshaped it into a more perfect phallic form.

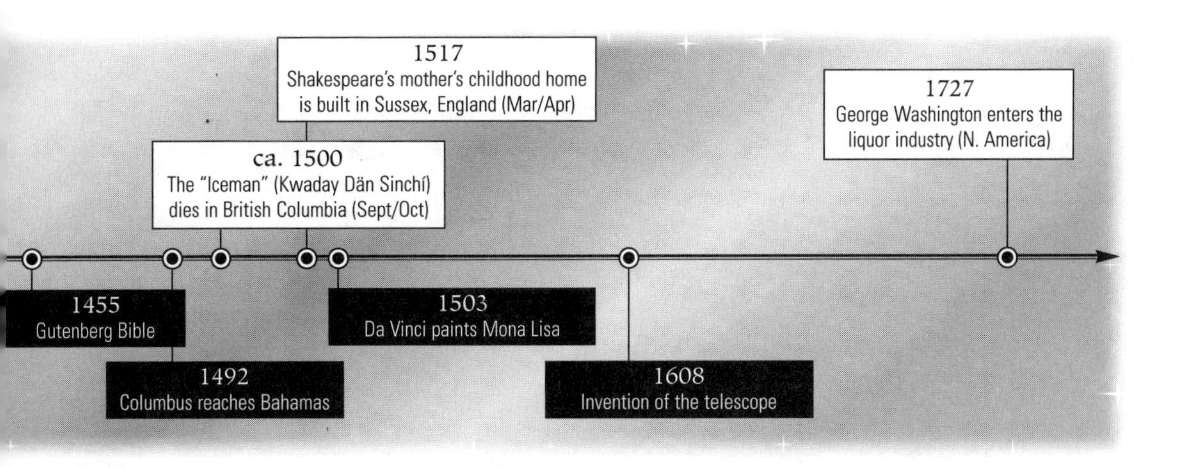

"The archaeological evidence strongly points to some mysterious, previously unknown cult activity, which may have been practiced in secrecy by the Illyrians," says Kaiser. "These cups and amphorae were among the finest of the day and their use in the cave underscores the gravity of the rituals enacted there."

The Illyrians are somewhat of a mystery to modern scholars, as only a handful of their settlement and burial sites have been excavated. Although described in Greek sources as warriors and pirates, the Illyrians had a soft spot for anything Greek, trading with or raiding colonists to accumulate pottery and other goods.

Nakovana Cave is now a nationally protected cultural monument. Kaiser's team will continue its excavations this summer.

—CAROLYN SWAN

May/June

Intolerance in Antiquity

LUXOR/TEL DOR—In the wake of the Taliban's destruction of pre-Islamic statues in Afghanistan, we are reminded that iconoclasm is not a new phenomenon. Archaeologists are currently debating whether to restore a 3,200-year-old colossal statue of Rameses II that lies in pieces within his temple at Luxor. It has been assumed that the 50-foot high statue collapsed in an earthquake around 27 B.C., but there is now evidence that it was deliberately cut up and pulled down by Christian monks in the fifth century A.D. "The face was attacked, as early Christians often did, and traces of hammering can be found all over the place, clearly showing that the destruction was willed," says Christian Leblanc of France's National Center for Scientific Research.

According to Leblanc, the issue of whether to return the pharaoh to his pedestal is unclear because "the statue's presence on the ground constitutes an historic event, and bears witness to the destructiveness of Christians."

Meanwhile, remains of a Greek temple excavated by a University of California, Berkeley, team at Tel Dor in Israel may be the first evidence of a crusade to destroy symbols

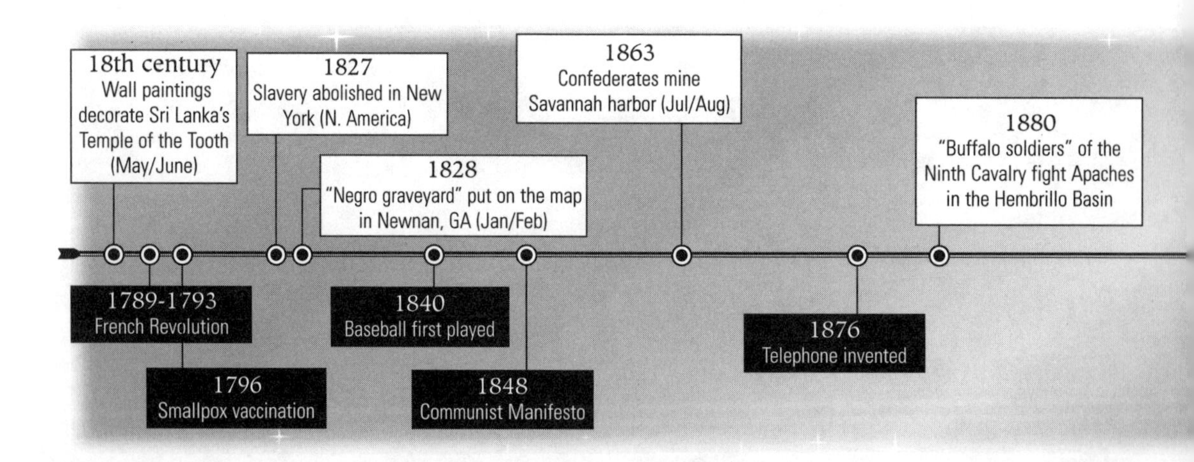

of paganism during a revival of Jewish traditionalism around 100 B.C. Temple columns, a headless statue of a winged Victory, and fragments of the temple's superstructure and mosaic floor were excavated from pits where they had been discarded in antiquity to create the foundation for another building. "This was part of a crusade by the Hasmonean dynasty to wipe out all pagan symbols," says archaeologist Andrew Stewart. The temple, dating to the second century B.C., is also the earliest yet discovered in Israel, and pushes back evidence of a considerable Greek presence in Palestine and surrounding territories by 200 years.

—KRISTIN M. ROMEY

Moche Madness

JEQUETEPEQUE VALLEY—Just when you thought you had seen it all from the Moche—gold and silver backflaps and necklaces strung with five-pound peanuts, ornate inlaid earspools, deadly war clubs, and magnificent pottery—still more material has come to light. The latest finds from the Peruvian culture, which flourished on the North Coast between A.D. 100 and 800, are from a series of elite burials found within an eroded mud-brick pyramid at Dos Cabezas (Two Heads), a 1,500-year-old site in the lower Jequetepeque Valley. Excavated by UCLA's Christopher Donnan and Alana Cordury Collins, the site has yielded the remains of eight individuals—three tall men, a teenage boy, a child, and three murdered female attendants—as well as sacrificed llamas. "What sets Dos Cabezas apart from all of the known Moche burial sites," says Donnan, "is the inclusion of miniature tombs, small chambers filled with offerings surrounding tiny figurines wrapped in textiles. The figurines were prepared for the afterlife in the same manner as the Moche lords." Donnan also believes that he has found evidence of a base-ten numbering system in the form of jars, bricks, and heads arranged in sets of five, ten, and 20. The Moche had no system of writing as we know it. Some 350 Moche burials have been excavated in recent years, the most famous being those discovered at Sipán in the late 1980s and 1990s (see ARCHAEOLOGY, November/December 1992, pp. 30–45).

—ANGELA M. H. SCHUSTER

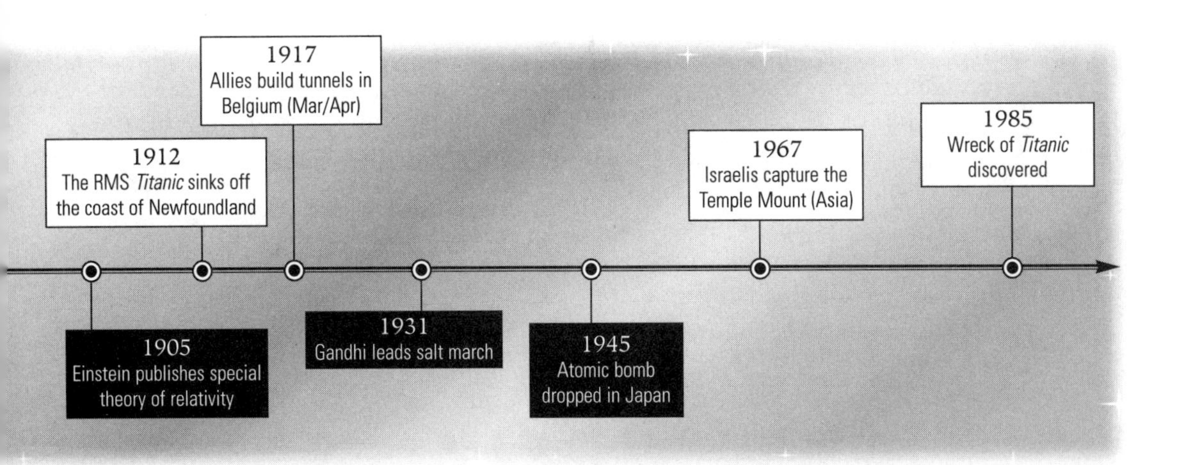

Brits Sign On

UNITED KINGDOM—The U.K.'s arts minister Alan Howarth announced March 14 that Britain will sign the 1970 UNESCO cultural property convention, which gives members the right to recover stolen or illicitly exported antiquities that surface in other signatory countries. "The importance of this for the protection of the world's cultural heritage and preservation of archaeological sites goes far beyond the fact that the U.K. is just one country among the 90-some who have already signed the treaty," says ARCHAEOLOGY's contributing editor Ellen Herscher. "Because England has long been a center for the trade in antiquities, British ratification—in concert with that of France and, expected soon, Switzerland—greatly strengthens the international controls among market countries."

—MARK ROSE

Ivan's Lament

MOSCOW—Moscow scientists can now confirm a rumor that has floated through the halls of the Kremlin for over 400 years: Anastasia Romanova, the beloved first wife of Czar Ivan IV who died suddenly at the age of 25, was poisoned.

Chemical analysis of the czarina's well-preserved braid, recovered from her sarcophagus in the cemetery of the Kremlin's Archangel Cathedral, contained unusually high amounts of mercury. In cases of acute mercury poisoning, contaminated sweat soaks the victim's hair, where the metal can remain for a long time.

Analysis of the remains of other ladies of the medieval court buried nearby revealed that many were exposed to lead, arsenic, mercury, and barium—present in makeup and medicines of the time—that may have caused an early death, but were not in themselves fatal.

The behavior of the devastated czar following the death of Romanova in 1560, allegedly at the hand of a rival of Ivan, earned him the moniker "Ivan the Terrible."

—KRISTIN M. ROMEY

Art Attack

SRI LANKA—A suicide truck bomb was a "blessing in disguise" for Sri Lanka's holiest Buddhist shrine, the sixteenth-century Temple of the Tooth. While the 1998 bombing by separatist Tamil Tigers blew the roof off the shrine, which houses a tooth belonging to the Buddha, it also took away layers of plaster that covered previously unknown eighteenth-century wall paintings depicting a ceremonial pageant.

Although the porous walls of the temple absorbed the shock of the explosion, which killed 16 people, restoration work on the UNESCO World Heritage site took nearly three years and $1.5 million to complete. "We have now completed 99 percent of the restoration work," said Neranjan Wijeyeratne, chief lay custodian of the temple. "Today, we have a living miracle."

—KRISTIN M. ROMEY

Marrow Meals

GLOUCESTER—While the British have never been known for their culinary skills, a recent discovery in a Gloucester cave may make even aficionados of mushy peas take pause. According to Bristol University archaeologist Mark Horton, 2,000-year-old human remains found by local cavers, including a femur that had been split and its marrow scraped out, provide the first "irrefutable evidence" for cannibalism in northern Europe.

The area was an important center for underworld cults during the later Iron Age, and a Bristol excavation team believes that the site may also have been the scene of mass human sacrifice. The remains of at least seven other victims, some possibly disfigured or disabled, show evidence of murder.

Only five percent of the cave has been excavated so far, but Horton anticipates that more than 50 victims will eventually be uncovered.

—KRISTIN M. ROMEY

July/August

Georgia on My Mine

GEORGIA—A backhoe operator inadvertently dug up a cast-iron Confederate "torpedo" while excavating a trench for a pipeline on Elba Island, near Savannah, Georgia. Two-and-a-half feet long, weighing 200 pounds, and encrusted with rust, the weapon, which operates something like a modern-day mine, would have been attached to a fixed pole in Savannah harbor sometime in 1863. Jeff Reed, a historian at Fort Stewart, Georgia, says the mine is an excellent example of the improvised munitions of the period. "Confederate weapons weren't always made in foundries. During the war, small laboratories specializing in munitions sprung up in Savannah." Fort Stewart's 38th Explosive Ordinance Disposal Company, an army bomb squad, was called in to recover the artifact. They heard water inside the shell, leading them to believe that its gunpowder was probably soaked. Nonetheless, historians at Fort Stewart aren't taking any chances. "In the worst case scenario, we'd render it inert. We'd blow it up," says Reed, who would prefer that the mine be left intact for further study. "A good portion of it might survive."

How do you curate an artifact that might blow your arm off? While the Fort Stewart Museum negotiates a minefield of red tape in an attempt to answer that question, the torpedo awaits its fate on a bed of sandbags in a concrete bunker.

—ERIC A. POWELL

Attacking Malta's Past

MALTA—Some 60 megaliths at Mnajdra, a 5,000-year-old Neolithic temple complex on Malta, were toppled by vandals this past April. Chief suspects are bird hunters, whose access to the area has been challenged by Malta's museums department in recent years. The Maltese islands, between Africa and Europe, are frequented by migratory birds that hunters have long trapped from small stone shelters that dot the landscape around the temples. The practice has come under increasing criticism by environmentalists as well as the museums department, which views the shelters as incompatible with the archaeological park intended for Mnajdra and Hagar Qim, a nearby temple complex.

The attack came after years of political wrangling about the need for greater protection of Malta's Neolithic monuments, which are collectively listed by UNESCO as a World Heritage Site (see Plate 1). The vandals cut through a fence to gain access to the site, which is in a rural area of Malta; a lone night guard was at Hagar Qim at the time of the attack. Security has been stepped up at Mnajdra, with construction of a guard house and the installation of lights and a new fence. Assessment of how to restore the temple complex is now underway.

—MARK ROSE

Vintage Footage

SUTTON HOO—Recently discovered film footage of an excavation that took place more than 60 years ago is offering archaeologists a fascinating new look at Sutton Hoo, the richest Anglo-Saxon ship burial ever discovered in Britain.

Elaborate gold jewelry and the remains of an 89-foot-long vessel were among the finds from an early seventh-century B.C. burial mound at the site, believed to be that of the Anglo-Saxon king Raedwald.

Excavations began in 1938 by landowner Edith Pretty, who recruited her chauffeur and gardener to help investigate the mound. A team from London's Science Museum, led by Charles Phillips, took over once the significance of the discovery became apparent.

Phillips' brother Harold filmed the cleaning and documentation of the ship during the final days of excavation. Harold later emigrated to Canada, where his grandson Jeremy Gilbert discovered the film, which is said to be of exceptional clarity.

"The excavation record made by the Science Museum was destroyed during the Blitz, so this film along with one other and some photos are the only record we have of this priceless discovery," says National Trust archaeologist Angus Wainwright. Excerpts from the film will be shown at the new exhibition center at Sutton Hoo, which will open in spring 2002.

—KRISTIN M. ROMEY

DNA Round-Up

EAST ASIA—Did modern humans coming out of Africa stick to themselves or get together with earlier humans, such as *Homo erectus* in Asia? A new study based on DNA from the Y chromosome, which is passed only from fathers to sons, looked at the DNA from more than 12,000 men from 163 populations in East Asia, checking for differences among them. What they found was a surprising degree of uniformity, indicating that little or no mixing took place in regions where *H. erectus* persisted the longest.

In another study, genetic fingerprints of people from Sweden, Nigeria, and Central Europe were compared. Conclusion: modern Europeans may be descended from no more than a few hundred Africans who entered Asia, then continued into Europe as recently as 35,000 years ago.

If DNA seems to be the answer to all archaeological questions these days, hold on. For early human fossils, such as Neandertal remains, DNA may be preserved only in extremely unusual circumstances, and low temperatures are critical according to a new study. So don't grind up that bone and assume you'll get results every time, the recent successful recovery of DNA from the Mezmaiskaya and Feldhofer Neandertal specimens notwithstanding.

—MARK ROSE

September/October

Cave Art Nouveau

SOUTHERN FRANCE—Rare representations of birds and unknown animals shown with elongated muzzles and open mouths are among more than 200 newly discovered Upper Palaeolithic engravings in Cussac cave in southern France. The site is also unique for the size of the figures—some are 13 feet in length—which include mammoths, rhinoceros, deer, and, in greater numbers, horses and bison. Also depicted are women in outline and schematic vulvas. Most of the figures were engraved with stone tools, some simply by finger, in the clay on the cave walls; there are no paintings.

The find was made last September by Marc Delluc, a caver prospecting in the Buisson-de-Cadouin area of the Dordogne region. After a few dozen yards inside the cave, he found the passage blocked by stones. Removing them, he revealed a large gallery beyond with ancient engravings on its walls. Following a second visit, Delluc notified authorities and by late November the ministry of culture had declared the site a historic monument.

It seems likely that the Cussac engravings were made during the Gravettian period (28,000–22,000 years ago), named for the nearby site La Gravette. Early in the twentieth century, archaeologist Denis Peyrony excavated in the entrance of Cussac and found Gravettian tools—but Peyrony had no idea of the prehistoric art deeper in the cave. The date is consistent with the age of engravings at another cave, Pech Merle, which, according to Palaeolithic art specialist Michel Lorblanchet, are similar to those at Cussac.

Remains of at least five people were discovered in three places in the cave. Bones of an adolescent were found in a depression in the cave floor thought to be a hollow originally dug out by a bear for hibernation. In another hollow were remains of at least three adults, but, oddly enough, no skulls. Elsewhere there was a nearly complete skeleton of an adult lying on its stomach. Neolithic people often placed their dead in caves, but there are no associated artifacts, such as pottery, with the burials that would point to a Neolithic date. One of the bone deposits may lie on a bed of red ochre, which would be more characteristic of an Upper Palaeolithic burial. Direct dating of the remains will be done to determine if they are contemporary with the engravings.

This is the third important cave art find in France within a decade, following the painted caves of Cosquer (1992) and Chauvet (1994). It suggests that there is even more such prehistoric art to be found.

—BERNADETTE ARNAUD

More Bones, More Claims

ETHIOPIA—Debate over whose fossils represent our earliest ancestor continues, the newest contender being the 5.2–5.8-million-year-old fossils—a right mandible, four teeth, two arm and finger bones, one collar bone, and a toe bone—found between 1997 and 2001 in the Middle Awash region of Ethiopia. Just reported in the journal *Nature* by paleontologist Yohannes Haile-Selassie of the University of California at Berkeley, the bones have been dubbed *Ardipithecus ramidus kadabba*, a subspecies of *A. ramidus*, already known from 4.4-million-year-old fossils.

In the Afar language, *kadabba* means progenitor. The name was chosen because the fossils are close in time to the divergence of the ape-chimp and human lines, estimated on genetic evidence to have happened 6.5 to 5.5 million years ago. It also reflects Haile-Selassie's belief that his finds, and not the six-million-year-old *Orrorin tugenensis* discovered recently in Kenya, are on the human line (see page 33 [Ancient Ancestors]). Haile-Selassie claims that his Ardipithecus postdates the split but is close to the last common ape-chimp and human ancestor. *O. tugenensis*, he contends, could be the last common ancestor, an ape and chimp ancestor, or the ancestor of a dead-end evolutionary line.

—MARK ROSE

Marathon Blunder

MARATHON—Lazaros Kolonas, head of the Greek Archaeological Service, has requested that the Olympic water-sports complex under construction at Marathon be moved farther south, following the discovery that an ancient cemetery extended into the building site. More than 15 graves from the fifth and fourth centuries B.C. had already been excavated just 200 yards from the site when it was realized that the cemetery's boundaries were more extensive than previously supposed. An ancient road and remains of a wall have also been found at the site. Minister of Culture Evangelos Venizelos had stated that if antiquities were found within the construction site the project would be moved, but he has refused to bring the matter before the Central Archaeological Council.

The water-sports venue—parking lots, grandstands, and a 1.4-mile-long artificial lake—has been opposed from the start by environmentalists, who say it will damage a rare dune pine forest and bird habitat, and by archaeologists, who are concerned with preserving the ancient battlefield landscape where the Athenians defeated invading Persians in 490 B.C. (see ARCHAEOLOGY, July/August 2001, p. 6).

—NIKOS AXARLIS

Fertility Figure Found

TEL AVIV—A construction crew digging a trench under the Trans-Israel highway near Tel Aviv has unearthed a 6,000-year-old burial chamber containing the first Chalcolithic period (ca. 4000 B.C.) fertility figurine to be discovered in the region.

"There is no parallel in the country for this figurine," says Ianir Milevski, a research archaeologist with the Israel Antiquities Authority (IAA) and the leader of the excavation. Milevski notes that while Chalcolithic figurines have been found in the northern Negev, they are different in style, probably reflecting a strong Egyptian influence.

Three pieces of the eight-inch-tall figurine were found in an ossuary: the head and the upper part of the torso, the lower part of the torso and legs, and the left arm.

The missing right arm and hand may have covered the penis, as on similar figurines found in Egypt, Greece, and parts of Eastern Europe.

The tomb contained more than 30 ossuaries and several burial jars, as well as bowls, an oval goblet with an elongated pointed base, and other small objects, some of which were damaged by past use of the cave. Human bones were found in both the ossuaries and burial jars and were scattered throughout the cave.

The figurine, restored by the IAA, will be displayed at the Israel Museum. Tests are currently being done to see if it originated from outside the region.

—Sydney Schwartz

Old Canuck No Kennewick Man

BRITISH COLUMBIA—A DNA study now under way in British Columbia may link a 500-year-old man with his modern descendants. Popularly known as the "Iceman" or Kwaday Dän Sinchí ("Long Ago Person Found"), the headless body was discovered at the foot of a melting glacier on the border of British Columbia and Yukon in 1999. The Iceman's tribal affiliation is unclear, though his clothing offers tantalizing, if contradictory, clues.

An intricately woven spruce root hat found with the body is in the style of the coastal Tlingit people, many of whom live in what is now Alaska. But the Iceman also wore a robe of gopher fur from the Canadian interior. Pollen found on the robe comes from both the coast and the interior mountains.

Though the inland Champagne and Aishihik First Nations had custody of the body, researchers probing the Iceman's origins in Victoria, British Columbia, are analyzing DNA samples from both them and the Alaskan Tlingit. Results are expected by the end of the year.

The high degree of cooperation between the native groups and scientists studying Kwaday Dän Sinchí contrasts sharply with the seemingly endless Kennewick Man controversy in the Lower 48 (see ARCHAEOLOGY, September/October 2001, p. 65). A group of scientists is suing in federal district court to prevent reburial of the 9,500-year-old skeleton, which a coalition of Indian groups claims as an ancestor. At press time, a ruling was still pending, but if the losing side appeals, expect the legal wrangling to last into next year, if not longer.

While the ultimate fate of Kennewick Man's skeleton is up to the judge, the Iceman's remains have already been cremated. This July, during a traditional potlatch feast near the glacier where the remains were found, the Champagne and Aishihik joined with the Tlingit in scattering their ancestor's ashes to the wind.

—Eric A. Powell

Working-Class Stiffs

HIERAKONPOLIS—The earliest evidence for mummification in Egypt has been found in a cemetery of working-class inhabitants at Hierakonpolis, the largest site of the Pre- and Protodynastic period (3800–3100 B.C.), 390 miles south of Cairo. One plundered and two intact burials, all of women and dating between 3600 and 3500 B.C., show clear evidence that the forearms, hands, and base of the head were padded with linen bundles and then wrapped in resin-soaked linen bandages. Although the bodies weren't fully wrapped like later mummies, they are 500 years earlier than the next known example of mummification, a wrapped arm from the tomb of the 1st Dynasty king Den (ca. 2980 B.C.) found wearing four bracelets (and now in the Cairo Museum).

Why the head and hands were padded and wrapped is not certain. Perhaps the intent was to keep the body intact, especially the hands and mouth which would be needed for eating food in the afterlife. Renee Friedman, Heagy Research Curator at the British Museum and co-director of the Hierakonpolis Expedition, who directs the working-class cemetery excavations, notes that the jaw and hand bones tend to separate from the rest of the skeleton as a body decomposes or if a grave is disturbed. "This is not any kind of ad-hoc treatment," she says. "This is very carefully thought out, and you have the finest linen against the body, which gets progressively coarser as it goes out."

Examination of one woman's remains revealed that her throat had been slit. The position of the cut marks on the first and second neck vertebrae suggests the head had been tilted back at an unnatural angle, indicating that the cutting took place after death and a certain amount of desiccation. In all, seven bodies, both men and women, have lacerations to the throat, resulting in decapitation in two cases. There may be a link between this and the myth of the god Osiris, who was killed and dismembered by his brother Set, but was later reassembled and mummified in order to be resurrected as Lord of the Underworld. The earliest of Egypt's funerary texts, the Pyramid Texts, includes an obscure passage that reads, "put your head back on your body, gather up your bones," which may refer to this ritual act. "Perhaps they're laying the bodies out to dry," says Friedman, "then ritually decapitating, re-assembling, and wrapping them up."

Of an estimated 2,000 burials in the cemetery, 170 have been investigated. Other finds include the oldest preserved beard (well trimmed); a unique sheepskin toupee used to cover a man's bald spot; and, in a woman's burial (3500 B.C.), the oldest proven use of the plant henna to dye gray hair a dark reddish brown and the earliest evidence of hair weaving, in which locks of human hair were knotted onto the natural hair to produce an elaborate beehive-like hairstyle.

—MARK ROSE

November/ December

All That Glitters...

LIMA—Peru's Museo de Oro, one of the country's most popular tourist attractions and purported home to 20,000 artifacts of gold and silver, among other materials, has closed under intense academic and public scrutiny. Acting on a tip that pieces in the museum are fake, Peru's Consumer Protection Commission (INDECOPI) found that up to 85 percent of the museum's pieces may be knock-offs. This, in addition to the conspicuous failure of the museum to provide full provenience for many of its objects, brings the integrity of the museum's collection into serious question.

While archaeologists working in Peru have suspected for some time that many of the gold artifacts housed in the museum were fakes, no one said anything until talk spread of a plan to have the collection tour foreign countries. Hoping to avoid embarrassment for Peru and its cultural heritage, "those in the know decided they could no longer ignore the obvious," says William Isbell of the University of Binghamton.

Large numbers of people come to the museum every year to see what they assume are legitimately acquired, authentic artifacts from the Paracas, Chavín, Nazca, Moche, Huari, and Inca cultures, among others. According to a statement by INDECOPI, in order to maintain its museum status, the Museo de Oro must reclassify the pieces that are not originals using one of the three following definitions: "pieces of modern manufacture..., modern pieces using archaeological materials, and pieces pertaining to the archaeological heritage"—surely not quite as impressive as the former labels.

—COLLEEN P. POPSON

Early Arctic Adventurers

RUSSIAN—Archaeologists have long thought the inhospitable Russian Arctic was colonized by humans relatively late in the game, but new evidence suggests that modern humans—or perhaps even Neandertals—were present in the Arctic about 22,000 years earlier than thought.

The new date comes from a four-foot mammoth tusk excavated by Norwegian and Russian scientists from a riverbank above the Arctic Circle. Covered on all sides with regular cut marks, there seems to be no question that the tusk was modified by someone around 36,000 years ago. But just who remains unclear.

The earliest unequivocal evidence for modern humans in Europe dates to 35,000 years ago. Could the Arctic colonizers have been Neandertals? They were certainly capable of making the stone tools found with the tusk, but modern humans produced similar artifacts.

Regardless of who is responsible for the marks on the tusk, the finding comes as a big surprise. Neandertals are generally thought to have lacked the sophisticated social organization necessary to survive in the Arctic, while modern humans were not supposed to have gravitated toward northernmost Eurasia until the end of the last Ice Age, over 20,000 years after the tusk was cut.

—ERIC A. POWELL

Summer Sacrifice

CAUCASUS—By analyzing soil, pollen, and animal remains from four Bronze Age kurgans, or burial mounds, on the north Caucasus steppe, a team of scientists led by archaeologist Natalia Shishlina of the State History Museum in Moscow has been able to reconstruct the annual life-cycle of Bronze Age nomadic herdsmen in the region. The team was able to identify the main burial season, as well as summer and winter pastures.

One mound showed that a grave had been dug in early spring, after the frozen ground had been thawed with fire. The grave, however, remained open until April or May, when it was covered with hornbeam and elm logs. In early summer a 15-year-old girl was sacrificed near the burial ground and interred with a floral pillow comprised of carnations, roses, and wormwood. "Such [sacrificial] ritual is very rare," says Shishlina. "We have only three examples of human sacrifice from the area for the Yamnaya culture (3000–2300 B.C.); they were probably ancient Indo-Europeans."

—CHRIS HELLIER

Gold Rush Wreck

SAN FRANCISCO—The hulk of the sailing ship *General Harrison*—a long-forgotten but spectacular remnant of California's mid-nineteenth-century Gold Rush— was recently encountered in waterfront landfill in the heart of San Francisco's modern financial district during foundation work for a new hotel. The still-solid oak hull is a vivid reminder of San Francisco's dramatic birth some 150 years ago, when it began to grow into America's principal Pacific Coast metropolis.

Built in Newbury, Massachusetts in 1840, the triple-masted *General Harrison* was converted into a floating warehouse in 1850 and consumed to the water line in the great San Francisco fire of 1851. The charred hulk of the ship was partially salvaged, buried in waterfront landfill, and forgotten for the next 150 years.

Excavation revealed that when the ship was buried, it was holding numerous cases of imported red wine; bolts of cloth; supplies of tacks, nails, and other hardware; wheat; and a large quantity of Italian glass trade beads. Nearly a dozen of the wine bottles were found intact, still corked and sealed, filled with what was probably Bordeaux or Burgundy, possibly the last bottles from the vintage of 1849.

During the next year, an intensive program of historical and laboratory research by the contract firm Archeo-Tec, which excavated the ship, will complete the final voyage of the *General Harrison* and allow this once proud vessel to add her tale to the annals of the California Gold Rush.

—A.G. PASTRON

Nurturing Neandertals

SOUTHEASTERN FRANCE—A pathological human jaw from Bau de l'Aubesier, a rock-shelter in southeastern France, shows that early Neandertals cared for those who were incapacitated.

Designated Aubesier 11, the jaw is described by site director Serge Lebel of Université de Québec à Montréal and anthropologist Erik Trinkaus of Washington University in St. Louis in the *Proceedings of the National Academy of Sciences.* Based on thermoluminescence dates and faunal studies, the level in which it was found dates from 175,000 to 200,000 years ago, perhaps earlier.

Other than the worn root tips of the canine and a third premolar, few, if any, of the teeth were in place when the individual died. The rot and reabsorption of bone indicate serious infection, likely resulting from extreme wear of the teeth rather than dental disease. The individual (whether male or female is unknown) lived for a matter of months unable to chew food without considerable pain.

"This is the oldest example of someone surviving for some period of time without an effective set of chompers," says Trinkaus.

"If their social organization was based on small family units, loss of individual members could have catastrophic consequences and had to be averted," notes Lebel. "Meat was an important dietary factor, and we must envisage a preparation and selection of soft food, like marrow, by other group members."

—MARK ROSE

The Acquisitive Curator

MADISON—A former curator of anthropology at the Wisconsin Historical Society Museum in Madison has been convicted of pilfering the museum's ethnographic collection and awaits sentencing for stealing dozens of artifacts. Now the same curator, David L. Wooley, stands accused of removing objects from another Wisconsin museum, the Lac du Flambeau tribal cultural center.

The thefts were uncovered thanks to a tip from German anthropologist Christian Feest of Goethe University, Frankfurt, who saw a Ho-Chunk prophet stick in a 1998 auction catalog and recognized it as one he had photographed at the Historical Society Museum a decade earlier. He asked the gallery about the item's provenance and was told the stick was purchased for $28,500 from a dealer who had sold a number of items supposedly owned by Wooley. Feest's query led Wooley to arrange for the dealer to return the artifact to the collection, thanking the German for his efforts.

It might have ended there, but Feest mentioned the bizarre incident to the new museum director, Ann Koski, in the fall of 2000. Alarmed by the tale of the traveling prophet stick, Koski launched an investigation that resulted in a state charge of theft against Wooley, who had become director of the Lac du Flambeau Museum and Cultural Center in 1999.

Searches of Wooley's home and storage units led the curator to admit stealing 34 items from the Historical Society Museum valued between $120,000 and $185,000. Charged with 14 counts of felony theft plus three counts of failing to file state income tax, Wooley faces a maximum sentence of about 100 years in prison.

During the course of the investigation, Lac du Flambeau tribal officials and artist James F. Frechette, Jr., identified a $15,000 clan bear statue from photos taken in Wooley's apartment. A fresh count of felony theft was filed in August. The cultural center is currently reviewing its collection to determine if other items are missing.

—MEG TURVILLE-HEITZ

PART II:

AFRICA

1

ANCIENT ANCESTORS

Kenyan fossils complicate the picture of early hominid evolution.

by ANGELA M.H. SCHUSTER

UNTIL RECENTLY, PALEOANTHROPOLOGISTS SUGgested that only one ancient ancestor gave rise to what eventually became the human family line 3 to 4 million years ago. But, as two recent fossil finds from Kenya attest, this scenario is far too simple. They call into question the place of the australopithecines—long thought to be our ancestors—within the human family tree and the date the human line split from that of the great apes.

The discovery of a 3.5-million-year-old cranium near the Lomekwi River in northern Kenya is prompting a major reconsideration of the australopithecine branch of our family tree. Discovered by Kenyan fossil hunter Justus Erus and Meave Leakey of the National Museums of Kenya during the 1998 and 1999 field seasons, the skull, named *Kenyanthropus platyops*, is strikingly different in appearance from

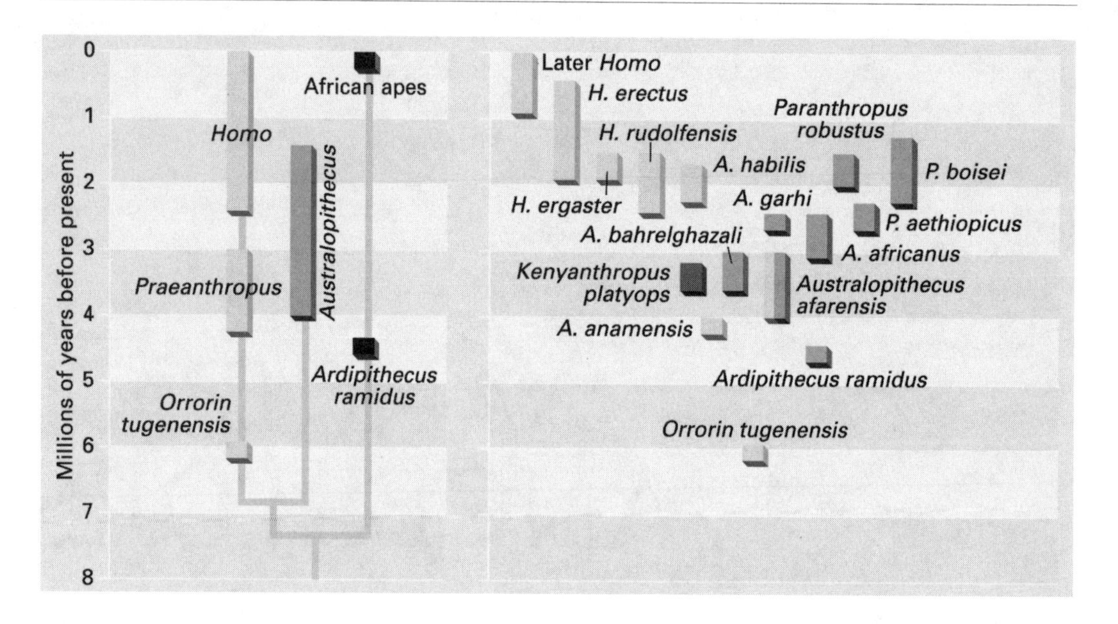

that of its contemporary and neighbor *Australopithecus afarensis*, the species to which the famous 3.2-million-year-old Lucy belongs. (The new fossil's name means "flat-faced man of Kenya.")

Though 40 percent of Lucy's skeleton had been recovered in 1974, her skull, aside from the lower jaw and a few cranial fragments, was missing, leaving unanswered questions about her dentition, facial architecture, and brain size. These questions were answered with the 1992 discovery at Hadar, Ethiopia, of a nearly complete 3-million-year-old male *A. afarensis* specimen, which had a small braincase, thick molars and large canines, and a heavy, protruding brow ridge.

While the newly found *K. platyops* is similar in brain size, it differs significantly in facial appearance, having a flat face and small teeth. These features, Leakey argues, appear more fully developed in *Homo rudolfensis*, a species that thrived in East Africa 2.4 to 1.8 million years ago, and which many view as the true beginning of the Homo line. "Based on the teeth alone," Leakey told ARCHAEOLOGY, "we believe that *K. platyops* exploited a different ecological niche, most likely subsisting on softer foods such as fruits and insects." *A. afarensis*, she believes, ate a coarser diet of roots and grasses.

That there was significantly more variation early in the australopithecine line itself would have been enough to make paleoanthropological news; a second Kenyan find, however, calls into question whether the australopithecines are even ancestral to modern humans.

Leakey's find came on the heels of the discovery of what may be the earliest-known human ancestor, a diminutive 6-million-year-old creature represented by a selection of fossils from several localities in what is known as the Lukeino Formation in the Tugen Hills of western Kenya's Baringo District. The date of the find, if accepted, pushes back the earliest-known ancestor by some 1.5 million years. Until this discovery, the oldest-known ancestor was the 4.5-million-year-old *Ardipithecus ramidus*, excavated at Aramis, Ethiopia (see ARCHAEOLOGY, March/April 1995, p. 13).

According to site excavators Brigitte Senut of the Musée National d'Histoire Naturelle in Paris and Martin Pickford of the Collège de France, the 13 fossils—jaw fragments with teeth, isolated upper and lower teeth, and arm and leg bones—represent five individuals of a species they have named *Orrorin tugenensis* (*Orrorin* means "original man" in the Tugen language). The antiquity attributed to the new finds is based on the ages of lava flows above and below the fossil-bearing layers.

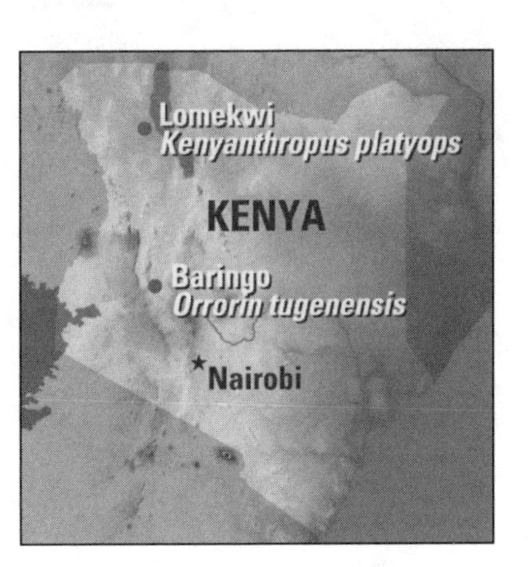

Based on the morphology of the limb bones, Senut and Pickford contend that *O. tugenensis* was a good climber and mostly lived in trees, but was bipedal when on the ground. Moreover, they say the creature had small molars with thick enamel, a feature that persists into the *Homo* line but is absent in the australopithecines, suggesting that a split between the two groups had already occurred by this early date. They believe the divergence of what would become the *Homo* line from the great apes may have taken place as early as 9 million years ago. Comparison of human and ape DNA has suggested the split occurred around 6 million years ago, the date of *O. tugenensis*. Australopithecines, say Senut and Pickford, simply came to an evolutionary dead end around 1.5 million years ago.

More controversial, however, are the circumstances under which the Tugen Hills fossils came to light. Senut and Pickford may have been digging without a proper permit in this hominid hot zone, a charge put forth by the National Museums of Kenya, which approves all excavation concessions in the country. Discord is not new to paleoanthropology, as witnessed by the long and often heated feuds between various researchers and their sponsoring institutions (see ARCHAEOLOGY, May/June 2001, pp. 74–77). However, this battle would appear to be more acrimonious than most. The whole matter has quickly deteriorated into a he-said-she-said scenario with allegations of malfeasance and misfeasance emanating from nearly all involved. Perhaps it is the fact that the stakes are so high, given the date of the find, that has brought out the worst in everyone.

2

FAKING AFRICAN ART

A five-year investigation reveals that most West African terra-cotta sculptures are fakes that have fooled specialists, sold for hundreds of thousands of dollars, and ended up in some of the world's most prestigious museums.

by MICHEL BRENT

ON WEDNESDAY, NOVEMBER 20, 1991, SOTHEBY'S New York auctioned the Kuhn collection, a well-known assemblage of African objects. On the cover of the auction catalog was the collection's masterpiece, a West African terra-cotta ram. Since thermoluminescence (TL) tests—a primary means of authentication—had indicated the figure was between 570 and 1,000 years old, there was no suspicion about the piece's age. A little before noon, the animal was sold for $275,000. The Kuhn ram has not been the object of much discussion in the years since the sale, except in Mali, its country of origin. There, rumors have it the piece may have been faked.

Since the 1980s, nearly 80 percent of the allegedly antique terra cottas that have left Mali have been counterfeit. Unlike most African countries, Mali is the source of both finely crafted ethnographic objects such as masks and fetishes, as well as archaeological artifacts such as bronze sculptures and terra-cotta statues. The latter may represent the spirits of people who flourished here for some 1,000 years, between the A.D. ninth and nineteenth centuries. Prized by collectors, Malian terra cottas have been looted from hundreds of archaeological sites on the middle Niger River. As these pieces have become increasingly scarce, Malian antiquities dealers have sought faked pieces from local potters. The resulting trade has seriously corrupted the art historical record: in most cases it is now simply impossible to tell if terra cottas published in scholarly works on West African art are genuine.

Confessions of a Forger

One day in 1995, while investigating a story on West African cultural heritage, I saw a terra-cotta animal leg, remarkably similar to those of the ram sold in 1991, in the backyard of a Bamako antiquities dealer's house. I had a sudden and inexplicable feeling—born of years of staring at these objects—that this leg had been fashioned by the same hand that had made the Kuhn ram. I decided to find out whether my intuition was correct.

Early in 1997, after persistent inquiry, I was put in touch with a man named Amadou, a Bamako potter with long, stick-like fingers who stands more than six-and-a-half feet tall. From our first meeting, it was clear I would have to pay Amadou, and pay him dearly, for any information about the leg. In the following weeks, I negotiated a price for an interview, an ethically dubious practice for a journalist. What credit, after all, could be given to the testimony of a crook?

Our meeting took place in March 1998 in the courtyard of a modest Bamako hotel. I asked Amadou if the Kuhn piece was real or fake. "It's a fake," he answered. "At least part of it. I was the one who made it." Amadou told me that back in October 1986, in the village of Dary, a hamlet along the Niger River, erosion caused by seasonal rains had exposed several pieces of terra cotta at an abandoned village site. The villagers soon engaged Baba Niagando, a Bandiagara antiquities dealer, to hunt for terra cottas at the site. The villagers, usually wary of outsiders, were friendly with Niagando because he occasionally hunted crocodiles in the area.

A distant relative of Niagando's, Amadou was summoned to help dig. Niagando also shared the project with Mamadou Traore, another local antiquities dealer, and they hired both Dary and Bandiagara villagers. The clandestine excavation lasted six months, but only three intact animals emerged from among the hundreds of terra-cotta fragments found at the site. It was here, according to Amadou, that an intact piece of the Kuhn ram was found—front legs, chest, and head—the rest of the animal was missing.

"From the three intact animals I was able to make more than 100 fake terra cottas," says Amadou. "As for the [Kuhn] piece, I was able to fashion it from nose to hindquarters." His handiwork from this prolific period also ended up in the Belgian count Baudouin de

Grunne's celebrated collection, as well as in Geneva's Barbier Muller Museum. The stomach of the Pregnant Ewe on display at the Museum of Fine Arts, Boston, was also found among the fragments in Dary and the entire piece refashioned by Amadou.

Proof that Amadou Wasn't Lying

Once I heard Amadou's story, I hurried to Dary, some 450 miles northeast of Bamako, to find out if the villagers' version corresponded with the forger's. The village has a population of about 200. There are no roads leading to it, and three months out of the year when the Niger River overflows there is no overland access at all. There are no phones here, no electricity, and no running water.

When shown Amadou's photos of the intact pieces that had emerged from the site, Denba Traore, the village chief, quickly grasped that I knew what had gone on there nine years before. For several hours I sought information from people in various parts of the village. Those who had taken part in the digging confirmed Amadou's story, corroborating the names of the antiquities dealers involved in the digging, the time they spent at the site, the number of intact pieces recovered, and how the pieces were transported out of the bush in jute bags on a donkey cart. They also provided details concerning the authentic fragment of the Kuhn ram (its findspot and the depth at which it was buried) as well as the stomach of the Pregnant Ewe at the Museum of Fine Arts, Boston. Everything checked out; Amadou had told me the truth.

How to Circumvent Thermoluminescence Tests

Having partially reconstructed the history of the Kuhn ram—its export to the United States by antiquities dealer Samba Kamissoko and its acquisition by New Orleans dealer Charles Davis—I wanted to learn how Amadou faked objects that deceived experts in African art. Even if Amadou were capable of reproducing the ancient terra cottas, how was he able to circumvent thermoluminescence dating tests?

These forgers apply a number of techniques to age their terra cottas artificially.

In addition to joining larger authentic pieces to fabricated parts, Amadou explained that he digs "holes into the clay where I can bury fragments of authentic terra cotta found at the [looted] sites; I do this after firing the new clay. As far as the piece [the Kuhn ram] you showed me is concerned, I put ancient fragments in the two hind legs and other pieces in the stomach." Amadou's explanation was believable; I had heard about the technique a few years earlier from an Italian restorer, who described it to me as "both risky and infallible—infallible because TL can't distinguish an inserted part from the rest of the object...and hazardous because it's necessary that the TL technician choose to test in an area where authentic pieces were inserted."

I was interested to find out if this method worked, so I traveled to Daybreak Nuclear and Medical Systems, Inc., the Guilford, Connecticut, TL lab that had tested the Kuhn ram. I hoped I'd be able to see the test results. After a good amount of hesitation (client documents are generally confidential), Victor Bortolot, the lab's director, agreed to search his archives for dossier 201A36. Judging the object to be authentic, the technician at the time had taken only a single sample, from under the left front leg, an authentic part of the piece. Hence the favorable test results published in the Sotheby's catalog, hence the high price fetched by the piece. "But don't forget that this file dates to March 1988," Bortolot said. "At the time our practice was to make only one test if we felt the object was good. But now, with the great number of fakes circulating, it's necessary to make at least two."

Other Fakers in the Hot Seat

I met with eight other Malian forgers to learn more about their methods. They agreed on several important points. First, Amadou's technique of concealing authentic fragments is widely practiced, but only when a large, well-preserved piece is available that can be the basis for a reconstruction, as was the case with the Kuhn ram. They also use authentic fragments to fill inconspicuous areas likely to be drilled so as not to mar the piece's appearance. These practices explain why most African antiquities dealers are so well stocked with apparently useless fragments of genuine terra cottas.

Second, these forgers apply a number of techniques to age their terra cottas artificially, like multiple immersions of an object in baths of different sorts to enhance their patina. Amadou dips his pieces in water mixed with potassium and authentic fragments; he keeps a fire burning under the bath for a week or more. Issa Kone of Bougouni, another forger, soaks his objects in water for two months, or until the liquid evaporates. Seyni M. Karabenta, a specialist in terra-cotta fakes in the Bankoni style of southern Mali, adds to his bath mixture dried birds' nests found on the walls of many Malian houses. Forgers also obtain a desired patina by painting the terra cottas with a substance derived from either the bark of a tree or plant or colored stones. Some forgers cover their pieces with a layer of clay cooked at a low temperature that can be brushed, scraped, or otherwise modified to convey an aged look. Another technique involves burial in soil. Amadou says the Kuhn ram was buried for ten months. Forgers moisten their burial plots with various liquids: urine, waste water, acid products, animal dung. The more corrosive, the faster the artificial aging process.

One can assume the African forgers learned about the TL tests and the means to circumvent them from complicit European dealers. My sense is that these shady characters must have lived in Mali or still do, and that they are the middlemen who buy from local forgers to sell to European clients. When a fake terra cotta leaves Mali, it has probably been modified several times by dealers and middlemen. Over the years, I'd suspected that multiple faking was practiced, but I didn't have real proof until I discovered the photo of the Kuhn ram at the Daybreak Laboratory in Connecticut. The ends of all four of its legs had been mutilated (even though Amadou says he delivered it intact) to better simulate the passage of the centuries.

Extent of the Traffic

Assembling disparate pieces was the first sort of faking to become popular in West Africa beginning in the 1970s. Since intact artifacts were rare, dealers, mostly from Mali, patched together fragments of authentic terra cottas from looted sites. A head, arm, or hand here, a foot or leg there—it was up to an artful restorer to compose an intact piece. The practice was never a secret among European gallery owners, who in time realized the assembly work would be more efficiently carried out in European workshops. Helène Leloup, a well-known Paris dealer, recalls seeing photos of pieces of African terra cottas newly arrived at European galleries; no one knew which limbs belonged to which figures.

The first doctored Malian terra cottas came from Sévaré, near Mopti in central Mali, where antiquities dealer Boubou Diarra has lived for more than 60 years. Since 1968, Diarra has sold looted terra cottas and exported them illegally to European colleagues such as the Belgian dealer Émile Deletaille and French merchant Philippe Guimiot. As demand increased and fewer intact terra cottas were being recovered, Diarra started selling fakes. Naturally, he wasn't the only dealer doing this for long. By the early 1980s, a countrywide network of dealers and forgers was in place—Youssouf Cissé in Mopti, Mobo Maiga in Djenné, Adama Ouloguem in Bamako, among others. Often dealers would scour the countryside for talented young potters, promising them lodging, food, and bicycles or scooters for faked terra cottas. Sometimes they would uproot potters with a knack for faking, moving them far from their families to villages where their production could be easily monitored.

The government has also had an indirect hand in the spread of fakes. Malian legislation forbidding the export of archaeological objects may have been passed to encourage faking discreetly; how otherwise to explain a 1994 government directive allowing local dealers to acquire "50 ancient-looking copies inspired by archaeological or ethnographic objects."

Another factor favored the spread of fakes: publication during the 1980s of monographs, art books, and auction house sale catalogs devoted to West African terra cottas. Seyni M. Karabenta of Kourikoulo, who began working for Boubou Diarra in 1978, told me that once catalog photos of African terra cottas started appearing in Mali, he began producing nearly 100 fakes annually. In fact, he made so many forgeries over a 15-year period that insiders started calling his fakes "Karabentos." Mobo Maiga, one of the two major Djenné dealers, confirmed that each time an authentic local piece was brought to him, he hired local sculptors to make several copies. Forgers no longer had to wait until new looted pieces emerged to copy them—they just worked directly from photos. Faking was simpler this way and the range of objects to copy wider. According to the forgers, to whom I showed a fair number of art books such as Bernard de Grunne's *Ancient Terra-cottas from West Africa* and catalogs including that of the Menil Collection in the United States, the most important published African terra cottas have been copied several times, and the copies sold as ancient.

Finally, a new class of collectors, less knowledgeable than their predecessors, has emerged who view authentic African art as a good financial investment. African dealers have now installed themselves in the United States, a huge market with potentially limitless profits. And American buyers are considerably less careful than their European counterparts in distinguishing authentic from fake.

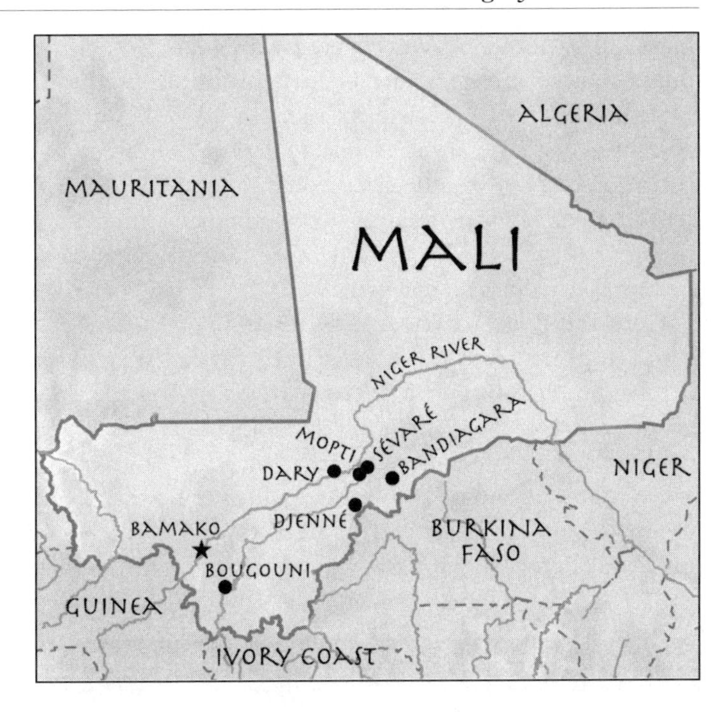

The Most Recent Cons

Early on, forgers were freewheeling in their use of materials. Several specialists told me they'd seen African terra cottas made from plaster or powder ground from ancient fragments. Francine Maurer, a collector and proprietor of ASA Laboratory and Expertise in Paris and Wadgassen, Germany, recalls with amusement that, shortly after founding her company in 1986, she fell in love with a lion's head purportedly created in Djenné in the twelfth century, which she bought for nearly $4,000 at the Gallery Drouot Montaigne in Paris. Back home, the object fell to the ground, breaking into several pieces; it had been fashioned from a termites' nest!

Today, West African forgers are counterfeiting Nok and Ife statues from Nigeria and Benin in response to trends in collecting. Their techniques have changed, however, since buyers have become more suspicious. Asian forgers are credited with a fairly recent innovation in counterfeiting: mixing authentic fired clay with resins, pastes, and acrylic gums or epoxies of all sorts. This mélange is used not only to coat pitted surfaces but also to make pieces from scratch. The result is practically undetectable and satisfies everyone—forgers and dealers—but not, understandably, their clients.

Gigi Pezzoli, a connoisseur of African art and member of Milan's Center for the Study of African Archaeology, was involved in a revealing misadventure. After having had a TL test conducted on an Ife head and receiving confirmation as to its authenticity, he gave the object to his restorer. Examining the object closer, the restorer sensed something fishy. The Ife head, which TL tests determined to be authentic, was covered with an outer coating meant to hide centuries of wear and tear and elevate its price. The object was genuine, but was probably in poor condition before it had been doctored. After spending years putting fragments of authentic pieces in fakes, counterfeiters are now putting fake patinas on real pieces!

Here and there I've heard stories about super-sophisticated faking methods that involve bombarding terra cottas with X or gamma rays to produce a false TL reading. I doubt that this is a common practice since it is too expensive and time consuming. For an object to pass TL tests, it would need to be uniformly bombarded by X and gamma rays. But it's nearly impossible to irradiate a terra cotta uniformly without spending a great amount of time in the laboratory turning the object so that all of its sides are exposed. Another problem is calculating the X- or gamma- ray dose required to mimic a certain age, something that would require the complicity of technically sophisticated partners.

An Obsession with Ancientness

There's no question that some African forgers are geniuses at what they do. Malian and Nigerian dealers have often told me how difficult it can be to distinguish fake from

The Limits of Thermoluminescence

Thermoluminescence dating of a ceramic requires two steps. The first consists of gauging the accumulated radiation (or "archaeological dose") absorbed by crystals in the ceramic since its firing. Buried terra cottas are irradiated by radioelements in the objects themselves and by those in the soil in which they are buried. To measure accumulated radiation, one tracks the thermoluminescent properties of the crystals—when heated, they release stored radioactive energy in the form of light. Technicians generally drill out small samples from a piece; only an ounce or two of material is necessary for the test. The second step consists of determining the amount of radiation absorbed yearly by the crystals. Dividing the "archaeological dose" by the "annual dose" gives the age of the terra cotta.

Thermoluminescence tests are an important factor when dealers and collectors judge authenticity. But TL has its limitations. First, in order to insure profitability, commercial labs often limit the number of samples they take from terra cottas for analysis, generally drawing them from only two parts of a piece. Scientists who run the labs say this number is insufficient in view of the con game now taking place with terra cottas.

Then there is the matter of who takes the samples. Since TL testing is a global business, it is impractical for directors of commercial firms to take all the samples themselves. Firms like Daybreak Nuclear and Medical Systems, Inc., in Guilford, Connecticut, and Oxford Authentication Ltd. in Wantage, England, employ a worldwide network of representatives who travel wherever the artifacts happen to be. While we have no reason to doubt the honesty of these representatives, the art world in which they operate is not always concerned with professional ethics. Dealers are capable of bribing the experts. Three times during my research I visited African dealers in Bamako who showed me terra cottas accompanied by certificates of authenticity from the largest commercial labs in Europe. They were fake terra cottas and, apparently, fake certificates.

Finally, there's reason to doubt the reliability of certain measurements of radiation attested in com-

genuine when terra cottas arrive at their doorsteps. If those in the trade have such doubts, the deck is obviously stacked against their clients. Furthermore, West African terra cottas represent a relatively new market. It was only at the end of the 1960s that European collectors first started buying these pieces. The very "newness" of the art leaves the door wide open for forgeries.

Also regrettable is the obsession among Western collectors with ancientness; white dealers who sell to them often disdain works of art younger than 100 years old, even when copies of wooden effigies made in Malian villages earlier in the twentieth century are sometimes better executed and more beautiful than the originals. Contemporary African art is flourishing, with Zimbabwean sculptors and Congolese bronze sculptors showing the way. While some forgers have created lucrative businesses selling their own wares, many more like Amadou are waiting for the time when they can step out of the shadows and own up to their considerable skills as legitimate creative artists.

mercial certificates. Annual doses are crucial to determining an object's age. "They are extremely difficult to obtain," says Max Schvoerer, a professor at the University of Bordeaux 3 and founder of the Center for Research in Applied Physics and Archaeology at the university. "In general, research scientists determine it by comparing measurements taken in the lab with those [from soil samples] at the place where the object was found. Because of the time and costs involved, commercial firms don't have the opportunity to do this. They thus either have to extrapolate from published reports about [the geology of] the region the object under analysis came from, or only measure the internal radiation of the object, which can sometimes result in considerable margins of error. In this case the test becomes merely an indication of antiquity, not a method of precise dating."

Directors of TL labs try to address these issues. They recognize, for example, that it would be preferable to take more samples. If there is serious doubt about an artifact, they will take further samples if the client requests. As for the wisdom of using representatives to take samples, Doreen Stoneham, director of Oxford Authentification Ltd., simply replies that "It's more practical." Lab directors refuse to discuss the possibility of corrupt practices, jealously guarding their employees' identities and qualifications. Victor Bortolot, director of Daybreak Nuclear, would say only that his team is composed of a dozen people, most of whom are art restorers.

As for the method used to measure annual doses of radiation, commercial labs recognize their weaknesses vis-a-vis university labs: the precision of their work cannot be compared with that of scientists who actually travel to the site where the artwork was found. Nonetheless, they say their calibrations still guarantee antiquity, which is usually all clients want. However, to avoid misunderstandings, most commercial labs have stricken the word "dating" from their brochures.

Commercial labs stress that TL tests are only one step in assessing an artwork's authenticity. Art market professionals, however, have every interest in promoting TL certificates as the final word. One couldn't dream of better support for a sales pitch.

–Michel Brent

PART III:

EGYPT

3

SACRED SANDS

Exploring the tombs and temples of ancient Abydos.

by DAVID O'CONNOR *and* DIANA CRAIG PATCH

DARK, RUGGED CLIFFS FLANK THE MIDDLE reaches of the Nile River. Between them is a fertile floodplain and beyond a vast expanse of desert rich in archaeology. For more than 5,000 years, the Egyptians prospered in this landscape, constructing towns, temples, and memorials to their dead. It was here that Egypt's earliest rulers were interred, Egypt's first writing appeared, and the cult of boat burials was born. It was also here that the New Kingdom pharaoh Seti I built an impressive mortuary complex and temple dedicated to himself and the god Osiris, master of the underworld. Today, these age-old ruins lie beneath the wind-blown sands of a place we know as Abydos, some 300 miles south of Cairo.

For more than three decades, Abydos and its environs have been the focus of an archaeological campaign undertaken by an expedition from the University of Pennsylvania Museum, Yale University, and New York University's Institute of Fine Arts in cooperation with Egypt's Supreme Council for Antiquities. Collectively, these projects, co-directed by William Kelly Simpson, have revealed much about the dawn of the pharaonic age and the course of Egyptian civilization.

During the Palaeolithic period, a moist climate kept most settlement off the valley floor, but by the early fourth millennium B.C., decreasing annual rainfall and the introduction of domesticated plants and animals encouraged people to adopt a new, sedentary life-style on the floodplain. To understand this change, we undertook an extensive regional survey in 1983 [directed by Diana Patch], locating low desert cemeteries dated between 3850 and 2150 B.C.—from the earliest Predynastic times to the end of the Old Kingdom. The first cemeteries were located primarily on the river's western bank, at the edge of the floodplain. Burials are uniform—bodies were placed in a pit in a flexed position, often wrapped in matting, and pottery was deposited around them, usually at the head and feet. Simple adornments, such as a necklace, bracelet, hair pin, or comb, were placed in the grave along with small lumps of lead ore or malachite and a stone palette used to grind them into eye makeup. On rare occasions, offerings of figurines, weapons, and amulets were also included.

Prehistoric Egyptians seem to have been organized in communities headed by chiefs, some of whom became regional rulers, laying the political groundwork for Egypt's eventual unification. The economy combined herding and agriculture with trade in finished goods and raw materials along the

A Landscape of Empty Tombs

During the last part of the nineteenth century and the beginning of the twentieth century, Abydos was literally mined for stelae, statues, and offering tables—many from the Middle Kingdom (1975–1640 b.c.)—for the collections of museums such as the Egyptian Museum in Cairo, the Louvre, the British Museum, and the Egyptological Museum, Leiden. The general area from which these antiquities derive is known, but their archaeological and architectural contexts have never been determined. From texts on some of the stelae, it is evident that these memorials were set up in chapels in an area at the south side of a processional route to a royal tomb of the Dynasty I (2950–2775 b.c.) pharaoh Djer. The tomb's identity was later forgotten and it became associated with the burial of the god Osiris. The texts describe elements of the ritual of the procession whereby a bark was transported to the tomb and a mock battle staged against those aboard carrying an image of Osiris.

Objects bearing the name of the same individual clearly belonged within a single chapel. For example, the general Ameny is represented by a large granite stela in the Louvre and two large matching limestone stelae, one in Cairo and the other in the British Museum. It seems likely that the Louvre stela was placed against the center wall of a structure and the limestone stelae on opposite walls. On all three monuments, Ameny is shown with "his beloved wife," but the ladies mentioned in the inscriptions have different names—a case of polygamy rather than successive wives.

Recent excavations show that these monuments were never used for burial. They were cenotaphs, or empty tombs, built to link the deceased with the Osiris cult.

—WILLIAM KELLY SIMPSON

Nile and beyond. The religion of the Egyptians at this time is poorly known, but the graves attest a uniform burial practice.

By 3450 B.C., increasing numbers of burials in the cemeteries indicate that four of the settlements using them—Thinis (location unknown), Mahasna, Abydos, and el-Amra—had grown dramatically. This expansion coincided with the appearance of specialized crafts, the construction of large religious structures, and evidence of increased contact between the populations of Upper and Lower Egypt. Cemeteries dating to this period contain numerous small tombs and several very large ones, the latter containing abundant grave goods, some of a rare and expensive nature such as lapis lazuli and gold jewelry, indicating an emergence of an elite class.

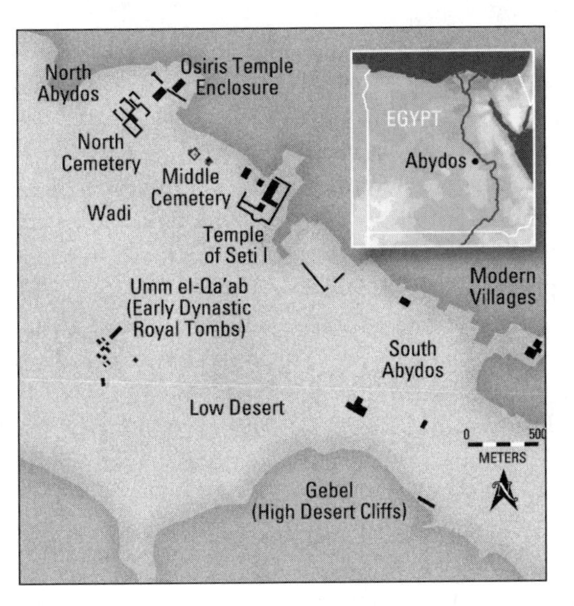

The most important finds from this period have been excavated by Gunter Dreyer of the German Archaeological Institute, at a site known as Cemetery U near Umm el Qa'ab, at the foot of the cliffs to the west of Abydos. Among the graves here, one contained numerous ivory and bone tags bearing Egypt's earliest-known writing. As the tags, which were used to label foodstuffs, cloth, and other items, are almost contemporary with the birth of writing in Mesopotamia, the prevailing view that writing was invented in the Near East needs to be reconsidered. The same tomb contained jars of wine imported from the southern Levant and a scepter, indicating the man buried there may have been an early king.

By the time of the unification of Upper and Lower Egypt at the beginning of the third millennium B.C., the seat of government had been firmly established at Memphis, near modern Cairo. Egypt's pharaohs, however, still preferred to be buried at Umm el Qa'ab until Dynasty IV (2575–2465 B.C.), when they began constructing their tombs at Giza. Each of the Umm el Qa'ab royal tombs consisted of a massive substructure packed with jewelry, stone vases, and supplies for the afterlife and capped by a subterranean mound. Small subsidiary graves for courtiers and servants, perhaps sacrificed during the king's funeral, surrounded each tomb.

We have investigated a group of contemporary mud-brick enclosures adjacent to a temple dedicated to the god Khentyamentiu, protector of the royal tombs, about a mile north of Umm el Qa'ab. Each enclosure housed a chapel used for the mortuary cult of one of these early kings. While the royal tombs themselves were comparatively small (3,200 square feet on average), their associated enclosures, which sometimes had walls more than 36 feet high and 16 feet thick, covered as much as two acres. These walls were originally whitewashed. An early enclosure is associated with what has been hailed as some of the most important finds excavated in recent years—14 well-preserved ships, buried side-by-side, each encased in a mud-brick, boat-shaped superstructure.

We believe that during the Early Dynastic period (2920–2649 B.C.), Abydos became a sacred precinct, dominated by a ritual route that connected the royal tombs at Umm el Qa'ab and Khentyamentiu's temple and its associated enclosures to their north. Initially used for royal burial processions, this route may have been followed by priests placing offerings at the royal tombs.

Khentyamentiu's temple remained important through the Old Kingdom (2575–2150 B.C.). Royal chapels dedicated to the ka, an individual's life force, were built next to it by a number of kings, and a large town developed nearby. South of the town was an imposing elite cemetery surrounded by commoners' graves. Officials buried there were of high rank and included Weni the Elder, whose long-lost tomb has been rediscovered by Janet Richards.

By 2000 B.C., worship of the god Osiris had taken hold at Abydos. According to myth, Osiris—killed by his envious brother, Seth, and brought back to life magically by his wife, Isis—ruled the dead, while his son Horus, who avenged his murder, ruled as king of the living. The legitimization of the living king, identified with Horus, was derived from his dead predecessor's identification with Osiris. Iconographically, Osiris melded with Khentyamentiu to become Abydos' patron god, and an annual festival was held in his honor. The identity of a tomb at Umm el Qa'ab belonging to the Dynasty I king Djer had been forgotten and it subsequently was believed to be the final resting place of Osiris.

In the Middle Kingdom (1975– 1640 B.C.), Osiris' temple flourished and many pilgrims set up memorial chapels nearby. A vast cemetery developed north of the processional route, itself kept free from tombs: according to a royal decree of the Dynasty XIII king Neferhotep (r. 1741–1730 B.C.), those who built tombs on the processional route were punished by burning. Janet Richards' excavations have revealed a socially diverse population buried in the Middle Kingdom cemetery, which continued to be used throughout the New Kingdom and later by both rich and poor alike.

Josef Wegner of the University of Pennsylvania is excavating a beautifully decorated temple built for the mortuary cult of the Dynasty XII king Senwosret III (r. 1836–1818 B.C.) at the floodplain edge in the southern part of the site. Deep in the desert a vast tomb served as Senwosret's real or symbolic burial place, mirroring that of Osiris, with his desert-edge temple and remote tomb at Umm el Qa'ab.

Even greater royal attention was lavished on Abydos during the New Kingdom (1539–1075 B.C.), attested by Stephen Harvey's excavation of the site's southernmost monument, built for the early Dynasty XVIII king Ahmose (r. 1539–1514 B.C.). It incorporates a temple and pyramid—the last royal pyramid built in Egypt. Unique scenes in the temple commemorated Ahmose's victory over the Hyksos, Canaanite invaders of Egypt. A distant desert tomb, real or symbolic, again echoed the plan of the Osiris temple and tomb. Both Senwosret and Ahmose appear in this way to be identified with Osiris and experience his regenerative powers.

The greatest of Abydos' New Kingdom monuments, a vast temple in central Abydos for Seti I (r. 1290–1279 B.C.) of Dynasty XIX, and a smaller one for Seti's son, Ramesses II (r. 1279–1213 B.C.) were built nearby (see Plate 2). Seti's temple, about an acre in extent, is the best preserved in Egypt of its period. Much of it is still roofed, and

Secrets in the Skeletons

Disease and deformity attest the hazards of daily life.

If Abydos is known for anything, it is its cemeteries. So far, we have excavated and analyzed more than 100 burials and huge concentrations of disturbed and commingled human remains. Already some surprising specimens have come to light.

In 1991, six burials of infants and young children were discovered under the floor of a house dating primarily to the First Intermediate period (2134–1797 b.c.). Three were newborns interred in pots. Another burial was of a newborn lying atop a toddler about 16 to 18 months old, both beneath a bowl. Cross-sections of this infant's arm and leg bones, which are normally tubular, showed no marrow cavities; they were completely solid! An infant without space for bone marrow cannot produce red and white blood cells and cannot survive. A rare congenital disease, this condition is known as osteopetrosis, or "stone bones."

Burials from the nearby Middle Cemetery provide further evidence of congenital abnormalities among the First Intermediate period residents of Abydos. One young woman displays a suite of anomalies—absence of permanent second premolar teeth, fusion of two bones in each foot, an extra right rib, an unusual sternum (breastbone), and only 23 vertebrae in her spine rather than the usual 24—suggesting she may have suffered from a congenital syndrome that contributed to her death in her late teens. A woman in her thirties buried nearby had an extra pair of ribs (see Plate 3). Known as cervical ribs, they occur in only 0.5 to 1.0 percent of modern humans. Thus, I was astonished to find two cases in two weeks' time. The abundance of developmental defects in the burials implies that the townspeople were exposed to as-yet-to-be-determined environmental hazards that triggered abnormalities or had a high degree of genetic relatedness.

Middle Kingdom burials from the North Cemetery have also yielded a wealth of information. Particularly disturbing are the remains of a Middle Kingdom woman who died in her early thirties. There are healed fractures in her left hand, right wrist, and both sides of her rib cage. Possible trauma to the right side of her jaw caused arthritis in her temporomandibular joint. Most of the fractures are well healed, and she lived long after those injuries. An infected fracture of her right wrist, however, was a more recent trauma. This type of fracture occurs in a fall when the outstretched hands absorb the impact. The final injury—a stab wound to her left ribs—was one she did not survive. Under magnification, the wound's edges show only slight evidence of new bone formation. This lack of healing indicates she died within days of the stabbing. The cut on her ribs and the pattern of fractures suggest the woman was battered throughout much of her life and, ultimately, may have been murdered.

–Brenda J. Baker

many beautifully carved and painted scenes and texts are well preserved. In addition to the standard cult scenes, they include a rendition of the Osiris myth and a famous king list, naming many of Egypt's rulers over a 1,700-year period. Immediately behind Seti's temple is a unique "Osirieon," a huge subterranean chamber dedicated to the worship of Seti-as-Osiris (the king was actually buried at Thebes) and reached by a corridor decorated as a royal tomb.

Royal ka-chapels continued to be built on the scarp overlooking the Osiris temple. A large one was dedicated to Ramesses II, and a smaller but beautifully decorated one, for Thutmosis III (r. 1479–1425 B.C.), has been discovered by Mary Ann Pouls Wegner. The latter had a unique plan, seemingly oriented toward Osiris' tomb at Umm el Qa'ab.

Abydos continued to flourish for another 1,500 years. Although the monuments of south Abydos were abandoned, the site's core area, which included Osiris' temple, Umm el Qa'ab, and the Seti I temple, remained an important religious center. The annual processional festival continued until the route was blocked by a Roman cemetery. A new Osiris temple was built in the fourth century B.C. and remained active well into the early centuries A.D. At the Seti temple, an "oracle" cult of the ugly but popular protective god Bes thrived well into the fifth century A.D., long after most of Egypt was Christianized. Since Abydos lost importance with the onset of Christianity, its innumerable structures decayed and sank into the desert sands.

Today, the vast expanse of Abydos seems largely devoid of ancient towns and villages, but in fact major and minor ones once flourished here. Our excavations, as well as those of Gunter Dreyer, are revealing archaeological riches that earlier excavators often missed, though the work of some—such as Flinders Petrie—has enduring value. Continued research will no doubt illuminate the lives of those who built this sacred landscape of Egypt's first pharaohs.

4

QUEST FOR WENI THE ELDER

An Old Kingdom cemetery yields the tomb of a "True Governor of Upper Egypt."

by JANET RICHARDS

EVERYONE WHO HAS STUDIED ANCIENT EGYPTIAN history is familiar with the autobiographical inscription of Weni the Elder, an enterprising individual who lived during Dynasty VI (ca. 2323–2150 B.C.) of the Old Kingdom. The inscription, carved on a limestone slab, describes Weni's service under three kings, culminating in his appointment as governor of Upper Egypt. Scholars have hailed it as one of the most important texts from ancient Egypt and have used it to illustrate the rise of a class of self-made men in the Old Kingdom, whose upward mobility rested on their abilities and not on noble birth. The slab bearing the inscription had been excavated on behalf of the Egyptian government by Auguste Mariette in 1860, from a tomb in the low desert, in an area which he called the "Middle Cemetery." Until recently, however, the precise location of the middle cemetery had never been determined, and thus the location of Weni's tomb remained unknown.

In 1995, the Abydos Middle Cemetery Project, of which I am director, began surveying an area we believed to be the most likely candidate for Weni's burial. Our surface survey documented numerous Dynasty VI ceramics and ruined mud-brick mastabas (surface chapels), including one we thought had promise as belonging to Weni. It was badly damaged, in a manner consistent with the removal of architectural elements, such as those taken by Mariette. Armed with that information and a survey of Mariette's finds in the Egyptian Museum, Cairo, we returned to the site in September, 1999.

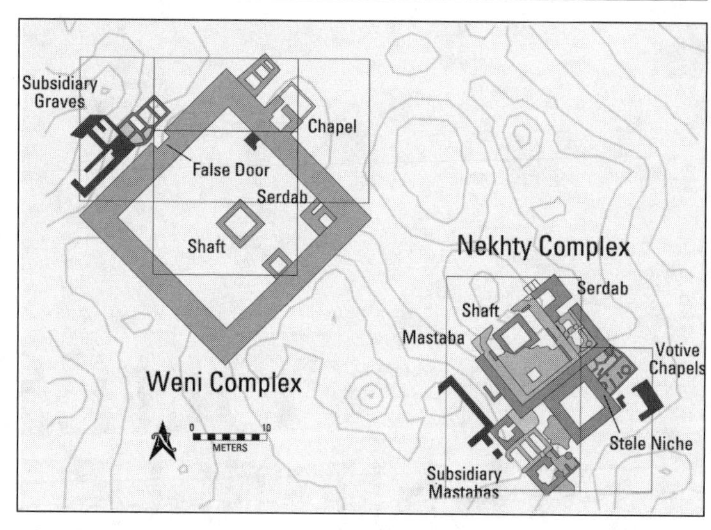

The rediscovered remains of two tomb complexes shed light on Old Kingdom burial practices.

Excavations revealed that our promising mastaba did not belong to Weni. Instead, the grave was that of a prince and chief priest, Nekhty, and it was the focus of a large complex and a number of subsiderary monuments constructed around it in the late Old Kingdom, the First Intermediate Period, the Middle Kingdom, and the Late Period. North of Nekhty's complex, however, lies an even larger structure, and it was here that we found the most compelling evidence for Weni the Elder (see Plate 5). In 1996, we had documented a mud-brick structure 53 feet long on its north face. Excavation revealed it to be a massive enclosure 95 feet on each side, ten feet thick, and more than 16 feet high. Within this enclosure was a great burial shaft along with two smaller shafts, and the whole structure would have been filled with clean sand and roofed over to give it the appearance of being a solid mastaba. The mound is situated at the highest point in the Middle Cemetery, and its visual impact on inhabitants of the town below would have echoed that of the great Early Dynastic funerary enclosures across the wadi in the North Cemetery.

Early in the season, we excavated inscribed relief fragments from this area bearing the name "Weni the Elder," and a title, "True Governor of Upper Egypt," the highest promotion recorded in Weni's autobiography. A damaged false door bore an inscription recording Weni's final promotion to the office of vizier. A series of shaft and surface burials, ranging in date from the later Old Kingdom to the First Intermediate period, lay north of this false door, suggesting that Weni's grave may have became the focus of a group cemetery—perhaps a kinship network.

Near the east face of the mastaba we discovered a massive limestone door jamb, inscribed for a vizier Iww. On one side of the jamb, a male relative presents offerings to Iww and is identified as: "His eldest son. The governor of Upper Egypt, Weni the Elder." So despite the stress laid by Weni in his autobiography on merit as the sole means of his upward mobility, it is clear that he was born into a powerful family—although he chose not to communicate this fact.

A small offering chapel with extremely thick walls was attached to the east wall of the great mastaba. Entered through a narrow doorway, the chapel was originally completely decorated with a painted reliefs depicting offering bearers; some had been removed by excavators and looters, others remained in situ. An exterior door jamb bore a standing representation of the tomb owner, preserved from the waist down. The top portion of the relief, which depicts Weni the Elder, is in the Egyptian Museum.

The final connection to Weni came from a rectangular *serdab*, or hidden chamber, in the southeast corner. This structure contained the deteriorated remains of more than 30 wooden bases for statues and statue fragments such as arms and hands, and limestone components of production scenes, including miniature basins capped with basket strainers for the production of beer. The best preserved and most significant artifact was a beautifully executed limestone statuette of the tomb owner as a young boy, identified by an inscription on its base as Weni (see Plate 4).

We believe the half-destroyed chapel is the source of Weni's autobiographical inscription. Upon his promotion to vizier at the very end of his career, he installed the false door recording that achievement along with another false door, found by Mariette. Both false doors align with the location of Weni's burial chamber, which lies north of the great shaft at a depth of more than 40 feet. We began excavation of the chamber in the spring of 2001.

5

NEW LIFE FOR THE DEAD

Atlanta's Emory University unveils a unique collection of Egyptian mummies and decorated coffins.

by PETER LACOVARA, SUE D'AURIA,
and THÉRÈSE O'GORMAN

ABRAHAM LINCOLN, GENERAL GRANT, EDWARD VII, and Theodore Roosevelt were among those who once admired the ancient Egyptian coffins and mummies displayed at the Niagara Falls Museum in Ontario. Brought to Canada in the mid-nineteenth century, the collection languished as fewer and fewer visitors patronized the museum, which in its final incarnation included the "Daredevil Hall of Fame" and was housed in an old corset factory. Despite the apparent quality of the individual coffins and mummies, no Egyptologist had ever studied them comprehensively and they were never published. Now, after nearly 150 years in Niagara Falls, the collection, reinstalled at the Michael C. Carlos Museum at Emory University, has been rescued from public obscurity and scholarly neglect.

The collection—over 145 items, including ten coffins and mummies along with funerary figures, canopic jars, amulets and jewelry, bronze sculptures, pottery, basketry, wooden objects, and relief fragments—dates from the 21st Dynasty (1070–946 B.C.) to the Roman period (31 B.C.–A.D. 395). Particularly well represented in this group, the 21st Dynasty was a period of great artistic achievement in funerary art. It marked the beginning of the Third Intermediate Period (1075–656 B.C.), a time of political turmoil and economic decline that saw control of the country split between pharaohs reigning in the Delta and the priesthood of the temple of Amun at Karnak ruling in Thebes. All the effort that had once gone into creating elaborately decorated tombs was now concentrated on coffins, the designs on which have been justifiably compared to stained glass windows in medieval cathedrals for their complex rendition of theological concepts in intricate, jewel-like colors.

Niagara Falls to Atlanta

The Egyptian Gallery contains a most interesting collection of Egyptian Antiquities and Casts of the principal curios ever discovered in that country. The Mummies are the only ones of Royal Personages exhibited in America. One of the three is the only perfect specimen in the world.

Brochures for the now-defunct Niagara Falls Museum touted not just its Egyptian collection, but also "The most interesting collection of deformities in the world. Some of the most wonderful Freaks of Nature you will ever have the opportunity of viewing, Etc." The museum, founded in 1827 by Canadian natural history enthusiast Thomas Barnett, was first housed in an old brewery. As it grew, it added to its holdings a shell and coral collection made by Harvard biologist Louis Agassiz, a humpback whale skeleton, a 77-foot diameter slab of a redwood tree trunk displayed at the 1901 Pan American Exposition, a saddle used by Wild Bill Hickock, a five-legged pig and two-headed calf, and barrels used by daredevils who braved the falls.

Most of the mummies and coffins were purchased in Egypt by a Montreal physician named James Douglas, who then sold them to Sidney Barnett, the museum founder's son, who acquired Egyptian objects to appeal to the public's growing interest in the land of the pharaohs. Douglas recorded in his 1860 journal that he dealt with Mustafa Aga Ayat. The consular agent for Britain, Belgium, and Russia, Ayat was a key figure in the antiquities trade at Luxor in the mid-nineteenth century. Taking advantage of his diplomatic immunity, he acted as a go-between for wealthy tourists and tomb robbers like the Rassul brothers, whose illicit discoveries included a cache of royal mummies at Deir el-Bahri near the Valley of the Kings.

Over the years, the museum changed hands and locations, its last home being the Spriella Corset Factory. But the introduction of casino gambling brought prosperity to Niagara Falls, and the property's increasing value led the museum's owner to sell it.

Emory's acquisition of the collection was made possible by public support from the Georgia community. In the fall of 1998, Canadian businessman Bill Jamieson, who had purchased the museum's collections, announced he was selling the Egyptian antiquities for $2 million. No Canadian museum stepped forward to purchase them, and that November we went to inspect them. We were amazed by the collection's extent and quality, and Anthony Hirschel, director of the Carlos Museum, and the board of trustees backed its acquisition. With a deadline of seven weeks to raise the money, we received a $250,000 grant early on from the Forward Arts Foundation, an Atlanta-based organization that supports the arts in Georgia. But we were running out of time and had to appeal to the public with the help of the *Atlanta Journal-Constitution*. Eventually more than 300 people contributed—from schoolchildren, to Atlantans who pitched in $10, to a museum docent who passed the hat among friends and netted $15,000. In March 1999, the sale was completed and two months later, the collection traveled to its new home.

Beneath the Wrappings

Over the past 25 years, the study of mummies has been greatly enhanced by new technologies such as CT scanning, endoscopy, and electron microscopy. Application of these techniques was a priority when the mummies arrived in Atlanta. We wanted to document how they were mummified, examine them for evidence of disease or trauma, and get a thorough understanding of their condition before proceeding with conservation measures. Between October 1999 and May 2001, nine of the mummies were taken to Emory University Hospital for X-ray and CT examination. Five of them—three men and two women, ranging in age from about 20 to about 40 at death—date to the 21st Dynasty, when the quality of mummification was at its height. Only two of them, however, had been treated carefully; most had numerous fractures, the result of rough handling during mummification. The body of a woman named Taaset was intact enough to be a candidate for endoscopy, in which a fiberscope was inserted into her body, enabling researchers to see inside her. The examination revealed a remarkably well preserved brain, lungs, and liver that had been left inside the mummy, and that provided tissue samples for later study.

The remains of two young children were particularly interesting. The mummy of one, named Hori, that had been buried in a miniature coffin during the 25th Dynasty (767–656 B.C.), was thought, because of its small size, to be a baby. X-ray images revealed that it was a child of about two years, whose legs had been amputated below the knee, perhaps to allow the body to fit an available coffin. The second child was about five years old, and there was evidence that he or she suffered from a cleft palate, a condition that can cause facial disfigurement, speech impediments, and, in severe cases, the inability to ingest food. There are several other documented cases of cleft palate from ancient Egypt, though they are not common. Two fractures, one of the skull, and a second just above the knee, may have been related to the child's death. Traces of gilding on the face of this mummy suggest it dates to the Roman period. Little disease, other than dental, could be found in the mummies, although the well-preserved body of a bearded man of the same era, who was at least 35 when he died, had evidence of tapeworms, parasites that can be transmitted by eating infected pork, a likely source of infection in ancient Egypt.

Conserving the Collection

With the acquisition of the collection came the responsibility to conserve the objects properly, and this amounted to a nearly $2-million undertaking. After being subjected to the extremes of Canada's climate for more than a century, many of the coffins and mummies had suffered considerable damage. Everything had to be carefully cleaned to remove the century-old layers of caked-on dirt and grime without harming the painted surfaces.

Perhaps the most intriguing mummy was an unwrapped body without a coffin; the body is extremely well-preserved.

In the case of Iawt-tayesheret, a lady-in-waiting to the Nubian princesses who resided in Thebes during the 25th Dynasty, it was also necessary to undo a badly botched nineteenth-century restoration of the eyes. Her image on both inner and outer coffins had originally been fitted with eyes made from either alabaster or limestone with glass or painted pupils. The eyebrows and lids were cast from bronze. The original eyes had been removed—probably stolen in antiquity—leaving bare wood eye sockets. In the late nineteenth century, the eyes were poorly and inaccurately restored with plaster. These restorations appeared much larger than the original eyes would have been, and their layer of varnish had yellowed significantly with the passing years. Fortunately, the nineteenth-century eyes were easily removed. Conservators fashioned new ones that more closely resembled those that had been created for these coffins in antiquity based on surviving ancient examples, using stable twentieth-century restoration materials to avoid any confusion for future scholars and conservators.

A Lost Pharaoh?

Perhaps the most intriguing mummy in the collection was an unwrapped body without a coffin (see Plate 6). Arne Eggebrecht of the Pelizaeus Museum in Hildesheim, Germany, was the first scholar to suggest it may be Ramesses I, the founder of the famous line that included Seti I, Ramesses II and his 50 sons, Queen Nofretari, and Ramesses III. This mummy will be the focus of a special exhibition entitled "Science, Scholarship and the Lost Pharaoh," opening in the spring of 2003.

The body is extremely well preserved. The man was probably over 45 years of age at his death and his arms are crossed over his chest, right over left, as is typical for royal mummies. The left hand was placed as though it had originally grasped an object, possibly a scepter. He also received the "royal treatment" in his careful and elaborate mummification, including the removal of the brain and internal organs. However, the heart, the seat of intelligence to the ancient Egyptians, had been left in place. Linen was placed into the back of the mouth and throat to restore their contours, which would have shrunk after the 40 days of dehydration during mummification. Five long, tightly rolled linen bundles were placed in the chest, abdomen, and pelvis. The phallus was separately wrapped, and the toes slightly splayed, indicating that they may have originally been placed in gold stalls.

If this is indeed a royal mummy, it might be one of those that had been sold out of the Deir el-Bahri cache before it was sequestered for the Cairo Museum. The cache had been discovered in Thebes in the mid-nineteenth century, when the Niagara Falls Museum was making its purchases. Whether this individual was indeed the founder of the 19th Dynasty (1292–1190 B.C.) or not remained unprovable until now. Comparative Y-chromosome DNA analysis, now under way, will allow us to match the mummy of Ramesses' son Seti I, in the Cairo Museum, to this one and could prove the identity of the putative Ramesses I once and for all. If he does indeed turn out to be the missing royal mummy, the Carlos Museum has already pledged that he will be returned to his rightful place in Egypt.

The most beautiful of the coffins belonged to the 21st Dynasty Lady Tanakhtenttahat.

Tahat and Taaset

The most beautiful of the coffins belonged to the 21st Dynasty Lady Tanakhtenttahat, a chantress in the temple of the god Amun at Karnak. Such women were usually of high rank and served in temples not as priests, but as chantresses, or singers, who presumably played instruments and recited hymns to the gods. On the coffin lid, Tanakhtenttahat, also referred to by the shorter version of her name, Tahat, is shown bedecked in a full wig surrounded by protective gods and symbols and adorned with her finest jewelry. On the sides of the coffin are delicately painted mythological scenes and depictions of Tahat being judged in the underworld and being reborn into eternal life.

Tahat's coffin belongs to the Third Intermediate Period, a time when fine wood, such as cedar of Lebanon, was not being imported and local softwoods were substituted. Such coffins were often coated with a thick layer of mud to correct defects in the wood and model the features of the body that could not be carved in its soft, splintery surface. A thin ground of fine, white gesso or plaster was then laid over the mud to form a canvas for the painting. Occasionally, as on Tahat's coffin, scarabs and other sacred images were modeled in plaster to give them the three-dimensional quality of actual jewels set into a coffin. After everything was painted, the whole surface was coated with a gleaming varnish to give it the appearance of gold.

Over the mummy was placed a coffin board, a device peculiar to the 21st Dynasty, which looked like and served as a secondary lid with more decorative elements designed to protect the deceased. The mummy found in Tahat's coffin had been carefully wrapped, but when she was examined at Emory Hospital, CT scans and X-ray images revealed that, against the custom of the period, her internal organs had not been removed. Why, in an era of elaborate mummification, this procedure was left undone was a mystery. Closer inspection of the inscriptions revealed that the coffin had been re-used, and Tahat's names had been partially erased and replaced with the name of a woman named Taaset. All over the coffin, older decoration and inscriptions had been covered up with new ones. Since Taaset could only afford a used coffin, it is no wonder that she didn't get a first-class mummification job. Such recycling seems to have been common in this period, from kings who re-used coffins and objects taken from the royal tombs in the Valley of the Kings for their own burials to private people re-using coffins and tombs.

After their long journey, the coffins and mummies will be unveiled in new galleries opening on October 6. Emory's museum is fondly known by many Atlantans as the "Mummy Museum." With these new acquisitions, the Michael C. Carlos Museum is indeed worthy of the name.

6

CASE OF THE DUMMY MUMMY

Psst!... Hey buddy, wanna buy a falcon?

by Bob Brier

FOR GENERATIONS, VENDORS ON LUXOR'S WEST bank, near the Valley of the Kings, have offered fake antiquities to tourists, who are warned by guides to bargain vigorously. It is all harmless fun. When the price of a carved pharaoh's head blackened with shoe polish drops from $200 to $20, everyone is happy. The traveler has his souvenir along with a good story to tell, and the seller has still made a huge profit. Forging Egyptian objects was also an ancient practice, a multi-million dollar industry in its time.

My first experience with ancient fakes came 20 years ago during a seminar that I was teaching on mummies. At the time, animal mummies were plentiful and could be legally taken out of Egypt. My classes would unwrap and perform an autopsy on a fish or bird mummy. Only once did we work on a cat, but it was too painful for cat lovers in the class. My students would form an archaeological team, one serving as photographer, another as artist. One would take the mummy to be X-rayed, another would analyze the linen wrappings, and yet another would conserve the bones.

One year, we unwrapped a falcon, or so we thought from its shape. A beak had been formed on the outside with a bit of resin, and a falcon's eyes had been painted on the wrappings. The X ray, however, revealed a jumble of bones. When the class unwrapped the mummy, it became clear that something was very wrong. The head was missing and there were not enough bones to make up a complete skeleton. The mummy was simply a random bunch of bones wrapped to look like a falcon.

I didn't think much more about this experience until two years ago, when I was filming a documentary for The Learning Channel. I wanted to X-ray a few mummies and show what was inside. Yale's Peabody Museum kindly loaned me a cat and an ibis. I contributed a friend's falcon mummy. The ibis came out beautifully, with its long beak clearly defined and all the bones perfectly in place. Then came the falcon's turn. I had selected a beautiful one, with markings carefully painted on elaborate wrappings. The X ray, however, showed no bones within—only rolls of cloth (see Plates 7, 8, and 9). We nicknamed it the "dummy mummy."

Animal mummification was a big business in ancient Egypt, and it seems as though a large portion of it was fraudulent. Ancient Egyptians mummified all kinds of creatures, from bulls to birds, and for different reasons. Some were pets, preserved to keep their masters company in the next world, but most were raised to be sacrificed as offerings to the gods.

When someone wished a favor from a god, he or she might leave an offering of a bronze statue, food, or an animal mummy in the god's temple. Cats were associated with Bast, a feline goddess. Cat mummies were still so numerous at the end of the nineteenth century that shiploads of them were sent to England to be ground into fertilizer. Cat cemeteries were located at Bubastis, the city of Bast in the Delta, and at other towns up and down the Nile.

Animal mummification was a big business in ancient Egypt.

More extensive than the cat cemeteries were the ibis and falcon galleries at Saqqara—miles of tunnels containing mummified birds. Carved into the walls of tunnels were thousands of niches, each with a mummified bird. When space in the walls ran out, the mummies were placed in ceramic pots and stacked floor to ceiling. The ibis was sacred to the god Toth, who was often depicted as a human with the head of an ibis. Toth was associated with the moon. The falcon was sacred to the god Horus, associated with the sun.

Along the route to the galleries were stalls where pilgrims could purchase mummified birds, many of which had been raised for that purpose. After a pilgrim selected one, it was placed in a ceramic pot and sealed. Priests of the gallery would place it in a niche and, for a small fee, say a prayer for the pilgrim.

A collection of the writings of Hor, a priest in charge of the ibis galleries around 200 B.C., explains that hundreds of people were involved in the animal mummification business at Saqqara. One of the more important jobs was that of the "doorkeeper," whom Hor says supervised the birds and their young, and was probably responsible for raising the ibises.

Unlike ibises, falcons cannot be raised in captivity, so there was no way that the supply of birds could meet the demand. Dummy mummies, like the one I X-rayed for television, were thus created out of fancy bundles of rags and sold to unsuspecting pilgrims. My colleagues Salima Ikram, who has studied animal mummies at the Egyptian Museum in Cairo, and Sue D'Auria, an assistant curator at the Huntington Museum of Art in West Virginia, confirmed our experience—many falcon mummies they have examined also proved to be ancient fakes.

Like the guides on the west bank of Luxor, Hor wanted to ensure that the pilgrims were not cheated. In one memo he wrote, "There must be one god in one vessel," or a bird in every sacrificial pot.

7

A THOROUGHLY MODERN MUMMY

Experimental archaeology—step by gruesome step, the Egyptian way.

by Bob Brier

FOR 3,000 YEARS THE ANCIENT EGYPTIANS MUMmified their dead, but no embalmer ever wrote down how he did it. Egypt was a nation of accountants who recorded almost everything—battles, offerings to temples, long lines of kings—but not a single papyrus exists telling how a human cadaver was prepared for the journey to the afterlife. For centuries mummification remained a closely guarded secret, that is, until Herodotus, the Greek historian and traveler, visited Egypt around 450 B.C. Herodotus described mummification in great detail:

As much of the brain as possible is extracted through the nostrils with an iron hook, and what the hook cannot reach is dissolved with drugs. Next the flank is slit open with a sharp Ethiopian stone and the entire contents of the abdomen removed. The cavity is then thoroughly cleansed and washed out, first with palm wine and again with a solution of pounded spices. Then it is filled with pure crushed myrrh, cassia, and all other aromatic substances, except frankincense.

The incision is sewn up and then the body is placed in natron, covered for 70 days, never longer. When this period, which may not be longer, is over, the body is washed and then wrapped from head to feet in linen which has been cut into strips and smeared on the underside with gum, which is commonly used by the Egyptians as glue. In this condition the body is returned to the family....

Modern research has confirmed much of Herodotus' account. X-ray images have shown that, for top-of-the-line mummifications, the brain was indeed removed via the nasal passages. It is also well established that the internal organs were removed. Chemical analyses of materials found within the bodies have shown that myrrh and other spices were used in the cleansing process.

Based on Herodotus' account and Egyptologists' research, the basics of mummification had been pieced together by the 1920s and scholars felt that little more was to be learned. In 1992, while writing a book on mummification, I began to realize just how wrong they were. There was a lot that we didn't know. Did the embalmers drain the blood? How do you remove a brain through the nose? What kind of tools did the embalmers use? How was natron used? What surgical procedures were performed? I realized that the only way to answer such questions was to actually mummify a human cadaver.

It would take nearly a year just to assemble the materials we needed. The ancient Egyptians used both bronze and copper knives. Michael Silva, a New York silversmith with a passion for archaeology, would manufacture ours, using a ratio of 88% copper and 12% tin, the same as found in ancient examples. He would also fashion a long coat hanger-like instrument that we could use to remove the brain through the nose. Herodotus said the embalmers used "a sharp Ethiopian stone" for the body incision. This meant obsidian, volcanic glass. My sister-in-law introduced me to archaeology graduate student James Eighmey at Arizona State University who could flake obsidian (a very difficult task), and he provided an assortment of blades, both fancy and crude.

The natron was the most difficult material to obtain. Natron is a mixture of sodium carbonate, sodium bicarbonate, sodium chloride, and some minor impurities—basically baking soda and table salt. The ancient Egyptians obtained their natron in an area they called "the salt fields" about 60 miles north of modern Cairo. Today it is called Wadi Natrun. It is an amazing place. Several small lakes, colored red by algae and brine shrimp, are rimmed by thick, white natron crusts. Natron, present in the soil, goes into solution when the water table rises each year. When the water table falls, the natron is deposited on the shores. Armed with a shovel and empty cement sacks, I went to gather my natron. I collected 400 pounds, breaking it up into small chunks which I would pulverize later. This was enough, I estimated, to comfortably cover one cadaver. I also picked up frankincense and myrrh at Cairo's spice market, imported, as in ancient times, from the Sudan, Yemen, and Somalia. Without doubt, one of the strangest ingredients we needed was palm wine, which according to Herodotus was used to wash out the abdominal cavity. Only one wine store in Cairo could get it for us, importing it from Nigeria. The label had a pyramid on it, which we took as a good omen, but the label also said "Shake well for full nutritional value."

BACK IN THE UNITED STATES, OTHER preparations had to be made. Several caches of embalmers' equipment—including linens, wooden ankh symbols, an embalmer's board, and jars used to store natron—have been found by Egyptologists. Herbert Winlock, a curator in the Metropolitan Museum of Art's Egyptian department in the 1920s, had discovered the most complete embalmer's cache on the west bank of Luxor. Using the Met's records of the find, we set to work to copy the natron storage jars. Soon Evan Rosenthal, a graduate student and master potter at the C.W. Post Campus of Long Island University, was making replicas of the ancient jars at the rate of two a day. He was so good at it that I asked him to make the four canopic jars in which the mummy's internal organs would be stored.

Without a doubt, one of the strangest ingredients we needed was palm wine.

As resurrectionists, Egyptians believed the body would literally get up and go into the next world, but to keep the mummy from decaying, they had to remove the internal organs. Because the body had to be complete in the afterlife, the internal organs were saved in four canopic jars. The word "canopic" derives from early Egyptologists, who linked the human-headed jars to Canopus, a Greek ship captain, according to Homer, deified after his death and worshiped in the form of a jar. Prior to the New Kingdom (before 1570 B.C.), jars had lids in the shape of human heads, representing the Four Sons of Horus (the falcon god), who watched over the internal organs. Later, three of the four human heads were replaced with animal heads: those of a jackal, an ape, and a falcon.

The ancient Egyptians were often buried with small magical statues called *ushabtiu*, ancient Egyptian for "answerers." If you were called upon in the next world to do work, the statues would answer for you and do the required task. They were often painted with magical spells to ensure that they would indeed do the job. A wealthy Egyptian could be buried with 365 *ushabtiu*, one for each day of the year. For a few weeks, C.W. Post looked like an ancient Egyptian funeral workshop, with the ceramic department cranking them out and my hieroglyph class painting them with spells.

Finally, we had all the materials except a proper embalmer's table. With the help of Tom Wood, a retired physics professor from the University of Pennsylvania and master carpenter, we made a replica of the board Winlock had found at Luxor in the 1920s. Using only hand tools, we pegged it together, but questions about the board that earlier Egyptologists had raised quickly resurfaced. At nearly six feet wide, it seemed far broader than necessary. Wood was scarce in Egypt, so there must have been a reason for the extravagant size. And what was the purpose of what looked like four railroad ties spaced across the width of the board? These questions would answer themselves once we began.

For the cadaver we used a body donor, someone who had left his body to science. We screened possible donors for health hazards, and eventually selected an elderly man who had died of a stroke.

I now had everything I needed, as well as a tremendous support team, of which the most important member was Ronn Wade, director of Maryland's State Anatomy Board and co-director of the project. His long interest in mummification began as a kid when he mummified a rat for a science project. Ronn is not only an anatomist, he is also a licensed mortician. His knowledge of anatomy and surgical skills would prove essential when the going got tough.

We would perform our mummification at the University of Maryland's School of Medicine in Baltimore. Would it work? We certainly had our doubts. The ancient embalmers were professionals at mummification with millennia of experience, while we were trying it for the first time. As Ronn and I discussed the impending surgical procedures, we agreed that the removal of the brain would be the most difficult. We were right.

Egyptology journals occasionally contain articles theorizing how the brain was removed through the nose. They describe a cadaver lying on its back while a long hooked tool is inserted into the nose and pushed through the cribiform plate (a thin, honeycombed bone behind the eyes) and into the cranium. A small piece of the brain adheres to the end of the tool and can be pulled out. The process is repeated until the entire brain is removed. That was the theory, but no modern researcher had ever actually done it. One week before we were to begin, Ronn and I tested this process on two heads obtained from body-donors, but could not get the brains out—they weren't viscous enough to stick to the tool. We finally hypothesized that if we used the tool much like a kitchen whisk inside the cranium, the brain would liquefy and then, if we inverted the cadaver, would run out through the nose. We would try this method on the donated body waiting to be mummified. We inserted a long bronze instrument, shaped like a miniature harpoon, inside the nasal passage and hammered it through the cribiform plate into the cranium with a wooden block. Then we inserted the coat hanger-shaped instrument into the cranium and rotated it for ten minutes on each side, breaking down the brain enough so it would run out when the cadaver was inverted. It worked. Using the coat-hanger tool, we then forced thin strips of linen into the cranium via the nasal passages and used them as swabs. With repeated swabbing they eventually came out clean. It was now time for the removal of the internal organs.

The first step was the abdominal incision. Herodotus wrote that a "sharp Ethiopian stone" was used. I had always thought that this must have been for ritualistic purposes (perhaps harkening back to archaic times when only stone knives were available). The Egyptians had bronze knives, which I thought would have been more effective surgical instruments, but, we quickly discovered that bronze knives were too dull for such a use. So when the time came for the abdominal incision, I made it with an obsidian flake.

Egyptian incisions were almost always on the left side of a mummy's abdomen, and, in preparation for this project, I had taken careful notice of the length of these incisions on existing mummies. They were surprisingly small, only about three and one-half inches long. Embalmers wanted to minimize damage so that when the body was resurrected it would look natural. That is also why the brain was removed via the nasal passages rather than opening the cranium itself.

Working through such a small abdominal incision created two problems. Only one hand fits inside, which makes internal cutting difficult. It is also impossible to see what you are doing, which raises a question about the anatomical knowledge of ancient Egyptian embalmers. It is often asserted that because they practiced mummification, the Egyptians were the most knowledgeable about anatomy in the ancient world. Not so. Working through such a small incision, embalmers weren't able to see the organs as they dissected them. Until the Greek occupation of Egypt (beginning in 332 B.C. with Alexander the Great) and the establishment of a medical school in Alexandria (during the Ptolemaic period, 332–30 B.C.), dissection of cadavers for the purpose of study was prohibited in Egypt. Indeed, even when a mummification took place, the man who made the abdominal incision—"the slitter"—was ritually pelted with stones "for he had defiled a human body." Additionally, there is linguistic evidence that the Egyptians did not know their anatomy. For instance, there is no word for "kidney" in the ancient Egyptian language and it is possible many embalmers were unaware that human kidneys existed or simply did not know their function. Hidden behind the peritoneum, a membrane in the abdominal cavity, and not easily reached through a small abdominal incision, the kidneys were often left inside mummies.

The hieroglyphs that normally come at the end of words to clarify their meanings (determinatives) suggest that much of Egyptian anatomical knowledge was based on animals, not on humans. Often the hieroglyphs in the words for both internal and external organs, the heart for example, depict nonhuman organs. So, when we began to remove the internal organs in our mummy, I had the feeling that although ancient embalmers were far more experienced at what they did than were we, Ronn and I certainly knew more about anatomy.

As we proceeded, a natural order for removing the organs emerged. The small intestine came out first and along with it the pancreas, followed by the spleen. Then we removed the kidneys. As we removed the bladder and stomach, I began thinking about the liver, which can weigh several pounds and requires two hands to hold. Could we remove it intact through such a small abdominal incision? We tried manipulating it from the outside, moving it to the opening, then trying to squeeze it through. The liver is composed of lobes and our idea was to push it out one lobe at a time. It didn't work. In the end, we lengthened the incision another half inch, and it popped out, much like a newborn. The lungs were next.

We cut through the diaphragm, which separates the abdominal and thoracic cavities. Just as in an ancient mummification, we removed the lungs but left the heart. The heart was the only organ intentionally left in place by the Egyptians. They believed that you thought with your heart and therefore would need it so you could recite magical spells when you were resurrected in the next world. Indeed, there is little evidence that Egyptians understood the function of the brain, which explains why it was the only organ they did not preserve at the time of mummification.

With the removal of the lungs, our surgical procedures were complete. We had established which tools were most likely used by the ancient embalmers, how the brain was removed, and the probable order in which the organs were taken out, but we were still far from finished. The body now had to be dehydrated in natron; just how it was done in antiquity has been the subject of considerable debate.

AT THE END OF THE 1932 BORIS KARLOFF movie, *The Mummy*, when the villain is preparing to mummify the heroine, an embalmer is shown stirring a large vat of natron. This scene was based upon the best available archaeological information of the time. Egyptologists Warren Dawson and Alfred Lucas of England had just published separate papers suggesting that the ancient Egyptian embalmers soaked their cadavers in solutions of natron and then dehydrated them. The theory that a solution of natron was used originates in a mistranslation of Herodotus. When describing how the natron was used, he employed a Greek word that means to preserve like fish. Fish of course can be either salted or pickled in brine. One of the earliest works on mummies, Englishman Thomas Pettigrew's 1834 *History of Egyptian Mummies*, relied on a translation that used the word "steep," and later scholars assumed the Egyptians soaked their mummies in a natron solution.

There are several compelling arguments against natron having been used in solution. First, it may have seemed counterintuitive to the ancient embalmers to soak the bodies in a liquid when the ultimate goal was to dehydrate them. Second, the Egyptians mummified millions of bodies over the centuries, so there would have been thousands of huge vats if this method was used, but none has ever been found. Third, Herodotus notes that the body cavity was packed with crushed spices and then placed in the natron. If it were in a solution, the spices would have washed out. All this suggests that the Egyptians used their natron dry.

From studying ancient mummies, we knew that the embalmers often placed small packets of natron inside the mummy to absorb internal body fluids. These packets were formed by cutting a square of linen, placing the natron in the center, and then gathering and tying the four corners together. One of the hieroglyphs in the combination that forms the word "natron," may even depict an embalmer's packet. The first four hieroglyphs are purely phonetic and indicate how the word was pronounced, something like *hesmen*. The last sign (actually two combined), the determinative, helps clarify the meaning of the word. On top is a banner or flag, the sign for "god" which suggests the religious use of natron. At bottom is a small pouch, a natron packet. We filled the abdominal and thoracic cavities with 29 packets. Then we were ready to put the body on the embalmer's board and cover it with natron to dehydrate it from the outside.

When we placed the body on the embalmer's board, we discovered the function of the planks running across it. When the heart stops beating, the only factor affecting the location of body fluids is gravity, so the fluids come to rest at the lower portions of the body. Since the natron is the primary desiccant, one wants it as close to the body fluids as possible, and this is the function of the planks—they held a considerable amount of natron in place beneath the body, near most of the fluids. Without the planks, the natron would slide out from under the body. We covered the board with natron to the height of the planks, set the body on top it, and then poured more natron over the cadaver until it was completely covered. Here we discovered why the board was so wide: to reach a height sufficient to cover the body a rather wide base was needed. We also determined that more than 400 pounds of natron, which we had, were required.

70 days was the period for the entire process, from death to burial.

The internal organs were placed in pottery dishes, covered with natron, and put at the corners of the board to dehydrate along with the body. The conditions in our mummification room were controlled to roughly approximate a tomb in the Valley of the Kings, with the humidity just below 30 percent and the temperature around 105 degrees Fahrenheit. The big question was how long to leave the body in this environment before removing it for wrapping.

No one knew for certain how long the body remained in natron. Ancient texts mention different periods. Herodotus wrote "They conceal the body for 70 days, embalmed in natron; no longer time is permitted for embalming." Diodorus, a later writer, says "they carefully prepare the entire body for more than 30 days.... " Other references indicate that Diodorus is closer to the mark than Herodotus. The Bible says that Joseph's father, Jacob, died in Egypt and notes that 70 days was the period of mourning, and that 40 of those days were for embalming. Some of those 40 days would have been taken up with preparations, so the body would have been in natron for something less that 40 days. The Rhind papyrus, one of the few ancient Egyptian texts that discusses mummification, indicates that the body was "at rest for 30 days in the Place of Cleansing." In an ancient Egyptian short story, a man named Neneferkaptah is mummified; we are told there were 35 days for wrapping and he was in his coffin on day 70. All of these clues suggested to us that 70 days was the period for the entire process, from death to burial, and that the body remained in natron for approximately 35 of those days, the amount of time we left our cadaver in natron.

Ronn and I wondered why a mummy looks like it does, shriveled and dark colored. Was it the result of thousands of years in a tomb or buried in the sand, or was it because of the mummification process itself? We would soon be the first people in 2,000 years to see what one looked like right after it was removed from natron.

When we entered the room after 35 days of waiting, there was a strong odor, but not of putrefaction. The smell was probably from the cedar, palm, and lotus oils used in the mummification. Around the body the natron had formed hard clumps stained dark brown from the body fluids they had absorbed. In some places the natron had congealed so firmly that a metal bar had to be used to break it up so it could be shoveled away. The natron beneath the body had not clumped, but was moist—the consistency of wet sand.

As the natron was removed and the hands, feet, and head emerged, we were struck by how similar they were to those of an ancient mummy—dark brown, with the hands and feet rigid, fingers and toes incapable of being flexed (see Plate 10). The head still retained the hair and though desiccated, the facial features were essentially unchanged. The process was responsible for all this, not the millennia in a tomb; mummies are brown probably because as the tissue and blood dehydrates, various elements, like iron, become more concentrated.

We then removed the natron packets with which we had filled the abdominal and thoracic cavities. They had nearly doubled in weight with the absorption of fluids. When the mummification began, the body weighed approximately 180 pounds, now it weighed about 77 pounds. There was still a bit of moisture in the larger muscles—the quadriceps of the thighs and the gluteus maximus of the backside; these areas were still soft to the touch. There was no doubt that if we replaced the wet natron beneath the planks with dry natron and replaced the mummy in the "tomb" (the climate-controlled mummification room) it would dehydrate quickly. We also had the option of wrapping the mummy and placing it in the tomb without natron. We chose this second option because we would learn more. The official 70 days of mummification were over, but undoubtedly there were times when ancient embalmers wrapped bodies while they were still a bit moist; we would see what happened in these cases.

We did a preliminary wrapping and placed the mummy in its tomb on the blocks of the embalmer's board, but with no natron, where it remained for more than four months. When we entered the tomb for the second time, once again there was no smell of putrefaction. The moisture remaining in the body had not caused it to decay. The body had lost an additional 28 pounds, and now almost all the moisture was gone. We took tissue samples from the organs we had removed and also from different parts of the body so we could later determine the efficacy of our dehydration method. It was now time for the final wrapping, and our big surprise.

Using pure white linen we wrapped the individual fingers and toes and then the limbs and torso. We intended to cross the arms over the chest, in a manner similar to mummies of the pharaohs of the New Kingdom, but were shocked to find it was impossible. The fully dehydrated body was too inflexible, the arms could not be bent without breaking them. Rather than damage the mummy, we placed the arms at the sides with the hands over the pubis and completed the wrapping. Our inability to cross the arms may have been our most important finding. We had assumed that the goal of placing the body in natron was total dehydration. This, we now see, is probably wrong. When the body is totally dehydrated it can't be positioned for wrapping. The goal of the embalmers was to remove as much fluid as necessary to prevent decay, but to leave just enough so the arms and other parts could be placed as desired. After 35 days in the natron, we could have positioned the arms.

It has been five years since we began our experiment, and up to the present our mummy has been kept at room temperature at the State Anatomy Board in Maryland. Periodically we check the body for signs of decay and so far have detected none.

Our mummy may help to answer a question that has been puzzling researchers, namely, why has it been so difficult to reproduce long sequences of DNA from ancient Egyptian mummies? Has the DNA degraded over the thousands of years? Or is its absence the result of the mummification process itself? Tissue samples are frequently requested by colleagues for their studies on various aspects of tissue preservation; currently, laboratories around the world are attempting to reproduce the DNA from our mummy. If they are successful, we will know it is the thousands of years and not the process that makes DNA replication so difficult. DNA studies in mummies may also hold the answers to many Egyptological questions—we may be able to establish the origins of the Egyptians, and we may also be able to identify unknown royal mummies by comparing their DNA to that of mummies who are positively identified.

Since the mummy project, both Ronn and I have tried to resume normal lives. Ronn still directs Maryland's State Anatomy Board. I am back to teaching Egyptology at the C.W. Post Campus of Long Island University, and am currently conducting research on the mummies of the frozen Inka sacrifices, three children, recently found on Mount Llullaillaco in Argentina. A major part of our task regarding the mummy Ronn and I made now lies in bringing information about our work to the attention of the public. When we give lectures, one of the most frequently asked questions is: "Did the body donor know he would be mummified?" No, he didn't. Body donors don't know to which scientific project their bodies are going. So our mummy will be very surprised when he wakes up in the next world.

PART IV:

ASIA & THE MIDDLE EAST

9

SAGA OF THE PERSIAN PRINCESS

In a dangerous corner of the world, uneasy neighbors clamor for the gilded remains of a mummified noblewoman. Trouble is, she's a fraud.

by KRISTIN M. ROMEY *and* MARK ROSE

THE BIZARRE TALE OF A MUMMY ADORNED WITH a cuneiform-inscribed gold plaque identifying it as a 2,600-year-old Persian princess, perhaps, according to one translation, a daughter of the king Xerxes, began trickling out of Pakistan this past October. Found during a murder investigation, the mummy, an amalgam of Egyptian and Persian elements, had evidently been for sale on the black market for a cool $11 million. While archaeologists in Karachi tried to make sense of the mummy, a dispute between Iran and Pakistan broke out over its ownership. Afghanistan's Taliban regime hinted that they, too, might claim it. Then, one November day, thousands of miles from where the mummy lay in Pakistan's National Museum under the watchful eye of armed guards, ARCHAEOLOGY was shown documents identifying the Persian princess as a fraud.

According to newspaper reports, Pakistani authorities learned of the mummy in mid-October, when they received a tip that Karachi resident Ali Akbar had a video tape showing a mummy he was selling. After interrogation, Akbar led police to the remains, which were being kept in the house of tribal leader Wali Mohammad Reeki in Quetta, capital of Pakistan's southwestern Balochistan Province, which borders Iran and Afghanistan. Reeki told police he had received the mummy from Sharif Shah Bakhi, an Iranian who allegedly found it after an earthquake in a nearby town. Reeki and Bakhi had agreed to sell the mummy and split the profits; Akbar's role is less clear. Reeki said an unidentified representative of an anonymous foreign buyer had offered 60 million rupees ($1.1 million) for the mummy, well below the 600 million rupee ($11 million) asking price. Reeki and Akbar were charged with violating Pakistan's Antiquity Act, which carries a ten-year maximum sentence; Bakhi remains at large.

The mummy was brought to the National Museum in Karachi as news of it spread quickly through the local and international press. In an October 26 press conference, clips of which appeared on NBC's evening news, archaeologist Ahmed Hasan Dani of Quaid-e-Azam University in Islamabad announced that the mummy, wrapped in Egyptian style and resting in a wooden coffin carved with cuneiform writing and images of the Zoroastrian deity Ahura Mazda, was that of a princess dated to ca. 600 B.C.

Museum officials shared results of a preliminary examination of the mummy and its inscriptions with a hungry press: her remains lay atop a mat coated with a mixture of wax and honey and were covered by a stone slab with additional cuneiform inscriptions; her name was Khor-ul-Gayan or Tundal Gayan; and she may have been the daughter of Karoosh-ul-Kabir, first ruler of Persia's Khamam-ul-Nishiyan Dynasty. Alternatively, Dani said, the mummy could be of an Egyptian princess, married to a Persian prince during the reign of Cyrus I (640–590 B.C.), whose body had been preserved following the custom of her own country. Various theories circulated about how it came to Quetta. National Museum curator Asma Ibrahim suggested it may have been looted from a tomb in the Hamadan region of western Iran or the southwestern Pakistani area of Kharan.

Shortly after the press conference, the Iranian Cultural Heritage Organization, claiming the mummy was of a member of the Persian royal family, said it would take legal action through UNESCO for its return. Salim-ul-Haq, director of Pakistan's Archaeological Department's Headquarters, retorted that the mummy was found in Kharan in Balochistan Province, "which is one hundred percent Pakistani territory. The mummy is property of Pakistan." At that point, Iran said it was cooperating with Interpol for the mummy's return. Pakistan's foreign minister warned against politicizing the issue, while the Taliban, the rulers of most of Afghanistan, demanded that their archaeologists play a role in deciding its ownership.

There were divisions even within Pakistan. A petition filed with the Balochistan High Court asked for the return of the princess to Quetta, claiming the police raid in which it was seized had been illegal and that the action had "spread panic among the people of Balochistan, who felt deprived of their cultural, historic, and valuable heritage." The Awan tribe of Balochistan, saying the inscriptions proved the princess belonged to the Awan royal family of Hika Munshi, asked that the mummy be moved immediately to the local Kallar Kahar Fossils Museum.

There were signs the Pakistanis were not sure exactly what they were keeping under guard at their National Museum.

While the conflict continued, there were subtle signs the Pakistanis were not sure exactly what they were keeping under guard in their National Museum. The local press reported that insurance companies were reluctant to cover the mummy until its legitimacy was proven. Dani insisted it was of Egyptian origin, pointing out that mummification was not practiced in Iran or Iraq, and conceded that the cuneiform inscriptions may have been added by smugglers after the body was taken out of Egypt.

Possibly in response to Dani's assertions, Iran fired back, claiming that an Italian archaeologist had translated the inscription, presumably through examining photographs, and confirmed that the mummy was of a member of the ancient Persian royal family.

TWO WEEKS AFTER THE DISCOVERY FIRST hit the press, Oscar White Muscarella of the Metropolitan Museum of Art and author of *The Lie Became Great: The Forgery of Ancient Near Eastern Cultures*, visited ARCHAEOLOGY's offices, where we asked for his thoughts on the Persian princess. While unaware of the recent find, Muscarella volunteered that its description sounded remarkably similar to photographs of a gold-adorned mummy sent to him last March by a New Jersey resident on behalf of an unidentified dealer in Pakistan—in fact, they were the same.

Muscarella had received four photographs of a mummy in a wooden coffin, replete with golden crown, mask, and inscribed breastplate. An accompanying letter stated that the mummy was owned by a Pakistani acquaintance and was brought by Zoroastrian families many years ago from Iran to Pakistan. The author claimed that the mummy was the daughter of the Persian king Xerxes, referring to an attached one-page translation of the cuneiform inscription on the breastplate. The owners, he wrote, had a video of the mummy—most likely the same video found with Ali Akbar in Karachi—that could be sent to New York if the museum was interested in purchasing the princess.

Muscarella, who suspected immediately that the mummy was a fraud, contacted the translator of the inscription, a cuneiform expert at a major American university, and found out that the dealer's New Jersey representative had not given him the complete analysis of it. The inscription does indeed contain the line "I am the daughter of the great king Xerxes," as well as a sizeable chunk lifted straight from a famous inscription of the king Darius (522–486 B.C.) at Behistun in western Iran. The Behistun inscription, which records the king's accomplishments, dates to 520–519 B.C., substantially later than the 600 B.C. date proposed for the mummy. The second page of analysis listed several problems with the mummy's inscription that led the scholar to believe that its author wrote in a manner inconsistent with Old Persian. The inscription, he concluded, was likely a modern falsification, probably dating "from no earlier than the 1930s."

Convinced that the scholar's twentieth-century date was incorrect, the dealer's representative apparently sent a small piece of the wooden coffin to a carbon-dating lab. The results indicated it was approximately 250 years old "which cannot be called modern," sniffed the representative in a follow-up letter to the cuneiform expert.

Muscarella politely broke off communications with the man. Seven months later, police raided the house in Quetta and the Persian princess surfaced again—this time under the glare of the international press.

ARCHAEOLOGY has submitted Muscarella's documentation to federal authorities, who have forwarded the matter to Interpol. Hopefully, by the time this article goes to press, the dispute between uneasy neighbors in a dangerous corner of the world will be resolved. While the Persian princess may be a fraud, perhaps a genuine Egyptian mummy with forged Persian additions, she is a reminder of the powerful emotions that can be sparked by unprecedented, or unbelievable, archaeological discoveries.

Note: On April 17, 2001, after many months of controversy, Pakistan's National Museum curator, Asma Isbrahim, issued an 11 page report declaring the mummy a fraud, and possibly a murder victim.

10

BIBLICAL ICONOCLAST

Israel Finkelstein tilts with colleagues over the history of Early Iron Age Palestine.

BY HAIM WATZMAN

NO ONE IN THE FIELD OF BIBLICAL ARCHAEOLogy likes the smell of battle better than Israel Finkelstein. When the director of Tel Aviv University's Sonia and Marco Nadler Institute of Archaeology gets up to speak at the institute's annual seminar on Early Iron Age Palestine, a ripple runs through the audience—the listeners know that within a few minutes they'll either be seething or cheering. In 2001, Finkelstein, 52, in white jacket and blue-and-yellow checked tie, saunters up to the stage with the usual impish grin that, together with his clipped beard and intense gaze, make him look like a natty young Elijah with a sense of humor.

His talk centers around Goliath. Deconstructing verses from Samuel that portray the giant warrior, Finkelstein maintains that the description is of a Greek mercenary in the Egyptian army of the seventh century B.C. rather than of a Philistine fighter from three centuries earlier. "The story of David and Goliath," he declares, "reflects the period in which it was written, not in which it supposedly took place."

That makes Goliath yet another literary creation that Finkelstein attributes to the reign of King Josiah (r. 639–609 B.C.), the time that Finkelstein believes the biblical account of Israel's origin and history was first drafted. According to that account, the Israelite nation is descended from Abraham, a tent-dwelling herdsman to whom God promised the land of Canaan. In an attempt to escape famine, his grandson Jacob and his family traveled to Egypt, where their descendants were enslaved. Moses led the Israelites back out of Egypt to Canaan, which they conquered under the leadership of Joshua.

Until relatively recently, archaeologists and historians attempted to match this story with the evidence provided by excavations and documents discovered in Egypt, Syria, and elsewhere in the Near East. Most, though not all, now believe that this biblical account is primarily mythical. There is little independent evidence to corroborate the stories of the patriarchs, the enslavement, the exodus, and the conquest, and what exists is ambiguous at best.

The archaeological record confirms that from 1200 to 1000 B.C.—corresponding to the period covered by the Bible's Book of Judges—a collection of small settlements appeared in the eastern part of the highlands of Palestine, in the area now called the West Bank or, by Israelis harking back to biblical history, Samaria and Judea. The population of these settlements displayed cultural elements that lead most scholars to identify them with the Israelites of the Bible (for example, an absence of pig bones, an animal not eaten by the Israelites). As the Israelite population grew in number and moved westward, according to the Bible, it developed into a loose confederation of 12 tribes that had neither the unity nor organization to ward off military threats, particularly from the Philistines, so they united first under Saul of the tribe of Benjamin, and then under David and his son Solomon, from the tribe of Judah.

Traditional chronology dates David and Solomon's united kingdom from ca. 1000 to 928 B.C. The Bible depicts it as a local empire that expanded beyond tribal borders, carried out extensive public works, and achieved great wealth. But the kingdom split after Solomon's death in 928 B.C., with his son and descendants of the Davidic line ruling Judah in the south with their capital in Jerusalem, and a series of usurpers ruling the northern tribes. The northern Kingdom of Israel was conquered by the Assyrians in 722 B.C., while the southern Kingdom of Judah survived until its conquest by the Babylonians in 586 B.C.

Archaeologists and historians long accepted this story of a glorious united kingdom, followed by a north-south split. Many still believe that it is fundamentally true, even if the Bible exaggerates the grandeur of David and Solomon's realm. But over the last three decades a growing number of scholars has begun to argue that archaeological finds previously taken as corroborations of the biblical story have, in fact, been misinterpreted.

Author and leading advocate of a new chronology for most of the major finds of

Early Iron Age Palestine, Finkelstein maintains that major construction projects at northern sites such as Megiddo and Gezer, which other archaeologists and historians assign to the time of the united kingdom of David and Solomon, actually date to the period of King Ahab, a century later.

According to Finkelstein, the united kingdom of David and Solomon—and much of the history of the people of Israel presented in the Bible—represents the political and theological interests of the court of King Josiah, which reinstituted the exclusive worship of the god of the Israelites, centered on the Temple in Jerusalem, and aspired to see their king reign over both Judah and the territory of the former northern kingdom. The intellectual and spiritual atmosphere of this new religious movement led its leaders to create a coherent narrative of Israelite history as an instrument of god's will. Finkelstein has now presented this theory in *The Bible Unearthed: Archaeology's New Vision of Ancient Israel and the Origin of its Sacred Texts*, a book written with archaeological journalist Neil Asher Silberman.

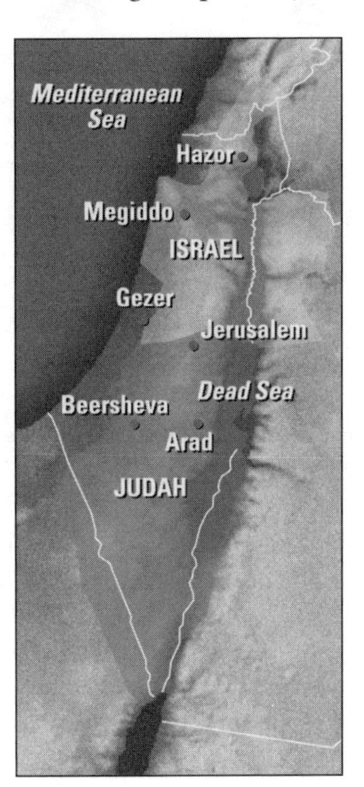

Finkelstein is sometimes classified as a member of the "biblical minimalist" school. Minimalists believe that the tales in the first five books of the Old Testament, called the Pentateuch, and the historical books of the Old Testament are fictions composed at a much later date than the events they claim to describe. In their view, the stories were meant to provide a mythical past for a Jewish people who achieved a national consciousness and unique theology only during the time of the Babylonian exile (586–538 B.C.) or perhaps even as late as the Hellenistic period (332–63 B.C.).

Among Israeli archaeologists, Finkelstein is considered a radical and a firebrand. To a large swath of the Israeli public, in particular those involved in the popular field of "Land of Israel Studies," Finkelstein is worse—they call him an anti-Zionist out to aid Israel's enemies. By challenging the truth of the Bible's version of history he is, they say, supporting the Palestinian claim that Jews are not really natives of their own land. Rabbi Yoel Ben-Nun, a leading figure in the West Bank settler community, said at a conference last year that the claims of Finkelstein and his like-minded colleagues are "really all an argument about Zionism."

Finkelstein rejects such charges: "I'm sick of people saying that we're putting weapons in the hands of Israel's enemies. We're strengthening Israeli society. The debate we're conducting testifies to the resilience of Israeli society."

In fact, Finkelstein disassociates himself from the minimalists, even if like them he rejects the "conservative" or "traditionalist" view that the stories of the period of the judges, the united kingdom of David and Solomon, and the early monarchy of Judah are fundamentally true and based on accounts compiled close to the time of the events they describe. He thinks that minor chiefs named David and Solomon founded the dynasty that later produced Josiah, but he is certain that their power never extended beyond the territory of Judah. He argues that demographic and material evidence produced by archaeological survey of the central highlands, the territory that was the cradle of the emerging Israelite nation, also show that Judah was a sparsely populated and economically backward chiefdom. Only when it absorbed refugees following Assyrian conquest and control of the north from 715 to 642 B.C. did Judah achieve the attributes of a state.

Megiddo is a key site in the debate over the historical veracity of the Bible.

Finkelstein, who lives with his wife and two daughters in Tel Aviv, wasn't always such an iconoclast. Articles written in his younger days, when he began his career excavating at Beersheva, show him following the traditional pattern of trying to identify archaeological finds with peoples and events described in the Bible. As recently as the late 1980s, he asserted that the kingdom of David and Solomon was a full-blown, mature state that controlled a large territory extending from the Galilee in the north to the Negev in the south. At that time he believed, along with most of his colleagues, that excavations at important sites as far-flung as Beersheva and Arad in southern Israel and Hazor and Megiddo in the country's north had produced ample evidence of major building projects dated to the tenth century B.C., the period that both biblical and modern historical chronology identify with the united kingdom. But soon thereafter, during a 1992–1993 sabbatical at Harvard, he began a major rethinking of his work.

"I sat quietly at home and the picture began to clarify. And the picture was cyclical," he explains. Surveys and excavations showed a recurring Bronze Age pattern of a populous and prosperous northern highland region—the one that would later be the Kingdom of Israel—and a southern hill region, later Judah, that was largely pastoral, tribal, and lacking in influence. If geography and climate dictated such a pattern in the Bronze Age, would it not have done the same in the Early Iron Age, the period of Israelite settlement?

MEGIDDO IS A KEY SITE IN THE DEBATE over the historical veracity of the Bible (see ARCHAEOLOGY, November/December 1999). "It's one of the few places where text and archaeology cross," notes Baruch Halpern, a historian from Pennsylvania State University, who, along with Finkelstein and David Ussishkin of Tel Aviv University, is a co-director of excavations there. The Bible says that Solomon fortified Megiddo, and that King Josiah was killed here in an attempt to restore Judah's control over the northern territories that seceded after Solomon's death. "Everyone was basing their claims on the excavations at Megiddo," says Finkelstein. "I saw that if the chronology there didn't work, then the traditional view fell apart."

HALPERN'S EXPERTISE IN TEXTUAL STUDY dovetailed with Finkelstein's growing interest in the use of the biblical record to interpret archaeological finds. Unlike the minimalists, who generally argue that the Bible was written so late as to be nearly useless as a historical record, Finkelstein was impressed by work done by his Tel Aviv colleague Nadav Na'aman and Harvard biblical scholar Frank M. Cross, who noted that many details of the Bible's stories from Genesis through Kings seemed to reflect the political, geographical, and social realities of the late monarchic period, in the decades before the Babylonian conquest of 586 B.C.

Finkelstein's dating of palaces and structures interpreted as stables, as well as a six-chambered city gate at Megiddo to the period of Ahab, a century after Solomon's supposed reign, is one of the foundations of his later chronology. While he is convinced he is right and gives no quarter in arguments with his colleagues, the evidence is complex and open to differing interpretations. Archaeological chronologies are based largely on the interpretation of potsherds and, more recently, on radiocarbon dating of wooden beams from the site. Both can be ambiguous and imprecise. "You can argue them five ways from Friday," asserts Halpern, who disputes Finkelstein's chronology.

Finkelstein is not one to present a balanced survey of scholarly opinion. *The Bible Unearthed* is a polemic, setting out the case for his chronology and the Josianic origin of the biblical text with great vigor and little acknowledgement of other points of view. That infuriates many of his colleagues. In a recent review of *The Bible Unearthed*, University of Arizona Bible scholar and historian William G. Dever, a vocal conservative, calls Finkelstein "idiosyncratic and doctrinaire." Furthermore, he charges, the book's "discussion of exceedingly complex matters is often simplistic and therefore misleading."

Finkelstein is nonplussed. "This is a question of how you write a book and how you do research," he says. "I don't sum up previous scholarship. I stir up an interesting argument and then the issues are clarified. I believe in the efficacy of stimulation and thinking to push scholarship forward."

Halpern is generous. "He's taken a position that in archaeology is extreme but in historical studies is not and which in textual studies is moderate. He's made a case for it. I disagree with it but there's nothing illegitimate about it. It's real scholarship and should be dealt with as such."

Halpern also credits Finkelstein with bringing the biblical text back into the debate, noting that over the last two or three decades reference to the Bible has gone out of fashion in archaeology, even among the conservatives. "That," Halpern says, "was because archaeology used to look at the Bible very simplistically. Now Finkelstein is looking at it through the lens of critical scholarship. You've got to give him a lot of credit for that."

In fact, Finkelstein's advocacy of a Josian origin for the Bible has given him something that his opponents on both sides lack—a narrative. It's a conceptual framework (some of his colleagues would say an obsession) that allows him to present a coherent account of the history of the kingdoms of Judah and Israel and of the composition of the Bible.

In fact, at the 2001 seminar, Finkelstein was practically the only speaker quoting the Bible. His talk on Goliath was laced with references to chapters and verses, whereas "mainstreamers" like Amihai Mazar of the Hebrew University had stripped their talks of biblical imagery and were referring staidly to Iron Ages IA and IB. Ironically, Finkelstein is doing just what he did when he was younger—and what so many archaeologists in this part of the world did until just a couple of decades ago. He's linking up archaeological finds to the Bible's story. He just tells that story differently than they did.

Finkelstein is certain that a large-scale radiocarbon survey of Iron Age sites currently underway will confirm his later dating of monuments. Preliminary results presented at the seminar point in this direction, although they are still far from conclusive.

Despite that, Finkelstein expects resolution. "Within five, six, or ten years the picture will have stabilized" and his chronology will have been confirmed, he proclaims with an infectious enthusiasm that is more reminiscent of his Hasidic forebears than of the halls of academe.

Will archaeology be free of controversy then? "No," he says, grinning. "Then we'll argue over the details."

11

LETTER FROM ISRAEL

A fight over sacred turf: Who controls Jerusalem's holiest shrine?

by Sandra Scham

A NEWLY OPENED ISRAELI MUSEUM IN THE shadow of the hilltop known to Jews as the Temple Mount, and to Muslims as the Haram al-Sharif (Noble Sanctuary), aptly symbolizes the historical relationship between Israelis and Palestinians over that site. The museum is designed to give tourists the experience of being on the Mount during the time of Herod—the glory days of the Jewish Temple. The exhibits show the Israeli concept of the Temple Mount-Haram al-Sharif site, devoid of the Dome of the Rock and Al-Aqsa Mosque, both built by the Umayyad Muslims in the seventh century A.D. Only the newest of many such reconstructions in Jerusalem, they would hardly be noteworthy were it not for the fact that the museum was constructed within the walls of an Umayyad palace. The age-old impulse to build on, and to some extent obscure, the remains of a past culture is still very much at work in this region.

In a way, the joint U.S.-Israeli proposal put forward at Camp David last year that the hill could be "horizontally divided" between Israelis and Palestinians, with Palestinians controlling what is above the surface and Israelis what is below, makes historical sense given the nature of the site. It was, however, a major factor in the disintegration of the peace talks, according to negotiators on both sides. One Palestinian spokesman and his colleagues were "stunned" by this scheme since, as they put it, no Israeli government had ever brought up such a thing before. In discussing the failure of the Camp David negotiations before an Israeli audience in Jerusalem, former U.S. Ambassador to Israel Martin Indyk confirmed this. He told his incredulous listeners that the breakdown occurred because Israelis had not realized that Yasser Arafat could not negotiate anything short of absolute Muslim sovereignty over the Haram al-Sharif, and Palestinians had not realized that Israelis were deeply attached to the site.

Indyk's comments and the spirit in which they were received only highlights how little the Israelis and Palestinians comprehend each other's beliefs and ideas regarding this place. Almost as soon as the Israeli flag was hoisted over the site in 1967, at the conclusion of the Six-Day War, Israelis lowered it on the orders of General Moshe Dayan, and invested the Muslim Waqf (religious trust) with the authority to manage the Temple Mount-Haram al-Sharif in order to "keep the peace." In the 30 or so years that have elapsed since then, the Waqf has remained relatively independent of Israeli control.

Because of this informal understanding between Israel and the Waqf, Muslims have assumed that Israelis don't care very much about the place and their current interest is just another excuse to cheat Palestinians out of what is rightfully theirs. After all, the Haram al-Sharif, revered as the site of Mohammed's ascension to heaven, is one of the three holiest places in Islam (the other two being Mecca and Medina); Muslims would never simply "give" control of it to the followers of another religion. Nevertheless, the Temple Mount is Judaism's holiest site—so holy that many religious Jews will not set foot on the hill, lest they inadvertently tread on sacred and forbidden ground. Equally important, it is a site of great national significance. In the eyes of many Israelis, the "return to Zion" that Jews living in Israel believe they have effected was completed by the capture of the Temple Mount.

THE CULTURAL CHASM THAT EXISTS between Jews and Muslims over the site is not simply played out on the political level. Social conversations with Israelis and Palestinians on this subject demonstrate it as well. Among friends, a liberal academic, who is not religious, recently reiterated what is a commonplace sentiment in Israel—that the Temple Mount is "far more important to Jews than to Muslims." Noting that the site is mentioned in the Jewish Bible hundreds of times, he stated that he, himself, was "willing to fight and die for" Israel's sovereignty over the embattled property.

Palestinians, on the other hand, while insisting on the primacy of their claims, will often downplay the extent to which they need the site for political as well as religious reasons. They need it for the prestige it would lend their fledgling state. They need it because it establishes a vital connection between the Palestinian Muslims and their co-religionists elsewhere in the Middle East. Most of all, they need it for the same reason that Israelis do—because it represents an important link with their past and their history in the land, and also because it represents a religious and historical affirmation of their right to be there.

The seemingly mundane construction of an exit and stairway has become a reminder of the battle for control there.

A week before the current intifada, a Palestinian archaeologist told a mixed dinner group of Palestinian and Israeli friends that former prime minister Ehud Barak was "stupid" for bringing up the question of Jerusalem and the Temple Mount-Haram al-Sharif at Camp David. The Israelis present were somewhat shocked to hear him question what they believed to be a well-intentioned effort to confront and solve the most difficult issues in Israeli-Palestinian relations as part of a comprehensive settlement. What he meant was that any change in the status quo of Israeli secular sovereignty-Muslim sacred sovereignty that didn't hand the site over completely to Muslims would be perceived as a loss throughout the Arab world. In his estimation, it would have been better to have not discussed it during the negotiations at all.

AGAINST THIS BACKDROP OF HISTORICAL conflict, with hidden and not-so-hidden agendas, an archaeological drama has been unfolding. It incorporates many of the issues involved in the current battle over the Temple Mount-Haram al-Sharif. The seemingly mundane construction of an exit and stairway at the site, initiated by the Waqf, has become a reminder of the battle for control there. Some archaeologists and other prominent Israelis, including well-known Jerusalem archaeologists Gaby Barkai and Eilat Mazar, as well as author Amos Oz and former Jerusalem mayor Teddy Kollek, have styled themselves as the Committee to Prevent the Destruction of Antiquities on the Temple Mount (CPDATM), and vowed to stop this building program.

Begun in 1999 and now almost complete, this construction project possibly represents the most substantial alteration that the area has undergone in some time. It includes a new path to the Al-Aqsa Mosque, a recently renovated prayer hall in the area known as "Solomon's Stables" (now the Al-Marwani Mosque), a staircase leading from the top of the Haram platform to the Al-Marwani Mosque beneath it, and possibly a renovation of certain underground portions of the existing Al-Aqsa Mosque. "Solomon's Stables," like many such sites in the Holy Land, has nothing to do with its namesake. Primarily an Umayyad (seventh and eighth centuries A.D.) building, this pillared "hall" was reconstructed from earlier, possibly Herodian, remains. It was used as a stable by the Crusaders, subsequently destroyed by an earthquake and rebuilt again. The gates to this space have been blocked since the Mamluk period (thirteenth–sixteenth centuries A.D.). Access from the platform was via a long narrow tunnel which, in the event of an emergency crowd control situation (unfortunately, not an unusual occurrence there), was very dangerous.

Because the Waqf has a certain amount of independence from the Israeli bureaucracy, it has found it necessary only to deal "unofficially" with the Israeli police over security matters. The police gave permission, for safety reasons, for the construction of a new entrance and exit. Israeli protesters, however, are less concerned with the construction than with the earth removed to make way for it. Many Israelis believe that major portions of Herod's Temple and perhaps even the Temple of Solomon are beneath the surface of the Haram, and are irate over what they see as unnecessary destruction of important archaeological strata.

There is every reason to suppose that there are archaeological remains beneath the surface of the Haram, but evidence relating to what was on top of the hill for periods before the Umayyad is scant, although substantial archaeological work done in its vicinity has revealed evidence of Bronze and Iron Age occupations. Various earlier structures, in addition to the Kotel or Western ("Wailing") Wall, which is believed to be a retaining wall for Herod's Temple, surround the Haram.

"It is an archaeological site but, before that, it's a holy site," says Yussuf Natsheh, archaeologist for the Al-Qaf Administration, the Waqf's managerial arm. Its purpose "is to fulfill the spiritual needs of Muslims and prayer.... The conclusion was reached that this was not a safe place.... We removed the earth after doing an investigation, after doing some documentation." Notwithstanding, CPDATM member Barkai characterizes the work as an "archaeological tragedy...I say it not because I am Jewish but because I think it should be important to any civilized person in the world—and to Muslims."

Natsheh and Barkai do not disagree on the site's basic nature. Both recognize that it is still in use as a place of prayer by one of the religions that revere it, but they part company in what they consider to be archaeologically significant. Natsheh justifiably sees his mission as supporting and maintaining the values of the buildings visible in the Haram—almost all of them Early Islamic. As he explains it, "Archaeology is very important but the feelings of the people, human beings, the needs of the people should be taken into consideration when we discuss heritage and archaeology. The main thing is to preserve this area for Muslims and not to cause harm to other civilizations." In contrast, Barkai and his fellow Committee members, while appreciative of the site's present architecture, are also fully convinced that some of those "other civilizations" are of equal, if not greater, importance.

The Haram is visited annually by hundreds of thousands during the brief period that marks the Muslim holiday of Ramadan, as well as tens of thousands every Friday. Thus, it is difficult to dispute the Waqf's right to make some accommodations for these numbers of pilgrims—neither the CPDATM nor the Israeli Antiquities Authority (IAA) have tried to. According to Jon Seligman,

IAA's Jerusalem District Archaeologist, the real question for the Authority "was not 'if' but 'how.'" Both Barkai and Seligman agree that the work could have been done with proper archaeological supervision but that, in their estimation, it was not. Neither takes issue with Natsheh's abilities to do so—rather, they both claim he wasn't present at the time that the work was done. Natsheh maintains that the questions raised are not archaeological ones. "They [the protesters] have their own motivations," he says, "but archaeology is the least one.... Nothing was destroyed, no buildings, no walls, no capitals." Seligman argues that this is beside the point. "This is the very first time in which work has been done under the levels of the platform. In a case like that this really demands that you have to do it properly."

The new construction was undertaken primarily in the southeastern corner of the Haram but Barkai cites rumors, dismissed by Natsheh and Seligman, that further destructive projects are being carried out on and below the platform. Barkai also asserts that important strata "saturated with archaeological material" were removed and dumped in the nearby Kidron Valley and the village of Azzaria. Tests conducted at the dump sites by his students, says Barkai, found significant amounts of shards representing "all periods." Natsheh's survey of the area excavated before construction indicated that "all of this earth was filled during the Ayubbid period [beginning in A.D. 1187]," and that any shards from earlier periods there were in stratigraphically disturbed contexts and cannot, with certainty, even be considered from the Temple Mount-Haram al-Sharif itself. The IAA's tests report the majority of material at the dump sites was from the seventh to eleventh centuries A.D., with insignificant percentages from earlier periods.

The two Israelis also disagree about the separation of archaeology from politics in discussing what happened at the site. While Barkai firmly maintains that the debate must focus on archaeology, Seligman says, "The truth is it's both. I think it's not honest to the subject to separate them—the reason it's so potent is because of the politics."

These "potent politics" may be the reason why a number of Israeli archaeologists whom one might expect to take an interest in the affair have declined to do so and others have even taken a view in opposition to Barkai's and, to some extent, Seligman's. Meir Ben-Dov, who is recognized primarily for his Jerusalem excavations, has publicly supported the claims of the Al-Qaf Administration that construction in the Haram was properly carried out. He has also argued that the original Temple Mount was some 16 feet higher than the present day platform, suggesting that the remains from prior occupations of the site—of greatest interest to Israelis—have already disappeared or been displaced.

The Temple Mount-Haram al-Sharif is registered with UNESCO as a World Heritage site, but why the work was done without UNESCO involvement is closely linked to the politics of the region. "There is a problem with the UNESCO registration of Jerusalem. It was done without consulting Israel," says Seligman, referring to the registration of the site as "a separate entity" nominated by Jordan in 1982. The fact that the site appears on the list "without the consent of the sovereign power," to quote Seligman, and the fact that certain past dealings between UNESCO and Israel have been less than cordial, means that their intervention would not be a prospect Israel would enthusiastically embrace.

Natsheh has no problem with UNESCO observing their work and states that such a visit, while welcomed by the Waqf, was postponed three times by Israeli authorities. Consulting the IAA, however, was out of the question. "The Al-Qaf Administration, which is responsible for Muslim affairs and the holy places, never admits the Israeli occupation," says Natsheh. "We never applied for the permission from the Israeli authorities and we are not going to apply." Interestingly, he was somewhat less candid when asked if the site should be under the sovereignty of the Palestinian Authority. It is possible that the Waqf, not entirely anxious to be enfolded in the arms of a new and poverty-stricken nation-state, may prefer an autonomous position for management of the Haram.

Reflecting Israeli concerns about the site, Barkai charges that, "what goes on, on the Temple Mount, is outrageous...it's being constantly damaged," while Seligman states angrily, "Here we have a situation where, at one of the most important of World Heritage Sites, work has been done in a really charlatan manner, causing real vandalism and UNESCO has said nothing—zero." CPDATM has managed to persuade prime minister Ariel Sharon to appoint a panel of scholars and politicians to look into the matter, but the panel has yet to convene. The construction work has been almost completed, and the only course of action left to them is to seek to prevent similar occurrences. "We really have to make sure that this can't happen again," Seligman says. "There have to be some sort of safeguards." On the other side of the controversy, Natsheh voices the anxieties of fellow Muslims, "This area is a holy area for Muslims. It was made holy by God. This can't be changed.... We have fears, worries that all of these attempts will lead to the destruction of the Dome of the Rock. We are very nervous and worried about what is going on around us."

It is difficult to envision that Israeli participation in the Waqf's prospective decisions on maintenance or construction in the Haram could take place without a significant change in the archaeological management of the site, a change that would have to be preceded by a political agreement that is now more elusive than ever. Although no one would suggest that the current conflict in the Middle East is about the Temple Mount-Haram al-Sharif any more than it is about any other single issue, the site remains a powerful symbol of the past, the present, and possibly the future of Israeli and Palestinian relations.

12

CULTURAL TERRORISM

The world deplores the Taliban's destructive rampage.

by KRISTIN M. ROMEY

THE REAL GOD IS ONLY ALLAH, AND ALL OTHER false gods should be removed." This statement from the one-eyed cleric Mullah Omar sent a chill through the international community following an edict issued by Afghanistan's fundamentalist Taliban regime announcing that all pre-Islamic statues in the country were to be destroyed. That edict, and the resulting destruction, has been universally condemned as "cultural terrorism."

Among the targeted relics were the Bamiyan Buddhas, two enormous 1,500-year-old statues hewn out of a cliff in the valley of Bamiyan, 140 miles northwest of the Afghan capital of Kabul, that were once one of the country's most popular tourist attractions. Destruction of the Buddhas was said to be completed by March 12, 2001. A Taliban guard has also reported that the second-century B.C. Buddhist complex in Ghazni was razed two weeks before the edict was issued. Many areas where the destruction is occurring have been sealed off to outsiders, making independent verification impossible at this time.

The Taliban seized control of much of Afghanistan in the mid-1990s and has since enforced an extreme interpretation of Islamic law. Women cannot work or attend school and are not allowed out of the house without a spouse or male relative. Music, cinema, and photography of people and animals are among the hundreds of aspects of modern life that are banned.

While the regime insists that it is simply observing Muslim law against idolatry, its actions are generally considered to be a reaction against UN sanctions implemented in January, following the regime's refusal to extradite terrorist leader Osama bin Laden. The sanctions, which include the shuttering of all Taliban offices outside Afghanistan and a ban on international travel by the Taliban leadership, are exacerbating the near-famine conditions caused by Afghanistan's worst drought in 30 years; the UN estimates that up to 600,000 Afghans have been displaced or become refugees.

Several governments and museums offered to remove the statues from Afghanistan.

International reaction to the February 26 edict was immediate, with dozens of countries, including Pakistan, the Taliban's closest ally, condemning the decision. The Taliban remained resistant, reporting that everything from anti-aircraft missiles to tank fire and dynamite were being used to destroy the Buddhas. "The statues are no big issue," Information and Culture Minister Mullah Qadradullah Jamal told reporters. "They are only objects made of mud or stone."

Response from religious groups has been particularly furious and protests have occurred in most major Buddhist countries. Japan threatened to cut off all aid to Afghanistan if the statues were destroyed. Muslim nations have also condemned the Taliban's actions, insisting that the cultural heritage of other religions must be respected. Pakistan's leading daily paper, *The Dawn*, wrote, "Islam is a religion of harmony and peaceful coexistence...Buddha was an apostle of peace and non-violence. Certainly he deserves better treatment than what he has hitherto received at the hands of blind zealots in Afghanistan."

Several governments and museums offered to remove the statues from Afghanistan, and some suggested that the Buddhas could be sold to help Afghanistan's ravaged economy. The regime refused, insisting that they wish to be known as "destroyers of idols, not sellers of idols."

The Taliban also accuses the international community of clamoring to save the statues, while ignoring the ongoing humanitarian disaster in the country. "These living people deserve more attention than those non-living things," said Mullah Abdul Salam Zaeef, the Taliban ambassador to Pakistan.

The larger of the two Buddhas rose 174 feet above the valley floor and was the tallest standing Buddha statue in the world. The smaller Buddha, 125 feet high, was a half mile away. Both were carved into the cliff face sometime around the fifth century A.D., plastered, and painted. Cells once used by monks pockmark the cliff around the statues.

The size of the statues has long attracted attention; their presence was first recorded in 632 by Hiuan Tsang, a Chinese monk visiting Bamiyan, a major Buddhist center from the second century B.C. until the rise of Islam in the ninth century A.D. Tsang described the greater Buddha as "glittering with gold and precious ornaments." They survived numerous invasions, including those of Genghis Khan and Tamerlane, although the larger Buddha was attacked in the seventeenth century by a Moghul commander's artillery.

By the mid 1990s, the Bamiyan valley had changed hands repeatedly between Taliban and opposition forces, and the base of the larger statue was being used as an ammunition dump. In 1997, a Taliban commander trying to seize the Bamiyan valley declared that the monumental Buddhas were to be destroyed as soon as the valley fell into his hands. The resulting international outcry caused the Taliban high command to prohibit the Buddhas' destruction and promise that the cultural heritage of Afghanistan would be protected. In 1998, however, the smaller Buddha's head and part of the shoulders were blown off, and the face of the larger Buddha blackened by burning tires.

Although Afghanistan signed the 1972 UNESCO World Heritage Convention, it is unenforceable. However, additions to the Geneva Conventions in 1977 and 1997 prohibit the destruction of cultural property in internal as well as international wars, and convictions on these charges have been won in the international war crimes tribunal for the former Yugoslavia. The UN has said that it will not retaliate against the destruction.

Scorning the current famine, Mullah Omar, the supreme religious leader of the Taliban, has ordered the slaughter of 100 cows to atone for any delay in the ongoing destruction.

13

AFGHAN MUSEUM UNDER SIEGE

In 2001, before the United States went to war in Afghanistan, the Taliban was already making news worldwide with its destruction of the Bamiyan Buddhas and other important artifacts. But although 2001 marked a year of especially violent upheaval, Afghanistan's rich heritage has long been threatened. This article, reprinted from the March/April 1996 issue of ARCHAEOLOGY, *reflects the results of the on-going war and destruction, and catalogs some of the many treasures that have been lost or destroyed over the years. Its author, Nancy Hatch Dupree, is a distinguished archaeologist who has been deeply concerned for more than thirty years with the preservation of Afghan culture.*

Attacked and looted by warring factions, Afghanistan's National Museum has now been stripped of 70 percent of its collections.

by NANCY HATCH DUPREE

WHEN SOVIET TROOPS WITHDREW FROM Afghanistan in 1988, all but the capital of Kabul had fallen to the resistance, known as the mujahideen. When Kabul itself was taken in April 1992, ending the 14-year rule of the Democratic Republic of Afghanistan (DRA), mujahideen factions began warring among themselves for control of the city. Attacks were often launched from the south, and the National Museum in Darulaman, six miles south of Kabul, was often on the front line. Each time a new faction triumphed, it would loot the ruins. On May 12, 1993, a rocket slammed into the roof of the museum, destroying a fourth- to fifth-century A.D. wall painting from Delbarjin-tepe, site of an ancient Kushan city in northern Afghanistan, and burying much of the museum's ancient pottery and bronzes under tons of debris. Last November 16 another rocket hit the northwest wing of the museum, exposing storerooms to winter rain and snow and further depredations of the combatants. Despite efforts to mediate factional rivalries, the fighting and looting continues.

About 70 percent of the museum's collections are now missing. Most of its vast gold and silver coin collection, which spanned the nation's history from the Achaemenids in the sixth century B.C. through the Islamic period, has been looted. Also gone is a Greco-Bactrian hoard of more than 600 coins from Kunduz, in northern Afghanistan, dating to the third and second centuries B.C., including the largest Greek coins ever discovered. Pieces of Buddhist stucco sculptures and schist reliefs dating between the first and third centuries A.D. and Hindu marble statuary from the seventh and ninth centuries have been taken, as have carved ivories in classic Indian styles from Begram, site of the summer capital of the Kushan Empire in the early centuries A.D. Also missing are many of the museum's prized examples of the renowned metalwork of the Ghaznavids, whose sumptuous capital flourished 90 miles southwest of Kabul during the tenth and eleventh centuries. Many of these pieces are destined for sale in Islamabad, London, New York, and Tokyo.

Afghanistan's first national museum was inaugurated by King Amanullah in November 1924 at Koti Baghcha, a small palace built by the founder of Afghanistan's royal dynasty, Amir Abdur Rahman (1880–1891). In 1931 its holdings were transferred to the present building in Darulaman. By this time the collection had been enriched by the work of the Délégation Archéologique Française en Afghanistan, which began after a treaty was signed with France in September 1922. After World War II, numerous archaeological missions, including those of the Italians, Americans, Japanese, British, Indians, and Soviets, conducted excavations. The first Afghan-directed work was carried out at a Buddhist site at Hadda in eastern Afghanistan in 1965. Foreign archaeological missions were bound by agreements guaranteeing that all excavated objects would be deposited with the government of Afghanistan. In 1966 the Afghan Institute of Archaeology was established in Darulaman to receive these finds; exceptional items were placed in the museum. A unique feature of the museum was the fact that more than 90 percent of its exhibits were scientifically excavated inside Afghanistan.

Claims that the Soviets had carted off the museum's treasures to the Hermitage in Leningrad arose from the April 1979 removal of the museum's collections to the center of Kabul for safekeeping. They were returned in October 1980, when the museum reopened. British and American friends still living in Kabul checked the exhibits against the 1974 museum guide and found that only two small gold repoussé elephant masks, pilfered in November 1978, were missing. According to another rumor, Victor Sarianidi of the Soviet-Afghan archaeological mission, which had excavated a hoard of more than 20,000 gold ornaments from six burial mounds called Tillya-tepe, had taken the gold to the Soviet Union. The first-century B.C. to first-century A.D. hoard, however, was shown to an international conference on Kushan studies in Kabul in November 1978. The Kabul government also displayed it to the diplomatic corps toward the end of 1991, after which the gold was packed in boxes and placed in a vault of the National Bank inside the palace, where it is said to be today.

As unrest threatened Kabul in February 1989, following the departure of Soviet troops, the museum staff crated, packed, and stored the bulk of the collections in the museum's storerooms. Only objects too heavy to move were left in situ. Astonishingly, one of the largest and heaviest pieces, a 32-inch-high second- to fifth-century A.D. Buddhist schist relief from Shotorak, disappeared one night from an upper corridor. How thieves managed to steal it without being detected remains a mystery. Still, the museum survived the rule of the Democratic Republic of Afghanistan and the Soviet occupation relatively intact.

The subsequent breakdown of law and order has been disastrous for the museum. Although united in ridding the country of the Soviets and their DRA clients, the seven major mujahideen factions that founded the Islamic State of Afghanistan in April 1992 never formed lasting alliances, and the accord establishing the new government under President Burhanuddin Rabbani had little substance. With no common enemy, the factions have fought one another for power. In May 1993 Hezbe Wahdat, a group led by Abdul Ali Mazari, took control of the Darulaman valley. Museum staff—civil servants in President Rabbani's government—were forbidden to visit the museum because it was in enemy territory. One staff member, Najibullah Popal, risked a visit and found crates and boxes in place, but could not check their contents or that of the many cabinets. He noted, however, that two schist reliefs were now missing. The rocket attack came the following week as fighting between Hezbe Wahdat and Rabbani's government troops intensified. Popal returned and found the Delbarjin-tepe wall painting burned beyond repair. The boxes and crates of artifacts in the basement, however, seemed untouched. At the beginning of September, CNN and BBC reporters found that the seals on the basement doors were intact, but in mid-September Popal risked another visit and saw the remains of packing cases on the ground outside the museum. Shortly thereafter a BBC correspondent returned and noted that cases had been moved and emptied; a small Buddha head had been placed near a storeroom window where protective iron bars had been bent. Outside, tire marks led directly from the window.

In late September 1993, at the request of Sotirios Mousouris, the United Nations secretary general's special representative in Afghanistan and Pakistan, I flew to Kabul to investigate these reports. Mousouris then decided to seek the support of Mazari, leader of Hezbe Wahdat, so the museum could be protected and repaired. In November the United Nations Office for the Coordination of Humanitarian Assistance to Afghanistan (UNOCHA) requested the United Nations Center for Human Resources (HABITAT) to assess the museum's condition. Investigators led by Jolyon Leslie, head of HABITAT, found that cases stood open inside every room. Barred windows in a new wing were badly damaged, providing thieves easy access. Photographs of the interior showed artifacts strewn among the rubble, and filing cabinets of museum records and catalogs indiscriminately dumped, much of the paper badly charred. Hasps had been unscrewed and locks ripped off steel storage boxes, and drawers and crates had been methodically emptied onto the floor. It appeared that most of the storage rooms had been thoroughly ransacked. HABITAT recommended securing windows with masonry, weatherproofing the flooring over the storerooms, and fitting the rooms with steel doors and stout locks. Mousouris called an emergency meeting of experts in Islamabad on November 27 at which a contribution from the Greek government, earmarked for securing the museum, was announced. Two days later he flew to Kabul. Visiting the museum, Mousouris found all 30,000 of the museum's coins missing. He secured Mazari's support for immediate repairs, and, most important, Mazari assured Mousouris that security would be provided for museum staff and workmen. Work began on December 21, 1993, under the supervision of HABITAT and with assistance from UNOCHA.

In May 1994 I returned to Kabul. The work that had been done at the museum was impressive considering the appalling conditions—intense winter cold with no electricity or heating and only a small kerosene lantern for light. The building had been weatherproofed, windows blocked, steel doors installed, and all of the corridors cleared of rubble. Some 3,000 ceramic objects recovered from the debris had been placed in storerooms. One room contained charred, melted, mangled, and otherwise disfigured Islamic bronzes that will require extensive conservation.

As of July 1994 the staff had inventoried about 16,000 objects remaining in the storerooms. Many of these, however, are mere fragments. Some 70 percent of the finer objects were missing. The looters in 1993 were discriminating in what they took and apparently had both the time and the knowledge to select the most attractive, saleable pieces. For example, they removed from wooden display mounts only the central figures (depicting voluptuous ladies standing in doorways) of the delicate Begram ivory carvings. It is also telling that although some 2,000 books and journals remain in the library, volumes with illustrations of the museum's best pieces are missing. This suggests the museum was not plundered by rampaging gangs of illiterate mujahideen. In 1992, while the various factions fought for control of Darulaman, government soldiers guarded the museum. In early 1993 they were replaced by soldiers loyal to Hezbe Wahdat. One, or perhaps both, of these groups is probably responsible for the looting.

Some of the larger and more important pieces remain. These include a second-century A.D. statue of the Kushan king Kanishka and a Bactrian inscription written in cursive Greek, both from the temple at Surkh Kotal, 145 miles north of Kabul; a third-century marble statue of a bearded figure, possibly Hermes, from the Greek city of Ai Khanoum far to the northeast; and a large, seated, painted clay Buddha of the third to fourth century from Tepe Maranjan, near Kabul. Also in place is an eleventh-century A.D. ornamental wall panel from the Ghaznavid winter palace at Lashkari Bazaar in southwestern Afghanistan. Delicately sculptured stucco decorations with borders of Koranic inscriptions from a mosque, possibly added to the Lashkari Bazaar palace by Ghorid successors in the twelfth century, remain, but they are still partly buried by debris. A black marble basin, 50 inches in diameter and embellished with fifteenth-and sixteenth-century Islamic inscriptions, found in Kandahar, still dominates the foyer. About a dozen rare pre-Islamic grave effigies from Nuristan also survive.

Some 16 metal trunks containing artifacts were removed by the government to safe areas in Kabul before the mujahideen arrived. These are still untouched but their contents remain a mystery; lists of what they contain were burned in the fire caused by the 1993 rocket attack. The government assures us that the 20,000 or more gold ornaments from Tillya-tepe are still safely guarded within the presidential palace in Kabul, but because of the political instability no attempt has been made to examine these objects, although the temptation to do so is great.

SOON AFTER THE FALL OF KABUL IN 1992, rumors claiming that the museum had been systematically emptied by gangs of mujahideen began to circulate. The bazaars of Peshawar, Islamabad, and Karachi were reportedly filled with objects. At one time I was assured that the "entire" contents of the museum were in Chitral, Pakistan, awaiting the highest bidder, but a group of European travelers who went to Chitral reported seeing only "dreadful junk." I am frequently shown pieces, but most of those I have seen have been fakes; the genuine pieces are mainly from recently looted sites.

There is no doubt that the ivory panels excavated at Begram, located on the ancient Silk Route some 40 miles northeast of Kabul, are on the international art market. These extremely fragile pieces originally decorated various pieces of furniture dating from the first to the middle of the third century A.D. Ten small panels were shown by an unidentified Afghan to an eminent Pakistani scholar in April 1994 in Islamabad. The seller claimed to have others, including several large ivories known to be missing from the museum. The asking price for the ten panels was $300,000; later it was rumored they were being offered for $600,000 in London—or perhaps Tokyo or Switzerland. Last summer more Begram ivories were seen in Islamabad, but accurate information is nearly impossible to obtain since the highly organized Pakistani underground network for stolen art is naturally secretive. Last September the Karachi-based *Herald Magazine* quoted General Naseerullah Babar, Pakistan's Federal Interior Minister, as saying that he had purchased one Begram ivory carving for $100,000, which he would return when the political situation in Afghanistan had stabilized. The general's fondness for antiquities is well known. The magazine also reported that Prime Minister Benazir Bhutto of Pakistan intends to provide substantial funds for obtaining artifacts to be "returned to the Afghans as a gift as soon as peace is established."

While I have seen few museum pieces for sale in Pakistan, there are a number of artifacts on the market that have recently been dug up in Afghanistan. Mujahideen commanders in all parts of the country are involved in this illicit activity, most notably in the east near the Hadda museum. An important Buddhist pilgrimage site in the second through seventh centuries, Hadda has been totally stripped of its exquisite clay sculptures in the Gandhara syle, which combines Bactrian, Greco-Roman, and Indian elements. Looted artifacts from Faryab and Balkh provinces in the north allegedly include jewel-encrusted golden crowns and statues, orbs (locally described as "soccer balls") studded with emeralds and all manner of exotic ephemera, as well as fluted marble columns similar to those found at Ai Khanoum in the northeastern province of Takhar. These are being carted away to embellish the houses of the newly powerful, according to witnesses. As far as I know, no reputable archaeologist has examined any of these finds. According to reports, one stone figurine of a winged female is similar to the gold "Bactrian Aphrodite" from Tillya-tepe. This is particularly intriguing because such reports began surfacing last June, at the same time that ornaments from Tillya-tepe were said to be for sale in Islamabad and Peshawar. An expert in antique gold confirmed that the gold jewelry in Peshawar is of the same period as the Tillya-tepe ornaments (first century B.C. to first century A.D.). Are these artifacts from the museum? Are they from new sites? Could they be from the unexcavated, seventh mound at Tillya-tepe? We have no reason not to believe the Kabul government's assurance that the Tillya-tepe collection is safe, even though no experts have been allowed to examine it.

In Darulaman relative calm extended through the first half of 1994, but at the end of July a splinter group from Hezbe Wahdat overran the area and began a seesaw contest with Mazari's forces. At the same time, gunners of the Hezbe Islami faction, led by Gulbuddin Hekmatyar and headquartered at Chahrasyab 15 miles to the southeast, occupied the heights overlooking the valley. For the remainder of the year fierce battles destroyed the southern edge of Kabul. Then, last February, a new force calling itself the Taliban ("religious students") seized Chahrasyab, drove out Hekmatyar's forces, and captured Mazari, who was killed in Ghazni on March 13. Government troops routed Taliban on March 23, 1995. During these eight unsettled months guards were posted at the museum by whichever faction happened to be holding the area. With each changeover, the fleeing guards took what they could. Some of the guards may have been cooperating with dealers who capitalized on the fact that the guards had the opportunity to identify saleable pieces as the museum staff worked at sorting and organizing the objects.

Five months of relative calm followed, and the central government assumed responsibility for the protection of the museum for the first time. Last April representatives of the Society for the Preservation of Afghanistan's Cultural Heritage (SPACH), an advocacy group formed in Islamabad in September 1994, met in Kabul with Sayed Ishaq Deljo Hussaini, the Minister of Information and Culture. Hussaini acknowledged the government's commitment to moving the museum to safe premises in Kabul, and SPACH agreed to seek assistance for the preparation of an inventory. The Minister also announced that government police had recently recovered 28 looted pieces, including schist reliefs, packed for shipment to Pakistan. Four pieces—two schist reliefs and two stucco heads—had been purchased by Abdullah Poyan, the ministry's President of Art, for return to the museum. In Kabul the Commission for the Preservation of Afghanistan's Cultural Heritage was organized, consisting of Afghan members of the

National Museum, the Institute of Archaeology, the Academy of Sciences, Kabul University, the Ministry of Information and Culture, HABITAT, and Afghan experts. The commission advises the government, coordinates efforts with SPACH, and receives recovered artifacts, either through donation or purchase. Last September, 43 pieces, which had been purchased in Kabul, were presented to the commission by HABITAT head Jolyon Leslie. In addition to a Bronze Age steatite seal, schist reliefs, and stucco heads, this donation included four fragments of a large Bronze Age silver bowl combining Indian and Mesopotamian stylistic characteristics in depicting a frieze of bulls. The bowl is part of a hoard of five gold and 12 silver vessels found at Tepe Fullol in northern Afghanistan in 1966. Tepe Fullol, not far from the famous lapis-lazuli mines of Badakhshan, was probably on an early trade route. Badakhshi lapis adorns luxury artifacts of the same period found at Ur in Mesopotamian Iraq. The commission purchased eight additional pieces last summer with funds provided by the government.

Last June in Kabul a joint mission of UNESCO and the Musée Guimet in Paris arranged for museum specialists to spend September in Kabul preparing a photo inventory of the objects remaining in the museum. On September 3, however, the Taliban captured the western city of Herat, and security in Kabul crumbled once again. Instead of flying on to Kabul from Peshawar, the mission returned to Paris. On the night of October 10 the Taliban recaptured the military base at Chahrasyab, and rockets fell in the museum's narrow front garden. Miraculously the building did not take another direct hit. Outside the entrance, however, the head of a lion on a Kushan schist throne from the Buddhist site of Khum Zargar, 40 miles north of Kabul, was split in two. During the attack, according to an eyewitness report by Armando Cuomo, an archaeologist from the University of London, government soldiers frightened away the government police guarding the museum, blasted open doors, and ransacked the storerooms unmindful of being observed by a foreigner. Because of the ongoing fighting, the museum staff has been unable to ascertain what was taken then.

By the time of my last visit at the end of October 1995, government guards were once again on duty, and the commission was feverishly preparing its response to President Rabbani's order that the collections be removed to Kabul immediately. The professionals on the commission are against the move. Packing and moving cannot be done in a hurry without causing much damage, and most feel that it would take from two to four months to pack adequately. They also feel that Kabul is now no safer than Darulaman; on November 20, jets dropped two 1,000 pound bombs on the center of Kabul near sites under consideration for storage of the museum collections. Despite months of searching, the government has yet to decide on a suitable new location. Meanwhile, HABITAT has drawn up plans for further work to secure the museum in Darulaman, which can be carried out with additional funds contributed by Portugal and Cyprus, along with a second donation from Greece. The commission favors accepting an offer by the president of security at Khad, the secret police, to take over responsibility for protecting the museum. But the war continues; all plans are tenuous.

An Endangered Heritage

The following artifacts are among the stolen or imperiled treasures of the National Museum.

MIDDLE PALAEOLITHIC TOOLS *dating 30,000 to 50,000 years ago, along with a skull fragment with both Neandertal and modern human characteristics, excavated in 1966 in Badakhshan province; 20,000 Upper Palaeolithic flint implements and a 15,000-year-old sculptured limestone pebble, possibly representing a human face, recovered in 1962 and 1965 from Aq Kupruk in Balkh province. Several boxes of Palaeolithic artifacts have been found, but their contents have not been checked, and the carving of the face has not been found.*

FRAGMENTS OF FIVE GOLD AND 12 SILVER VESSELS *dated about 2500 b.c. found accidentally at Tepe Fullol near the ancient lapis-lazuli mines of Badakhshan. In 1966, before they were recovered by the government, the vessels were cut into fragments for distribution by the finders. The gold vessel fragments are missing; four pieces of silver vessels have been recovered.*

THIRD-CENTURY B.C. GREEK AND ARAMAIC INSCRIPTIONS *found at Kandahar in 1963 and 1967, including the westernmost Ashokan Edicts yet discovered. The edicts proclaim the Doctrine of Piety of the Indian emperor Ashoka (ca. 262–232 b.c.), including abstention from killing man or beast and obedience to parents and elders. Condition and whereabouts unknown.*

FOURTH- TO SECOND-CENTURY B.C. FINDS *excavated between 1965 and 1978 at Ai Khanoum in Takhar province, including pseudo-Corinthian capitals, marble and unbaked clay statuary, a gilded silver plaque, coins, Greek inscriptions, and a listing of Delphic precepts. The easternmost Greek city yet known, Ai Khanoum may have been established by order of Alexander the Great. Condition and whereabouts of most of the objects unknown; the site has been badly pillaged.*

MORE THAN 20,000 GOLD ORNAMENTS *dating from the first century b.c. to the first century a.d. excavated in 1978 from six burial mounds at Tillya-tepe, near Shibarghan, in the northern province of Jozjan. A seventh mound was left untouched when the war forced the excavators to close down their mission. Said to be in a bank vault in Kabul, but not seen since 1991.*

WALL PAINTINGS *with Greek, Buddhist, and Hindu motifs from Delbarjin-tepe, once a major Kushan city some 50 miles east of Tillya-tepe, excavated from 1970 to 1973. One painting destroyed when rocket hit museum in 1993.*

A COLLECTION OF 1,772 ARTIFACTS *excavated between 1937 and 1946 from Begram (ancient Kapisa, the summer capital of the Kushan Empire), in Parwan province on the fabled Silk Route that linked India and China with Rome. The finds, dating from the first to third centuries a.d., include carved ivories in classic Indian styles, Chinese lacquers, and a wide variety of gold jewelry, Roman bronzes, and Alexandrian glass. Some ivories remain; others are known to be for sale on the art market.*

A STATUE OF KANISHKA *(ca. a.d. 128), the greatest Kushan ruler, found at Surkh Kotal, in Baghlan province, where excavations began in 1952. Other pieces from the site include a long inscription in the Kushan language, written in Greek script, and Gandharan art works employing classical, Iranian, and Central Asian motifs. Statue* *of Kanishka, a clay fire altar, limestone capitals, and pilasters remain at the museum.*

HUNDREDS OF SCHIST AND LIMESTONE RELIEF SCULPTURES, *together with stucco and terra-cotta artworks that once adorned Buddhist monasteries throughout Afghanistan. Of note is the Dipankara schist relief from Shotorak (second to fifth centuries A.D.), a 33-inch-high relief depicting an encounter between the former Dipankara Buddha and Sumedha, a young Hindu ascetic, who would be reborn as the historic Buddha, Guatama. Large seventh-century A.D. painted sculptures from Fondukistan, made of unbaked clay reinforced with wooden frames and horsehair, illustrate characters from Buddhist mythology and scenes from the life of Buddha. Several schists taken, but some have been recovered in Kabul.*

MARBLE SCULPTURES *depicting various forms of Hindu iconography from the period of Hindu Shahi rule in Kabul, from the sixth to the ninth centuries a.d., and exhibiting styles unique in the history of Indian art. It is feared that many large sculptures now missing have been sawed into fragments to facilitate smuggling and sale. Some 5,000 bronzes, marble reliefs, ceramics, and frescoes from Islam's artistic and cultural flowering under the Ghaznavid dynasty, established late in the tenth century A.D. by a slave from Bokhara, and the Ghorid dynasty, from the central mountains of Afghanistan, that succeeded it in the twelfth century. Many of the bronzes were melted during the fire caused by the first rocket attack in May 1993.*

MORE THAN 30,000 COINS, *from the eighth century b.c. to modern periods, among the largest such collections in the world. An important group was a Greco-Bactrian hoard of more than 600 coins dating from the third to the second centuries B.C. found in 1946 near Kunduz, in Kunduz province. This cache included the largest Greek coins ever discovered, double decadrachmas issued by the Macedonian king Amyntas ca. 120 B.C. and weighing 3.4 ounces each. It also included hoards from Chaman-i-Houzouri near Kabul (Greek and Persian coins from ca. 380 B.C.), Tepe Maranjan (gold and silver Sasanian coins including 368 silver drachmas of the fourth century A.D.),*

15

ROOTS OF TIBETAN BUDDHISM

A U.S.-Chinese team hopes to clarify early Buddhist history in the high plateau of western Tibet.

by MARK ALDENDERFER

TIBET HAS BEEN CLOSED TO WESTERN SCHOLARS until very recently, and the Chinese have worked only sporadically there, mostly near Lhasa, the capital, and in the far eastern regions. What archaeology has been done has examined Neolithic or pre-Buddhist cultures. Research on the Buddhist period has focused on architecture of standing structures or the iconography of wall painting, statuary, or other portable art. Most Chinese archaeologists consider the Buddhist epoch part of historical archaeology, and, as such, excavation is often little more than the attempt to demonstrate the veracity of documentary sources. When conflicts arise between the sources, archaeology tends to be ignored.

Because knowledge of ancient Tibetan Buddhism is so scant, I felt fortunate to collaborate with Huo Wei and Li Yongxian, archaeologists from the department of history at Sichuan Union University in Chengdu, in excavations at Piyang, an important Buddhist temple in western Tibet built late in the tenth century A.D. (see Plate 12). To my knowledge, it is the first such collaboration between Chinese and Western archaeologists in Tibet. My interests have focused on how Buddhist monastic and temple centers in the region were supported, and how secular power influenced them. I am also interested in learning more about the role of trade in the growth of these centers and in reconstructing daily monastic life.

While my Chinese colleagues and I have differences of opinion on archaeological technique and historical perspective, we've been able to develop a mutually satisfying research program. Consistent with their interests, the Chinese are using archaeology to explore the sources of artistic tradition at Piyang in hope of untangling the influence of different Buddhist sects at the site through time. While they naturally study the style of standing structures and the iconography of the art found in caves at the site, they are also receptive to new archaeological methods, such as flotation recovery and geophysical techniques.

Scholars who study Tibet's past believe that Buddhism was first introduced into the central part of the country from India and China in the early to mid-seventh century A.D. Tibet's rulers adopted the religion and became its patrons, founding a number of temples, chapels, and monasteries, many of which still exist. As Tibet's political control over central Asian trade routes faltered, and as the kingdom itself collapsed around A.D. 840, Buddhism's fortunes waned. Few new temples were built, and existing institutions suffered from neglect.

BUDDHISM UNDERWENT A RENAISSANCE in the tenth and eleventh centuries in the unlikeliest of places: the barren stretches of far western Tibet. There, Ye-shes-'od, a regional ruler, became a central figure in the *phyi-dar*, or restoration of Buddhism. Around A.D. 985, Ye-shes-'od renounced his throne and was ordained a Buddhist monk. Using his royal position, and with the support of his family and leading nobles, he undertook the re-establishment of a purer form of Buddhism. The character of religious life in western Tibet following the collapse of the Tibetan empire in A.D. 840 is not well understood, but it seems probable that it was a mixture of Buddhist thought, remnants of Bon (the pre-Buddhist, indigenous religion of much of Tibet), and other cults. To Ye-shes-'od and his followers, much of this practice was degenerate. His reforms included laws that promulgated and protected Buddhist practice and its sponsorship, defined roles for the nobility and commoners, and created the basis for the establishment of communities of ordained monks.

The most important material expression of the reforms was the extraordinary building campaign that took place across western Tibet beginning in A.D. 996 through the early eleventh century. It was during this period that temples were built that became the primary centers of Buddhist teaching in western Tibet for the next 500 years. These buildings were filled with statuary, their walls painted with extraordinary art, strongly influenced, indeed painted by, artists from what is now Kashmir in northern India.

Party cadres were taken to major and minor sites, where they systematically smashed statues, defaced art and pulled roofs from buildings.

Although my Chinese colleagues and I are working on sites that are in some cases 1,000 years old, many have only entered the archaeological record recently. When the Italian art historian Giuseppe Tucci traveled through western Tibet and its borderlands in the 1930s, the temples and other buildings at Tholing, for example, were essentially intact. Other sites—like Tsparang, a capital of Guge on the Sutlej River near Tibet's modern boundary with India—were partly ruined, but unlooted. In 1965, China's Cultural Revolution spread even to this remote corner of Tibet. The results were devastating. Party cadres were taken to major and minor sites, where they systematically smashed statues, defaced art, and pulled roofs from buildings. Books were torn apart and burned, centuries-old sacred objects became mixed with materials of much more recent age, making contextual interpretation next to impossible. At Tholing, a small Mao pin was found in a deposit at the main temple, along with materials dating many centuries earlier.

Piyang is in ruins today, and many of our excavations have faced similar problems of context. The site is large, more than 14 acres, and includes buildings and caves of various sizes and uses in the surrounding hills. In addition to mapping the site, our work has focused on discovering evidence of the A.D. 996 building program. According to historian Roberto Vitali, who has extensively studied the texts of the period, a temple (or *lag-khang*) was first established at Piyang in A.D. 996. It is likely that a *chos-sde* (monastic community) was established there at that time or shortly thereafter. The records, however, are contradictory. Some texts state that only a temple was constructed and that a monastery was built later, well into the eleventh century. Consequently, our first efforts were directed at locating the remains of an early temple, and determining whether or not a monastic community was associated with it.

Fortunately, architectural studies of existing Tibetan and Buddhist temples provide us with a general model of what to expect. Anne Chayet, a French archaeologist and art historian, notes that early temples tend to be square or rectangular in plan and composed of three main parts: an assembly hall, ambulatory, and cella. The hall serves as a meeting and worship place, while the ambulatory is a circuit that a worshiper walks in clockwise fashion while in prayer. It usually surrounds the cella, an interior room that contains sacred images of the Buddha and other holy figures. The interior walls of these rooms are lavishly painted with sacred images and scenes from the life of the Buddha.

Piyang is divided by a small stream. The western half has buildings of relatively recent date (thirteenth through seventeenth centuries) and is the site of the modern village. The eastern side rests on flat tableland 100 feet above the valley floor of the Blackwater River, which drains into the Sutlej. Near the western edge of this plain lies a large, rectangular building that we named the Old Temple. Built of thick adobe blocks, its walls in some places stand more than 20 feet high. These walls are much eroded, but are marked with niches and holes for statues and supports for the roof. In the westernmost room we discovered a white platform with shell-like carved details resembling the seats upon which Buddhas and bodhisattvas reposed. Near the original floor of this room was a strip of decorative wall painting. A sample was radiocarbon dated to ca. A.D. 997. This room is almost certainly a cella, and, if so, the large open room to the east is an assembly hall. Whether we have an ambulatory, however, is uncertain. In published examples of early temples, the ambulatory is enclosed by the walls of the temple. At Piyang, it appears that if an ambulatory is present, it is not roofed; the exterior walls of the cella serve as the interior of the ambulatory. This configuration is supported by the discovery of wall painting at the base of south exterior wall of the cella. If this reconstruction is correct, and the dating secure, it seems probable that the Old Temple is indeed an example of the A.D. 996 building program.

The location of the monastic community remains unclear, but it is likely to be just to the north of the Old Temple, where more than 80 small caves were cut into the rock. The caves closest to the Old Temple are little more than single chambers with few, if any, wall niches. As one moves to the east, there are larger, more elaborate multiroomed caves with hearths, cooking areas, and many wall niches. These resemble later dwellings found at Piyang, and our working hypothesis is that those near the Old Temple are the earliest. How early remains a question. Since monastic life was very spartan, few material remains exist that can be used to determine just when the monks arrived in Piyang. Moreover, these communities were probably not self-supporting; Vitali notes that one of Ye-shes-'od's reforms ordered farmers of the region to donate to monasteries the production of a plot of land and a specific weight of seed (wheat or barley); herders were enjoined to provide equivalents in butter and other products. Thus, while it is unlikely that early caves will have much in the way of artifacts or features to help date them, they do have carbon sooting in the niches that probably held butter lamps for worship or lighting. We took small samples of carbon from both simple and complex caves, and we hope that dates from them will bear out our hypothesis.

One question that often arises in conversation with colleagues or those interested in Tibet is the matter of the Chinese presence there and the ways in which this has affected the development of archaeology in the region. Many Tibetans, of course, see this presence as an occupation of their formerly independent nation, and there are likely some who feel that Chinese-sponsored research is necessarily biased toward a pro-Beijing position. Not surprisingly, it is difficult to sample the opinions of Tibetans living there, although it is clear that those with whom I have had contact are pleased with the excavations taking place at Piyang and other sacred sites. They reason that the preservation of the tangible aspects of the Tibetan past is a worthy effort, and that any work toward that end is desirable, especially in the light of the excesses of the Cultural Revolution. Indeed, they seem especially pleased that a Westerner is part of the effort, because they are certain my presence will help to diffuse more widely an understanding of the Tibetan past.

There are signs that Tibetans are being encouraged to participate at a professional level in research into the Tibetan past. Although there have long been a number of Tibetan "paraprofessionals" with extensive archaeological knowledge who have worked for the Tibetan Bureau of Cultural Relics (TBRC), none have advanced degrees. Tibetans have now been enrolled in the undergraduate program at Sichuan Union University, with the goal that they return to Tibet and develop new research programs. And finally, the University of California at Santa Barbara, Sichuan Union, and the TBCR are currently engaged in negotiations that will bring the first Tibetan to the United States to obtain a Ph.D. in archaeology. All parties agree that this
is a very worthwhile project.

Although our work at Piyang is just beginning, we are reasonably certain we have identified an A.D. 996 temple, and possibly an early monastic complex. Movies such as *Kundun* and *Seven Years in Tibet* have promoted a sense that Tibetan Buddhism is timeless and eternal. For those who practice its tenets, this is true, but materially, Buddhism is not eternal; projects like ours are among the few that will preserve Tibetan Buddhist history for future generations.

MARK ROSE

PLATE 1: *The temple at Mnajdra, in Malta, before it was attacked by vandals in April of 2001.*

DAVID O'CONNOR/PENN-YALE-IFA

PLATE 2: *Abydos' most famous monuments were built during the New Kingdom, including a temple of Rameses II (r. 1290-1224* B.C.*), son of Seti I (r. 1306–1290* B.C.*).*

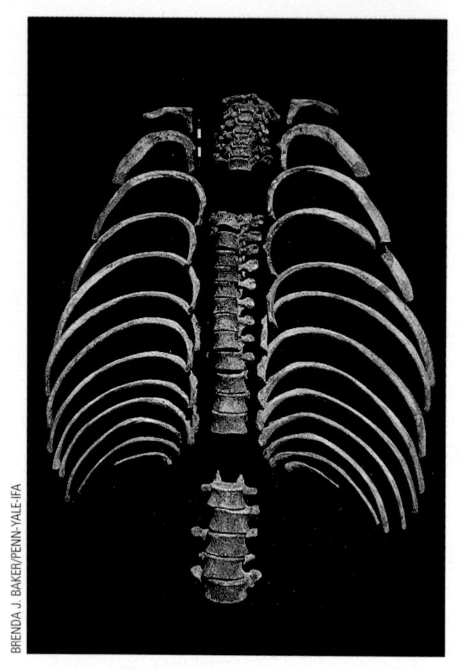

BRENDA J. BAKER/PENN-YALE-IFA

PLATE 3: *The skeleton of a woman in her 30s found at Abydos reveals an extra set of ribs.*

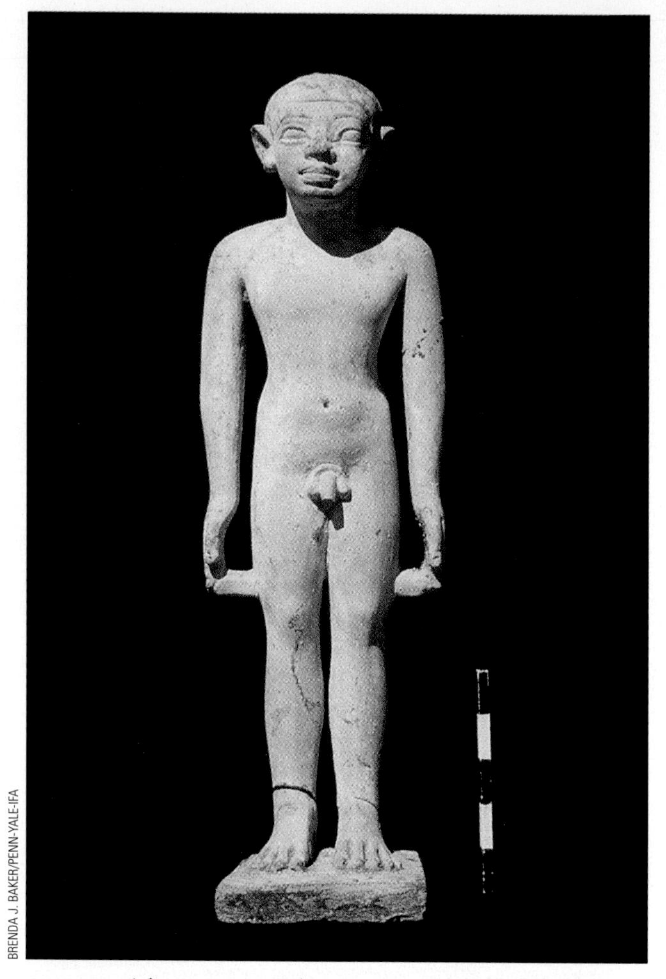

BRENDA J. BAKER/PENN-YALE-IFA

PLATE 4: *A limestone statue depicting Weni the Elder as a child was found in the southeast corner of his tomb complex.*

JANET RICHARDS/PENN-YALE-IFA

PLATE 5: *The interior of the mastaba of Weni the Elder. The shaft to his grave is visible in the foreground; the serdab, or hidden chamber, is behind it to the right.*

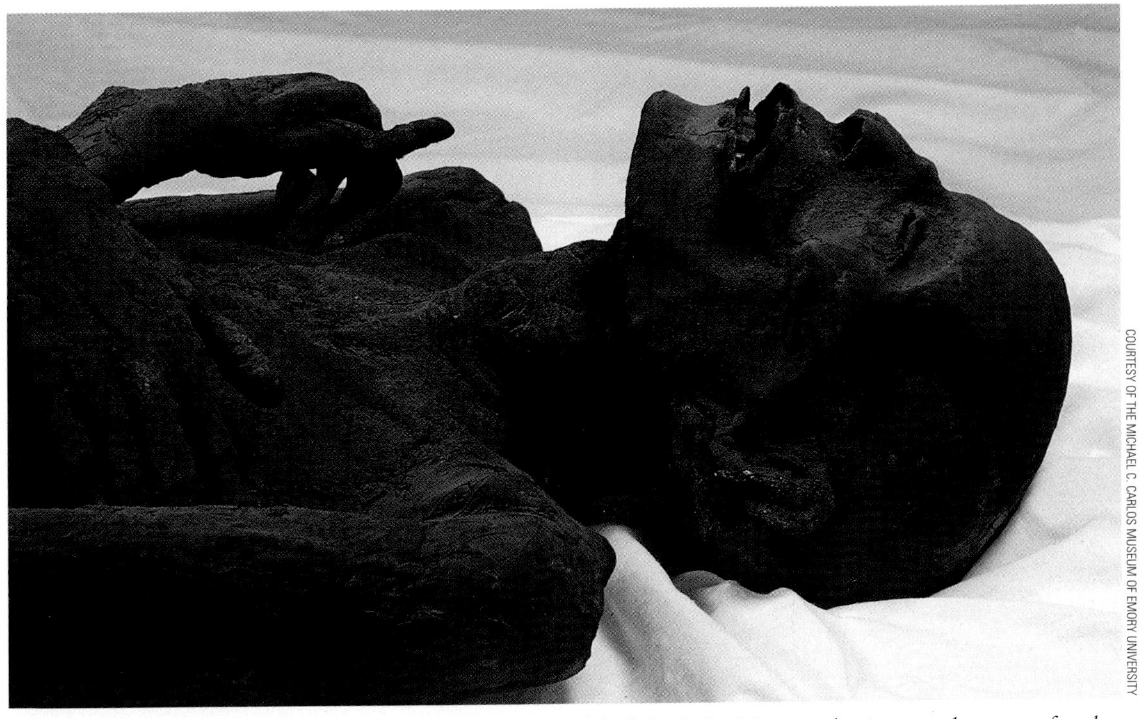

COURTESY OF THE MICHAEL C. CARLOS MUSEUM OF EMORY UNIVERSITY

PLATE 6: *An image of the possible Ramesses I mummy in the Michael C. Carlos Museum, showing crossed-arm pose found on 19th Dynasty pharaohs.*

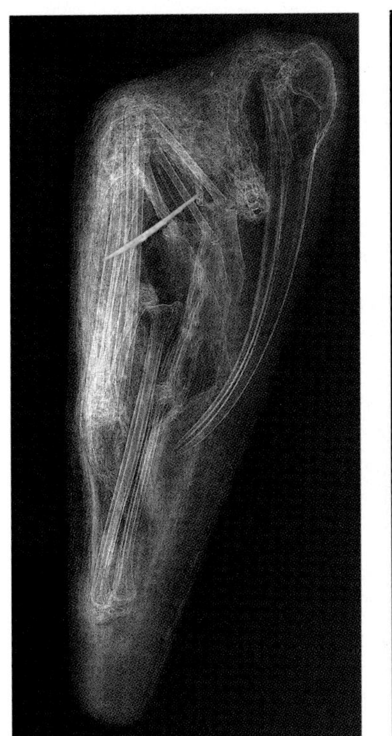

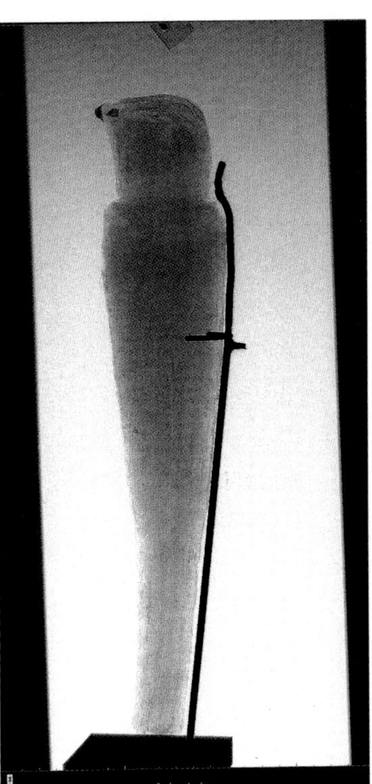

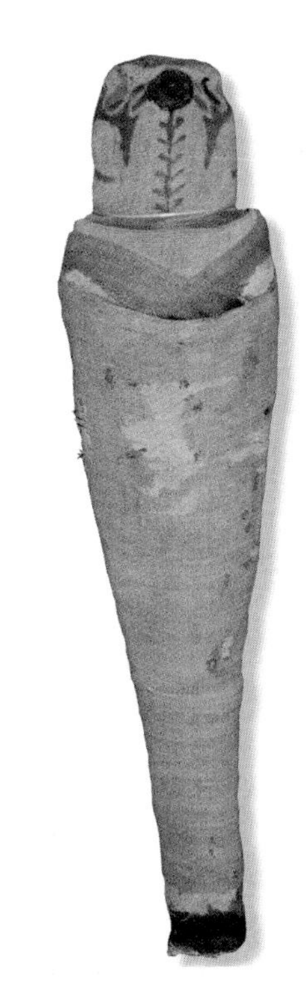

COURTESY BOB BRIER

(l-r) PLATE 7, 8 & 9: *X-ray examination of a mummified ibis, left, revealed the bird's intact skeleton, while the falcon mummy, middle, turned up nothing but a false bill of goods for some unsuspecting pilgrim. Far right, the fully wrapped falcon fake.*

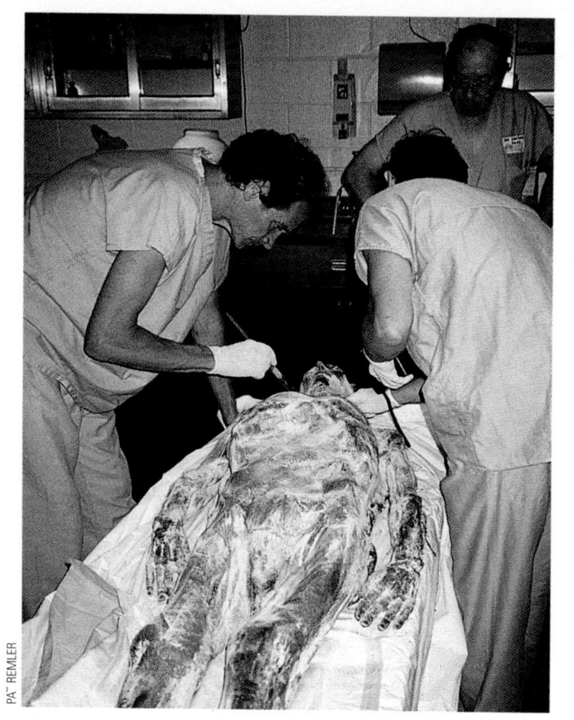

PAT REMLER

PLATE 10: *Once the natron has been removed, the author's mummy, like its ancient counterparts, is dark brown and rigid, and the arms are difficult to flex.*

MARK ROSE

PLATE 11: *Piers of the Ponte Fabricio, Rome's best preserved ancient bridge, were restored while soot was removed for the 2000 jubilee.*

MARK ALDENDERFER

PLATE 12: *The temple and monastic remains at Piyang. This portion of the site was used from the thirteenth to sixteenth century* A.D.

COURTESY KILMARTIN HOUSE TRUST, SCOTLAND

PLATE 13: *By A.D. 490, immigrants from Dál Riata, a petty kingdom in northeastern Ireland, had crossed to Scotland and established their family seat, the fortress of Dunadd in Argyll, shown here.*

COURTESY KILMARTIN HOUSE TRUST, SCOTLAND

PLATE 14: *Crucible and brooch mold excavated at Dunadd attest the manufacture of jewelry at the site.*

STEPHEN H. LEKSON

PLATE 15: *Pinnacle Ruin, atop a butte at the end of the Rio Alamosa gorge, was settled by Anasazi emigrants from the Four Corners region.*

STEPHEN H. LEKSON

PLATE 16 & 17: *Pottery styles point to connections between the Mesa Verde Anasazi and their descendants. Patterns on pottery from Pinnacle Ruin (left) are clearly derived from Mesa Verde ones (right).*

CHARLES ANDREW DITMAS, FROM HISTORIC HOMESTEADS OF KINGS COUNTY

PLATE 18: *An old photo shows the Lott house as a working farm, before the area around it was developed.*

COURTESY CATHERINE LOTT-DIVIS

PLATE 19: *Field hands are joined by a Lott family member, far left, to pick string beans.*

U.S. MILITARY ACADEMY

PLATE 20: *Portrait of Buffalo Soldiers: Sergeant Nathan Fletcher, standing far left, and Sergeant Robert Burley, sitting second from left, fought at Hembrillo.*

COURTESY ARIZONA HISTORICAL SOCIETY/TUSCON

PLATE 21: *Victorio, an Apache chief who led a two-year Apache uprising against the U.S.*

JAMES P. DELGADO

PLATE 22: *Visitors to the* Titanic *have left memorial plaques and a bouquet of plastic roses.*

PART V: EUROPE

15

LAND OF THE GOLDEN FLEECE

Legendary Colchis lives on in the Republic of Georgia.

by KRISTIN M. ROMEY

"WE'RE LOOKING FOR NAMARNU. CAN YOU HELP us?" The wizened, kerchiefed wo-man looked up from her garden, eyeing our red van. "Namarnu, Namarnu," she repeated slowly, as if it were an incantation, "Namarnu." She shook her head. "Medea's city," the driver offered, "Namarnu."

Hearing the name of the Colchian princess who helped Jason steal the Golden Fleece, the woman smiled. "Ah, Medea!" She pointed her finger toward the gutted remains of a nearby collective farm, framed by a vast expanse of barren fields and the rapidly setting sun. "Out there, past those buildings."

We inched the van down the dirt road pocked with potholes that could easily swallow one of the many water buffalo that watched us from the nearby riverbank and stopped far behind the farm. In the distance, several small, treed hillocks rose from the plain.

"It's been 12 years since I've been out here," muttered Guram, my guide. "I think that's the site, but in this light, I can't tell." The sky was birdless and still and turned inky black in what seemed to be a single moment. To the Greeks, Colchis lay at the fringes of the inhabited world. That night, I had to agree.

There are two sides to every story, but in the case of tales told by the ancient Greeks, by triumph of their early literacy and our later biases, usually only their side has survived. It was the pursuit of that other side of a favorite Greek tale that took me last summer to Georgia, a small former Soviet republic the size of South Carolina, wedged between the Caucasus Mountains and Russia to the north and Turkey to the south. Here in the country's western half, a region bordered by the Black Sea, is where Greek legend says Jason sailed up the river Phasis and stole the Golden Fleece from Aeetes, king of the Colchians.

Our earliest complete description of Jason's travels to Colchis, the *Argonautica*, was composed by Apollonius Rhodius in the third century B.C. The Hellenistic poet charmed his audiences with the tale of Jason and his crew aboard the *Argo*, determined to fulfill a seemingly impossible task demanded by Jason's uncle in exchange for Jason's rightful place upon his father's throne: to return to Greece the fleece of a golden ram that had long ago carried a young Greek prince across the Black Sea to safety on its eastern shore. The Argonauts enjoyed a series of minor Mediterranean adventures—including a quick retreat from an island of lusty women—before surviving a treacherous passage through the Bosporus and into the Black Sea, eventually anchoring along the marshy shores of Colchis. The potions of Aeetes' love-lorn sorceress daughter Medea enabled Jason to rise to the king's challenge and steal the fleece from its serpent guardian. Jason and Medea returned to Greece with the fleece and reclaimed the family's throne. (Other ancient authors provided this epic its unhappy ending, in which Medea poisons her children and Jason's new wife.)

Apollonius Rhodius' poem was not the first to celebrate Jason's adventures; the legend of the Argonauts' voyage is among the earliest of the Greek world. Homer alludes to it in both the *Iliad* and *Odyssey*, describing some participants in the Trojan War as the sons and grandsons of the Argonauts, which would place the arrival of the *Argo* on the eastern shores of the Black Sea some time in the Late Bronze Age (ca. 1700–1100 B.C.). While the archaeological record does not support a voyage at such an early date, there is plenty of evidence for Greek trading centers in Colchis from the mid-sixth century B.C. on. In their quest for gold, precious stones, and fine cloth, intrepid traders were lured to the farthest reaches of their known world, where, according to Greek writers, women practiced witchcraft, deadly creatures lurked in rivers, and unfortunate interlopers were flayed alive.

How did the Colchians, farmers and metallurgists who had lived in the region since the third millennium B.C., view the treasure-seekers who appeared on their shores? What sort of relationship did they develop with these strangers? Did they embrace the mythical legacy of cooperation between the two peoples that the Greeks brought with them to Colchis hundreds of years after the arrival of *Argo*? Georgian archaeologists have been working for more than a century to answer these questions, and their work continues despite the dismantling of their once-primary funding source, the Soviet state, despite civil wars, breakaway republics, and a near collapse of basic services.

In the Georgian capital of Tbilisi, I met Guram Kvirkvelia, an expert in Colchian archaeology at the Georgian Academy of Science's Center for Archaeological Studies, and Bato, our driver. Bato was particularly pleased to be associated with the trip; he hails from the western Georgian district of Mingrelia, whose population claims a direct descent from the Colchians.

We made our way west from Tbilisi over the Surami Mountains, which divide the country into eastern and western regions. For millennia, the Surami also divided the country culturally, with the eastern kingdom of Iberia maintaining closer ties to the Assyrian and Persian empires, while the Colchian west looked more toward the Mediterranean world. From the Surami, lushly wooded hills tumble down into and around fertile, subtropical lowlands that end on the marshy eastern shores of the Black Sea.

Our first stop was the temple city of Vani, the most significant Colchian administrative and trading center yet discovered. Far from the sea, on a strategic hilltop overlooking the plain where the Phasis (modern Rioni) and Sulori rivers meet, it is in Vani that the Colchian's legendary golden wealth is best demonstrated.

Unlike many other regions around the Black Sea, where the Greeks established colonies to exploit rich agricultural land, Colchis came within the sights of Mediterranean traders because of its abundant natural resources. The Greek geographer Strabo wrote about the lush forests that provided excellent shipbuilding materials, while the historian Herodotus mentioned the fine linen woven from local flax. The availability of gemstones in the region was reflected in a Greek belief that the first gem set into a ring was fashioned from the Caucasian mountain to which Prometheus was chained after stealing fire from the gods, but Colchis was best known for the rich deposits of copper and iron ores and gold.

Since antiquity people have speculated about the nature of that infamous fleece: Was it truly golden, truly a fleece? Or a symbol for something else? The most common explanation was put forth by Strabo and the Roman author Appian, who described how natives of the Caucasus hung sheepskins in mountain streams to collect gold dust suspended in the water. Other ancient authors contended that the golden fleece was a book on how to obtain gold by means of chemistry, or a technique for writing in gold.

Vani was founded in the eighth century B.C., a century during which Colchis witnessed a population explosion, most likely caused by significant innovations in iron production. The settlement atop the hill consisted of a collection of log buildings, the standard form of shelter in heavily wooded Colchis. From its inception, Vani appears to have been a center for cult activity, evidenced by caches of fantastic multiheaded clay animals buried there.

By the sixth century, Greek colonists from Miletus had established emporias along the sea coast to trade directly with their Colchian neighbors. Here in the hinterland, however,

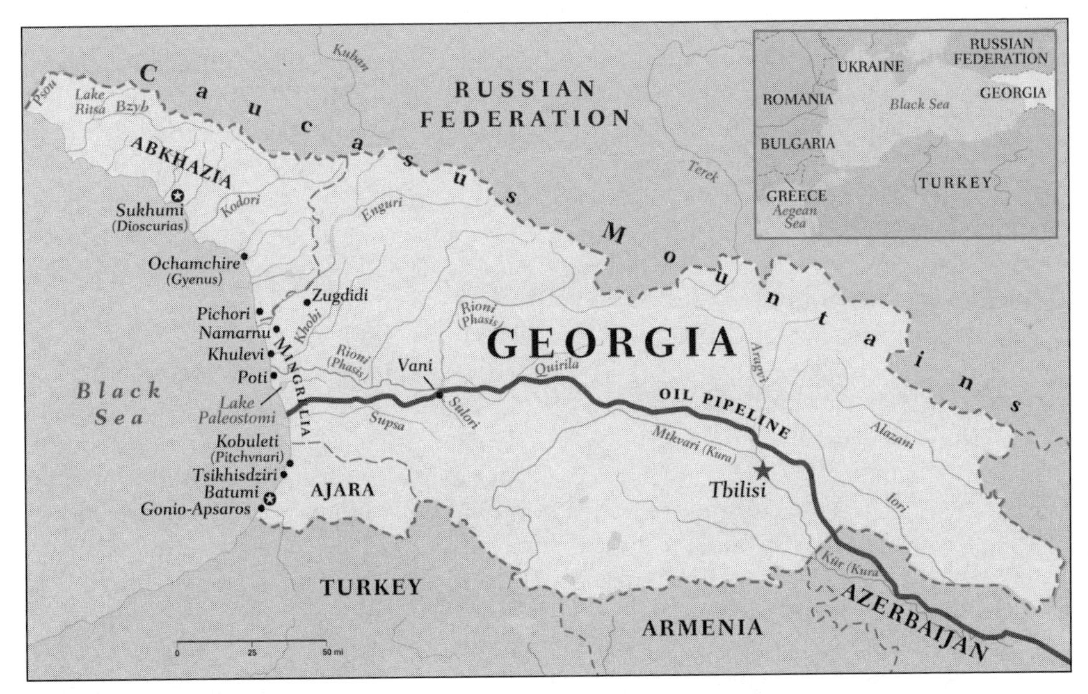

they preferred to trade only with local rulers, ferrying imported luxury items up the Phasis and its tributaries to exchange for raw materials. Rivers were the primary highways for trade, demonstrated by the fact that Greek pottery finds decrease in proportion to their distance from rivers. Profits from this trade created a Colchian elite at Vani that, while adopting Greek writing and monetary systems, resisted a more encompassing Hellenization for centuries. Local pottery styles, with wavy lines and chevrons, persisted; buildings retained the log-cabin design used in the region since the Bronze Age; human and horse sacrifice accompanied the most elite burials; and the jewelry remained beautifully and uniquely Colchian, a careful balance of Greek composition and Achaemenid Persian themes, together with a local fondness for animal forms, expressed in fanciful combinations of granulation and filigree.

By the Hellenistic period, the increasingly wealthy cult center of Vani may have appeared as a Greek city to an outsider, but closer inspection would reveal that Greek-looking stone temples lacked Greek-style interiors and Greek gods. Male figurines cast in iron and bronze and adorned with gold earrings and necklaces were buried in the foundations of buildings. A fragmentary inscription on a bronze plaque records, in Greek, local religious legislation; it is perhaps the only Colchian text that remains with us today: "Helios, Gaia, and Man [deities of the sun, earth, and moon] have witnessed this, and if anybody does not obey, the gods will...." Seals, grafitti, and stamped roof tiles reveal names written in Greek that are neither Greek nor Persian, but Colchian: Dedatos, Arsans, Melabes, Oradzo, and Khorsip.

As the city's altars and temples, and accompanying treasuries, increased in number, so did its fortifications. Vani's wealth may have led to its downfall. Strabo writes that the city was plundered twice, and archaeologists have uncovered evidence—including a battering ram on display at the Vani museum—of two destructions, most likely committed by Bosporan king Pharnaces and Mithridates VI in the first half of the first century B.C.

LIFE AT VANI TODAY REFLECTS THE GENeral political and economic crises facing the republic. Nonetheless, its archaeologists are surprisingly resilient. Guram, who has worked for many years at Vani, recalls the 1992 excavation season, when rebel forces loyal to deposed president Zvaid Gamsakhurdia attempted to seize Tbilisi and were stopped only miles outside of Vani. The archaeologists continued to excavate while shells exploded in the distance. Nowadays, energy supplies in the country are so limited that the electricity comes on for only a few hours at night, but Vani's museum remains open and its employees, who haven't been paid in many months, and aren't expecting a paycheck anytime soon, still come to work in a building that houses a treasury of gold coins and jewelry. No one here would dream of taking a single obol.

Preeminent Georgian archaeologist and Colchian specialist Otar Lordkipanadze, who has directed excavations at Vani since 1966, would later explain the reverence that Georgia's citizens hold for their history: "Colchian culture marked the beginning of Georgian statehood," he told me back in Tbilisi. This was a deceptively simple statement. Georgia is a country that has been at the crossroads of powerful empires—Assyrian, Persian, Roman, Byzantine, Ottoman, and Russian—for millennia, but has stubbornly resisted assimilation. Georgians are proud that they have retained their language, alphabet, and culture in light of so many trying circumstances; the concept of the Georgian state is a sacred one.

Even though it was June, up in the hills the air was cold and damp, permeating our clothes and lodging in our bones. So on our last afternoon at Vani, while our photographer was attempting to take pictures in the unlit exhibition hall, Guram and I huddled around the museum's acrid kerosene heater and discussed Vani's more recent history. Excavations have been going on here for over 100 years, ever since word spread of fantastic golden objects spilling out of the hillsides after heavy rains. I asked Guram how much of the city still lies beneath the farms that ring the hilltop. He shrugged. "During Soviet times, our expedition received over 40,000 rubles a year, and we excavated over seven sites in Vani each season. When the Union collapsed, all of our money disappeared. Now, we depend on the few foreign volunteers that come to Vani. If we have two, three, four people paying about $900 each to dig, that's enough to keep some excavation going. Not that I want the communists back," he adds quickly, nudging the kerosene heater with his foot, "Not for any reason."

For the past few years, the laying of an oil pipeline from the Caspian shores of neighboring Azerbaijan across Georgia to its central Black Sea coast provided funds for the Center for Archaeological Studies to excavate just ahead of construction. Oil industry money still trickles in, in support of salvage operations in areas where additional infrastructure is being built for an offshore oil terminal. The excavation of the Colchian settlement of Khulevi, at the mouth of the Khobi River on the Black Sea coast just north of the Phasis, is the latest beneficiary. The existence of a Colchian settlement at Khulevi was first established through test trenches dug in the 1970s, but a full excavation began last April, funded by a multinational venture that is building a harbor for oil tankers. Excavation director Rezo Papuashvili gave us a tour of the site, shouting over the combined roar of a stormy sea and, more ominously, the enormous earth-dredger eating its way into the riverbank.

To live comfortably on the marshy coastal plain, Colchians created artificial hillocks, often clustered or arranged in concentric circles separated by moats, on which they built their log houses. At Khulevi, the largest settlement yet found from the eighth and seventh centuries B.C.—the period of the Colchian population explosion—the five-acre hillock is encircled by a 90-foot-wide defensive ditch, with some smaller undefended settlements surrounding it. Papuashvili pointed out fragments of oak walls that stick out from trenches dug down below sea level. The Black Sea has risen considerably since the time of the Colchians, and Papuashvili speculated that a significant portion of the settlement may now lie off the coast. His team has yet to locate the town's necropolis, generally located on the outskirts of a settlement.

From the second half of the eighth century to the end of the sixth, local burial practice involved hanging the dead from trees until bodies were completely defleshed, a practice described in the *Argonautica*, when Jason and his crew sneak off the *Argo* into Colchian territory at night: "Here osiers and willows stand in rows, with corpses dangling on ropes from their highest branches." At some point—perhaps on a specific day of the year or when a certain number of dead had been reached—the bodies were gathered together, burned and buried in collective pits along with grave goods including beads, weapons, zoomorphic and anthropomorphic figurines, and agricultural implements such as hoes and scythes. Some collective burial pits have contained remains of over 250 individuals. Guram noted that such secondary burials still occurred last century in the republic's northern district of Abkhazia—but, oddly enough, only for people killed by lightning.

Perhaps the strangest fact regarding Colchian burial practices is that, although their settlements date back well into the second millennium B.C., not a single burial has been found that predates the eighth century B.C. Archaeologists seem reluctant to speculate why. "Maybe in earlier times they put their dead in the rivers or the sea," said Guram, "but that is very hypothetical at best." As contacts with the Greeks increased from the sixth century on, Colchians began to bury their dead, curling them up in a fetal position or interring them in large pots.

Papuashvili had until the end of the year to finish work at Khulevi. "We've known about this settlement for a while," he said, raising his voice as an oil company bulldozer lumbered by, "but only the oil money gave us the possibility to excavate it."

Highway travel in Georgia is consistently

hindered by the traffic police, who always manage to find some offense that can be easily remedied by cash. Driving from Khulevi to Poti, a port city on the coast near the mouth of the Phasis River, we were pulled over (for an imagined infraction) below a large sign featuring an image of the *Argo*. It was near Poti that the *Argo* first entered Aeetes' kingdom, and reminders of the Argonaut legend appear everywhere. A monument to the "Colchian Mother" stands in the center of town, and a fiberglass rendition of the *Argo* until recently served as a harborside café where one could purchase ice-cold bottles of Argo beer. Relatively quiet since Soviet naval forces left the port (taking with them everything they could and blowing up what they couldn't), Poti is pinning its hopes on the oil pipeline and trade with new regional partners. A promotional brochure for the city touts its long history as a trading center, beginning with the ancient city of Phasis.

ACCORDING TO GREEK TRADITION, A colony was founded at Phasis by the Milesians, who at first thought of their Colchian neighbors as cannibals who "stripped the skin off men"—perhaps a misunderstanding of their burial practices. The colony, believed to have been established around the mid-sixth century B.C., soon became a major trading center for the two cultures. The actual site of Phasis has yet to be positively identified, although many archaeologists believe it now lies beneath the murky waters of nearby Lake Palaeostomi. At a mid-sixth- to mid-fifth-century Colchian settlement 12 miles up the Phasis River from the coast, excavations yielded gold jewelry and imported Greek pottery in the remains of the Colchians' humble log cabins.

While kings named Aeetes were known to the Romans as late as the sixth century A.D. and the Roman writer Arrian claimed that the *Argo*'s anchor was on display in Phasis, oddly enough there is no reference to the expedition of the Argonauts in any Colchian or Greek material found in the territory of Georgia, with the exception of a Greek colony named after the Argonaut twins Castor and Pollux, brothers of Helen of Troy who were known as the Dioscuri.

The site of Dioscurias is located on the northwestern coastal fringe of Colchis, in the region of Abkhazia. Much of this area, rising above the marshy plains of the central coast, attracted larger and earlier Colchian settlements that were influenced by Scythians living north of the Caucasus. The Greeks had arrived at Dioscurias by the fifth century, and archaeological evidence shows that they lived in close proximity to their Colchian neighbors. Parts of Dioscurias now lie beneath the Abkhaz capital of Sukhumi, while a significant portion of the ancient city has fallen victim to the rising waters of the Black Sea. Excavations in the area have revealed Attic bronze helmets, amphorae from Chios, Attica, and Sinope, a statuette of Demeter, and a Greek funerary stele. South of Dioscurias is Gyenus (modern Ochamchire), the third Greek colony in Colchis, along with Phasis and Dioscurias, mentioned by ancient writers. Like Khulevi and Phasis, Gyenus was established on the coast at the mouth of a navigable river. Considerable Greek influence, reflected in large amounts of Ionian pottery, appeared here in the sixth century, but more excavation is needed to determine the extent of Greek settlement in the area.

Unfortunately, the closest most archaeologists can get to Dioscurias and Gyenus these days is the Enguri River, which marks the border between Abkhazia and the rest of Georgia. Between 1992 and 1993, ethnic nationalist Abkhaz forces attempted to separate from the rest of the republic and fighting ensued. Abkhazia's status remains in limbo, its territory occupied by Russian and UNOMIG (United Nations Observer Mission in Georgia) peacekeepers. Sukhumi and Ochamchire remain inactive war zones; the coast is littered with mines.

The coast is littered with mines.

Zugdidi, the largest town on the Georgian side of the Enguri River, lies within the 12-mile security zone maintained by peacekeeping forces on either side of the border. On our way to see the Colchian collection in the Zugdidi Museum, we passed into the zone, marked by a tank with a drowsy Russian soldier sitting atop, resting his elbows on the Kalashnikov assault rifle lying across his lap.

We were met at the museum by director Ilya Antelava and made small talk in his office while waiting for another official to escort us to the collection, a typical Colchian assortment of bronze and iron weapons, farming tools, and ornaments. Zugdidi is a city of refugees, its only industries UNOMIG and a Snickers factory, and the despair was obvious even here in the museum. Antelava, who is also head of the Mingrelian Scientific Center of the Georgian Academy of Sciences, spoke of his historical research. "I have no idea what's going on a half kilometer away," he said, gesturing towards the river, "so how am I supposed to know what happened there 500 years ago?" Hoping to break the uncomfortable silence that followed, I asked him if he agreed that the Mingrelians are direct descendants of the Colchians. Antelava smiled a sad smile. "Yes. That's the only true thing around here."

After our tour of the collection, we headed back to the van. "Bato asks if you want to see the border," said Guram. "Sure," I replied immediately, although I wasn't sure if the decision was fueled more by curiosity or the bravado resulting from numerous shots of *chacha* (Georgian moonshine) foisted on us by our host at breakfast that morning.

The border itself was a makeshift assortment of wood and barbed-wire barriers blocking a bridge across the Enguri. Armed Russian soldiers in bullet-proof vests walked in slow circles, occasionally pulling the barriers aside to let military vehicles and some cars and horse-drawn carts driven by Abkhazian citizens pass. A sign on one of the barriers read in Russian: "Stop. Or we will shoot you."

We stood there for a while and stared across the river at the verdant, unexpectedly quiet hills. "You know, there's a very interesting site right across the river there," Guram said, pointing from behind the barricades. "Pichori. It was occupied from the end of the third millennium until the fourth century B.C. Huge site, right near the sea. I identified it back in 1979, and we excavated there from 1981 until the war." He went on to describe the 25-acre Colchian city, consisting of a hill about 200 feet around and 15 feet high, surrounded by a moat and encircled by another ten settlement hills, surrounded again by another moat and another ten hills. Bronze-making workshops and a necropolis were also found, as well as a system of moats and a river connecting Pichori to two other nearby settlements. All together, this Colchian city covered almost 25 acres in size. Systematic excavations at Pichori, like at Dioscurias and Gyenus, stopped with the fighting.

A soldier began to shout at us for taking too many photographs. As we walked away from barricades, Guram took a final look over the river. "This is all so stupid," he sighed, "Before this damn war, we didn't have these problems. Abkhaz, Georgian, who cares, that didn't matter when you were excavating."

EVER SINCE VANI, GURAM HAD BEEN talking about a "very interesting charioteer" in a provincial museum that I absolutely had to see. I had no idea what exactly this "charioteer" was, but was eager to get out of the misery of Zugdidi. Soon we were humming down a straightaway when we heard the now-familiar shrill of a traffic police whistle. Bato rolled his eyes and pulled over, and a corpulent cop, hand on his gun, sauntered over and stuck his head in the van window to better survey our luggage and camera equipment. "Your turn signal is broken," he drawled. Guram translated and I tried to suppress a laugh. The last turn we had made was three miles back.

Bato tried a line he was having some success with: "There's an American journalist in the van."

The cop looked over at me. I smiled, raising my notebook.

His face reddening, the cop turned back to Bato. "I'll stop you again on the way back," he growled, "and then I'll fine you a hundred dollars!" And with that, the cop yanked on the brim of his Soviet-era hat, complete with hammer and sickle, spun on his heel, and marched away.

Thanks to the cop, we arrived at the museum just after closing time, and Givi Elliava, the 82-year-old museum director, was reluctant to let us in. "Please," pleaded Guram, "this lady has come all the way from America to see your charioteer!" Elliava frowned. "Come back in 45 minutes," he replied.

When we returned, the director was cradling a small cardboard box in his hands. Beaming, he removed the top, and inside I saw a small bronze figurine of a man, hands extended to clutch the reins of a chariot, maybe one-and-a-half inches high. It was found in 1975 during the excavation of a Colchian necropolis at a nearby village. The necropolis, dated to the second half of the eighth century–first half of the seventh century, contained standard collective burials featuring typical zoomorphic ceramics, beads, weapons, and bronze animal figurines.

"This charioteer is really unusual," Guram said. "Nothing like it has been found in Colchis or anywhere around it. But it is very much like Geometric Greek (eighth century B.C.) charioteer figurines from Greece. Professor Lordkipanadze believes that it may be a Greek import, maybe the earliest one in the entire Black Sea area."This came as a surprise to me—the general belief among scholars is that the first archaeological evidence for Greek contact with peoples living around the Black Sea did not occur until almost a century later, in the last quarter of the seventh century.

I asked Lordkipanadze about the possibility of Greeks in the Black Sea as early as the eighth century. "There was active contact during the eighth century, at least with the Colchians," he replied. "There are bronze bells and figurines from the eighth century found on the Greek island of Samos. They are definitely Colchian, and we have found the same items here. Greek fibulae and pottery forms and designs characteristic of Geometric art—these appear in Colchis in the eighth century. I believe there is a connection between the multiheaded animal figurines at Vani and very similar ones found at Olympus. And look at the literary evidence: already in the eighth and seventh centuries, the Greeks mention Colchis, they mention Phasis. The legend of the Argonauts is very popular at this time; the Greeks were very interested."

Did the Greeks actually travel across the Black Sea in the Late Bronze Age, as Homer would have us believe? Lordkipanadze smiled. "Of course, there is no archaeological evidence yet for such a trip. But I believe the myth of Jason and the Argonauts reflects the earliest Greek exploration. Troy wasn't a fantasy to the Greeks."

Our final destination was the southwestern region of Adjara, which had declared itself an autonomous republic within Georgia and festooned the main crossing point into the district with large concrete barricades and equally large "border patrol" officers who demanded our passports. A couple of miles past the checkpoint, an enormous Soviet-style statue of a bearded, cloaked man holding the reins of two equally enormous horses rose up from the side of the road. Guram pointed to it. "There's King Aeetes, and right behind him is Pitchvnari."

ALTHOUGH NOT MENTIONED IN THE ancient literature, the site of Pitchvnari had a considerable Greek community from the second half of the fifth century to the end of the fourth century, featuring the only Greek necropolis found so far in Colchis. Excavations at the necropolis have revealed the finest Athenian pottery, including a magnificent red-figure krater. Archaeologists have discovered the associated Greek settlement, but its waterlogged location—near the sea at the confluence of two rivers—would make its excavation an extremely expensive prospect. An enormous Colchian settlement existed nearby, and finds at its necropolis, only 300 feet away from the Greek one, show that the Colchians at Pitchvnari adopted some Greek funerary practices, including placing a coin under the tongue of the dead to pay Charon, the ferryman who carried their souls over the river Styx.

The finds at Pitchvnari tell a story of Greek colonization that is unusual for the Black Sea region. Outside of Colchis, particularly along the northern and western coasts, the Greeks exploited enormous areas of land and established powerful city-states, like Chersonesus in modern-day Ukraine, to regulate trade and local populations. The Greek "colonies" of Colchis, however, appear to be no more than small-scale trading posts whose presence did not radically alter the traditional life-style of the region. With the exception of the Vani aristocracy, Colchians continued to live in their log cabins, producing their traditional weapons and pottery and worshiping their local deities. Although Herodotus claims that the Colchians assisted Xerxes in his invasion of Greece in the fifth century B.C., there is no evidence of conflict between the native population and Greeks in Colchis.

We met Amiran Kakhidze, the director of excavations at Pitchvnari, in the Adjaran capital of Batumi. He showed us the new Batumi Archaeological Museum, of which he is also the director. Workers were busy renovating the building, a former Soviet cultural center, with funds provided by Adjara's leader, who refuses to turn over tax revenue from Batumi's busy port and its border crossing with Turkey to the central Georgian government. A large room houses the collections from Pitchvnari and the nearby site of Tsikhisdziri, where fifth-century burials have revealed large amounts of Attic red- and black-figure pottery and terra-cotta animal figurines. My eye fell on a small, blue basalt statuette of an Egyptian pharaoh, and I was immediately reminded of Herodotus' assertion that the Colchians were descendants of Egyptian soldiers who, following a campaign in the northern Black Sea, were unwilling to make the long trip home. "Yes, the pharaoh," Kakhidze smiled, "he was found during the construction of a house in a nearby village. Perhaps some Greek settler brought him here." What about Herodotus' idea of the Colchian's Egyptian origin? Kakhidze dismissed the question with a wave of his hand. "He was probably drinking too much wine when he wrote that," volunteered a bystander.

The Colchians had a long-standing wine-drinking tradition well before the Greeks arrived on their shores.

The Colchians themselves had a long-standing wine-drinking tradition well before the Greeks arrived on their shores. Some archaeologists suggest, only half in jest, that relations between Colchians and Greeks were cordial because of their mutual respect for the grape. Kakhidze extended an invitation to sample the local product at a traditional Georgian *supra*, or feast, he was hosting in the Apsaros fortress.

A couple of miles south of Batumi, the fortress was the perfect place to finish our expedition: a symbol of the beginning and end of the Colchian saga. According to Greek tradition, after Medea helped Jason steal the Golden Fleece, they fled on the *Argo*, only to be pursued by a Colchian fleet led by Medea's brother Apsaros. Medea invited her brother onboard, whereupon he was killed, chopped up, and thrown into the sea. The Colchians collected his remains and buried them, according to Roman writers, at this site. Perhaps this was an attempt by Rome to claim an association with the Argonauts; during the Third Mithridatic War (74–63 B.C.), Pompey routed Mithridates in Colchis and annexed the region, building forts along the coast and bringing Colchian rule of the region to an end.

THE FORTRESS WAS ESTABLISHED BY THE Romans in the first half of the first century B.C., and successive Byzantine and Ottoman forces enlarged and fortified the 11-acre complex. Its impressive walls and towers still stand, and during Soviet times its interior served as a citrus farm, growing oranges and lemons for party elite in Moscow. Today, parts of the fort are being excavated, revealing elaborate Turkish baths and Byzantine and Roman barracks.

It was on our way back to Tbilisi that Guram suggested we take a look at Namarnu, described as the "great barbarian polis" by a fourth-century B.C. writer and often referred to as "Medea's city." The 30-acre site, founded around the beginning of the first millennium B.C. between the Phasis and Pichora rivers, has been excavated only intermittently.

The site lies very far off the beaten path, and as we trundled along the rutted dirt roads, eliciting stares from those on the occasional horse-drawn cart, I began to review our trip, trying to align the mythical adventures of the Argonauts—their encounter with a barbarian king and his sorceress daughter, serpents guarding golden fleece in outdoor sanctuaries, dark swamps festooned with corpses—with the reality of life for the true Argonauts, trading painted pots and amphoras of food and drink from their small coastal settlements in return for metals and wood, quietly coexisting with the local "barbarians."

I was still trying to reconcile this when we finally stopped the van and peered out at the collection of hillocks said to be Medea's hometown. It wasn't until the last feeble rays of sun disappeared behind the hills that I realized how infinitely far away the Greeks must have felt from their own world, out here on the dark Colchian plain, with only the gleam of gold to light their way.

16

CELEBRATING MIDAS

Contents of a great Phrygian king's tomb reveal a lavish funerary banquet.

by ELIZABETH SIMPSON

AROUND 700 B.C. A GREAT KING—PERHAPS THE historical King Midas himself—died and was buried at Gordion, the capital of the ancient kingdom of Phrygia in what is now central Turkey. Whoever he was, the elderly ruler, then in his sixties, was surely one of the most powerful men of his day. His death wrought grief within his family and no doubt caused tension over the succession and division of wealth. Mourners included those who felt the king's loss keenly and others looking to advance their own influence. This unstable situation was mitigated by means of the traditional last rites, carefully orchestrated to maintain order within the community, while serving the spiritual needs of the deceased. These rites culminated in the king's burial, finalizing the passing of his authority, which profoundly affected not only the Phrygian kingdom but also the neighboring states.

This much may be surmised, but historical details are

lacking: the Phrygians, though literate, left no account of this momentous event. Remarkably well preserved remains from the tomb, however, allow the scenario to be envisioned. Fifteen pieces of fine wooden furniture buried with the king, along with nearly 200 bronze and pottery vessels—some containing food and drink residues—have enabled researchers to reconstruct the ceremony that was enacted and the setting in which it took place.

The king's burial mound was excavated in 1957 by a University of Pennsylvania team under the direction of Rodney S. Young. Called Tumulus MM by Young (for "Midas Mound"), the huge mound stood 175 feet high, with a diameter of nearly 1,000 feet. Deep within the tumulus was a 17-by-20-foot pine chamber; inside it lay the skeleton of the king, resting on the remains of an open coffin cut from a huge cedar log. Miraculously, the stable environment and low moisture levels within the burial chamber had preserved most of the tomb's furnishings. The chamber had no door, suggesting that the walls were built first and the burial goods then lowered in. After the objects were arranged inside, the roof was finished, and the structure was finally covered with the earth of the tumulus.

The parts of the coffin had been placed along the northern wall of the tomb chamber. The coffin body broke apart over time, its eastern end falling onto a small, plain wooden table. The table itself collapsed, spilling to the floor a bag of bronze fibulas (ancient safety pins). Seven similar tables, with boxwood legs and tops of walnut or maple, were found in the center and southeast corner of the tomb. All eight tables had tray-shaped tops, suggesting they were portable banquet tables that could be loaded with food and then carried, set down, and removed when the meal had been finished.

Ten large bronze jugs were found on the floor near the tomb's west wall, along with nine bronze-and-leather belts (a tenth belt was found on the king). The belts, along with many of the handled vessels buried with the king, had hung from iron nails driven into the burial chamber's walls and had fallen when the nails corroded.

In the tomb's northeast corner were remnants of three pieces of furniture, probably two stools and a chair or bed. Leaning against the east wall were two ornate inlaid objects that Young called screens, because of their screen-like faces. To the south of the "screens" was a carved and lavishly inlaid banquet table, named the "Pagoda Table" by Young because of its exotic design. The "screens" and inlaid table were well preserved when found by the excavators. Unfortunately, subsequent changes in the tomb's environment and early efforts to conserve the wood contributed to their deterioration.

The 15 pieces of wooden furniture recovered from Tumulus MM were originally recorded and drawn in the field by members of the University of Pennsylvania team; these drawings were featured in Young's final report, published posthumously in 1981, the result of a collaborative effort. It was my job to correct the original drawings, using Young's field books and excavation photographs. This proved difficult when the field drawings were found to contain errors that could not be corrected without reference to the objects themselves.

In 1981, I went to Turkey to study the

precious wooden objects, which had been housed in the Museum of Anatolian Civilizations in Ankara. Many of the pieces could not be handled, however, because the wood had begun to deteriorate. The University of Pennsylvania Museum immediately initiated a project to restudy and reconserve all the wooden artifacts from Gordion. This work, carried out over the past 20 years, has revolutionized our understanding of the arts of the Phrygians and revealed unprecedented information about funerary customs in the age of King Midas.

The first piece to be restudied was the inlaid table, one of the most intractable of all the wooden objects. The field drawing, which by then had been published several times, was more of an artist's rendering than a reproduction of the table as it had actually looked. Interpretations of other pieces of furniture suffered from the same approach. Further complicating the matter was the warped and shrunken state of the wood, which had to be envisioned in its original size and shape before the objects could be reconstructed on paper. Mistakes in the early drawings were caused, in part, by the limited amount of time available to the field artists, who had to work quickly while the objects were being studied and catalogued, removed from the tomb, treated, and stored. By comparison, my 1985 reconstruction drawing of the inlaid table in perspective took more than a year to complete; this included detail drawings of all 40 pieces of the table, which had to be finished before the perspective drawing could be begun. The new drawings reveal the true form of the table and accurately depict the geometric patterns that make up its complex inlaid decoration.

The other two pieces of inlaid furniture from the tomb, Young's "screens," had boxwood faces decorated with geometric patterns made from thousands of pieces of juniper inlay. The rosette at the center of each face is now recognized as a symbol of the Phrygian goddess Matar, supported by abstract versions of lion's legs that suggest her attendant lions. Comparison of the faces of the "screens" with several rock monuments in the Phrygian highlands to the southwest of Gordion supports this interpretation. The monuments are carved to replicate building facades, decorated in raised relief with geometric patterns. In the lower part of each facade is a carved doorway opening onto a niche, and in several of these niches are figures of the goddess. One of the most impressive, Arslan Kaya, preserves a figure of Matar in the niche, flanked by her two lions. If Arslan Kaya represents the shrine of the goddess, then the Tumulus MM "screens" are portable, wooden versions.

Young's "screens" were ceremonial but functional as well: they are now known to be serving stands, with walnut top pieces carved with open rings to hold small bronze cauldrons, ten of which were found nearby in the tomb. Also associated with the stands were two bronze ladles and two situlas (buckets)—one ending in a lion's head and one in the head of a ram. Other bronze vessels were recovered from the burial, including jugs, bowls with handles, 98 *omphalos* bowls, and three large cauldrons on iron stands. Many of these yielded organic remains: new research has shown that the pottery jars inside the large cauldrons contained a meat preparation, and the small cauldrons used with the serving stands held a special mixed beverage.

The two serving stands and nine tables found in the tomb were clearly banquet furniture, and food and drink had been buried with the king. Apparently these items were not intended solely as tomb furnishings—the king's coffin provided direct evidence for a funeral ceremony that took place before the burial. The ceremony apparently included a banquet, almost certainly involving sacrifice in honor of the deceased.

The remains of the coffin as disposed on the tomb floor showed that the parts had been disassembled before they were lowered into the chamber. Once inside, they had not been placed in their original positions, indicating that the assembled coffin had been used outside the tomb prior to the burial. This suggests that a funeral ceremony had taken place before the interment, with the king lying in state in his open log coffin.

The furniture found buried with the king must also have played a role in the ceremony: the tables held vessels, food, and drink, and the serving stands were used to transfer the beverage from the small cauldrons into the many bronze bowls that were found in the chamber. The meal should not be imagined in terms of a modern banquet, however, where feasting is the main preoccupation. This is clear from ancient literary references that are approximately contemporary with the Tumulus MM burial.

The custom of the funerary meal was widespread throughout the Near East and Greece in antiquity, and was tied inevitably to the ritual killing of the animals to be eaten. As recorded in the *Iliad*—perhaps dating to the eighth century B.C.—the funerals of the Greek hero Patroklos and the Trojan prince Hektor both included feasting and sacrificial ceremonies. The feast at the funeral of Patroklos involved the massive slaughter of oxen, sheep, goats, and swine. Elsewhere in the *Iliad*, the method of roasting the meat is described: animals are killed, cut into pieces, spitted, and roasted—but the meat is eaten only after the appropriate portions have been dedicated to the deities. Wine was sacrificed at the funeral of Patroklos as well, in the form of libations poured on the ground. The bones were interred and his tomb was covered with a mound. Writing in the fifth century B.C., Herodotus records a similar sequence for Thracian funerary ritual.

The Phrygians settled in the area of the Anatolian plateau in the late second millennium B.C.

The funeral of the great Phrygian king must also have included the ritual slaughter and sacrifice of animals. The many *omphalos* bowls found in the tomb suggest a drink offering as well: although there is no firm evidence for the function of these bowls in Phrygia, the Greeks, who adopted the shape from the Near East for their "phiale mesomphalos," used the phiale exclusively for the pouring of libations. In fact, a bowl is a frequent attribute of Matar, interpreted as a receptacle for the liquid sacrifice offered to the goddess by her worshippers. An image of the great funeral can thus be reconstructed, with mourners gathered around the body of the king and ceremonial furniture and vessels in use for the enactment of the ritual—all taking place in view of the tumulus, partially constructed in preparation for the final deposition.

Yet questions persist regarding the significance of the grave goods in the burial. Were they gifts for the king for his sustenance in the afterlife? Were they dedications to the goddess on behalf of the king, provided by his survivors? Votive offerings of bowls and fibulas were frequently dedicated in sanctuaries. Or were the remains of the impressive sacrifice put in the tomb to enable the king to perform the ceremony in perpetuity?

That Phrygian kings played an important role in sacrificial rites and ceremony is clear from ancient sources. The historian Diodorus Siculus, writing in the first century B.C., credits Midas with the establishment of the rites of Matar, and inscriptions on the largest rock monument in the Phrygian highlands, the so-called Midas Monument, link the king with the worship of the goddess. The possibility that the finds from Tumulus MM were the king's ritual equipment, and not mere possessions, has widespread implications for the interpretation of ancient burials—the contents of which are normally considered provisions for the dead in the hereafter.

One final question remains unanswered: who was the king buried in the Tumulus MM chamber? Proponents of the theory that he was indeed King Midas point to the size of the tumulus—by far the largest at Gordion—and richness of the burial, believing that this could only be the tomb of Phrygia's greatest king. They suggest that the date of the burial is approximately correct: King Midas (as King "Mita") appears in the annals of the Assyrian king Sargon II (721–705 B.C.), and Eusebios (ca. A.D. 260–339) records that Midas ruled between 738 and 696 B.C. Furthermore, objects from the chamber find parallels in those from the "destruction level" of the city mound, which is thought to be the result of an invasion by nomadic Kimmerians, reported to have occurred around 700 B.C. Strabo writes that Midas committed suicide at the time of the Kimmerian invasion.

Others argue that the tomb is earlier than 700 (or 696) B.C., and that if Midas had died as a result of the Kimmerian invasion, the raid would have left the inhabitants of Gordion without the resources to provide for such a magnificent burial. Recent dendrochronological research posits a date of 718 B.C. or earlier for the cutting of the logs of the outer casing of the Tumulus MM chamber. As the logs may have been cut significantly earlier than Midas' death, it therefore seems possible that the great king buried in the tomb is not Midas but his predecessor. But King Midas is again implicated even in this hypothesis: if Midas buried his father, it seems certain he would have officiated at the final rites.

Study of the inlaid table has produced one piece of evidence that is intriguing but remains ambiguous. Precious-metal fittings from the table were pried off, damaging the table and indicating a robbery—an inside job before the sealing of the tomb chamber, or plunder such as that which would have occurred during the Kimmerian raid. If the latter, then the burial could be that of Midas, interred with his somewhat diminished table, as he is reported to have died at the time of the invasion.

Whether the tomb's occupant was Midas or his father, aspects of the burial point to certain viable conclusions: the tomb furnishings belonged to Midas in some respect, whether they were placed in the tomb of his predecessor or in his own burial. The rare wooden furniture and other contents of the tomb included votives and ritual artifacts. The types of objects found and their disposition in the chamber indicate that a lavish funeral ceremony in which the king had lain in state took place before the burial. The ceremony included sacrifice and a sumptuous funerary banquet, the menu of which can be reconstructed. And none of this could have been ascertained without the careful, scientific excavation of the tomb in 1957 and the hard work of our many colleagues—archaeologists, conservators, artists, photographers, and scientists—over the subsequent years of study.

17

BACCHIC MYSTERIES

Spiritual life in antiquity.

by JAMES WISEMAN

CHRISTOPHER HAWKES, A PROMINENT OXFORD archaeologist of the mid-twentieth century, ranked trying to determine spiritual life from material remains "the hardest [archaeological] inference of all." It is easy, he argued, to reach conclusions about prehistoric technology and "fairly easy" to determine subsistence economics, but it is more difficult to draw inferences about social-political organization and hardest of all to reconstruct religious institutions and spiritual life. The reasons for the increasing difficulty are several, but the most significant are that modern analogy is often misleading for the third and fourth categories, and empirical testing very difficult for the third and impossible for the fourth. Both, on the other hand, are very useful in determining technology or subsistence economics. My own research has often led me into the problems of inferring aspects of ancient beliefs or interpreting symbolism within its social and political context, most recently in a study of the Roman

Imperial cult in Greek Macedonia. So I have followed with particular interest recent developments in the study of Greco-Roman religion, especially mystery cults.

Hawkes, we should note, was concerned in the comments above mainly with prehistory, the time before writing. The archaeology of historical periods, however, can draw not only on material culture, including art, but also on written records, even literature, for aid in interpreting ancient ritual, symbols, and ideology. Of course, the use of written texts has its own problems of interpretation, and works of art might reflect aesthetic tastes as much as ritual symbolism in decorative scenes. Still, multiple approaches to the past often allow inferences of one kind to reinforce conclusions from other paths of reasoning. A partnership of archaeology, anthropology, art history, history, and philology has been particularly successful in recent years with regard to the study of mystery cults of the Greco-Roman world, especially mysteries in honor of the god the Greeks knew as Dionysus or Bakchos, and the Romans as Bacchus.

It will be helpful to point out that in the polytheistic societies of Greece and Rome it was common for individuals to belong to more than one mystery cult. Initiates of the Eleusinian mysteries, for example, might also belong to mystery cults of Dionysus or Isis, or both. Only initiates (the word "mystery" derives from the Greek word *mystes*, meaning "initiate") were told the secrets—sacred tales, symbols, formulas, or promised benefactions of the god.

One of the most popular and most widespread mystery cults was that of Dionysus, the god of wine, who was also the god of drama and the mask. Dionysus inspired ecstasy and frenzy both in his female followers, known as maenads, and in men, and was concerned both with the living and the spirits of the dead. He is the god who appears—often, before revealing himself, in disguise—and then disappears. He was thought to be present even within his followers during their revels: both god and worshiper could be called *bakchos*, but only the god was called Dionysus. In one myth, he is the son of Zeus, king of the gods, who took human form to seduce Semele, mortal princess of Thebes. The ever-jealous Hera persuaded Semele, several months pregnant with Dionysus, to request to see her child's father as himself and was consumed in fire when Zeus revealed himself in his full, radiant glory. Zeus saved the baby from the flames and incubated him in his thigh, from which Dionysus, now immortal, was born when his term was full. He was thus called "twice-born." His dual nature is manifested also in other myths in which he dies and is reborn. In those accounts, he is the son of Persephone, goddess of the Underworld. As a child, he was enticed away by the Titans, who then tore him to pieces and ate most of him; Athena snatched away his heart, however, from which he was later brought back to life. Zeus, his father, destroyed the Titans with a thunderbolt, and it was from their ashes that humans were born. This myth became a central feature of the Orphic mysteries, which held Dionysus in special reverence and are named after Orpheus, the mythical musician who also had close ties to Dionysus.

In Greek art, Dionysus is often depicted with an entourage of maenads and the semi-divine, bestial spirits of the wild, young satyrs and older sileni. In vase paintings he appears in the sixth century B.C. as a bearded man, but by the fourth century he is shown as a youth, and over time he becomes increasingly effeminate in appearance. In Macedonia, his cult received royal favor from the fifth century B.C., and later, he was especially revered wherever Macedonian power extended. Plutarch wrote about the fascination Orphic and Bacchic rites held for Olympias, mother of Alexander the Great, and claimed that she performed the sacred dances with great serpents about her. In India, Alexander was himself said to have discovered Mt. Nysa, where Dionysus was said to have been hidden from Hera, and even came to identify himself as Dionysus. The importance of the Dionysiac cult in Macedonia is also attested by ample archaeological evidence. For example, Dionysus and his company appear on one of the masterpieces of metalwork from the fourth century B.C., the time of Philip and Alexander, a gilded bronze krater that had served as a burial urn in a tomb at Derveni on the outskirts of Thessaloniki. The krater, almost three feet tall, bears in relief on the main part of its body the marriage of Dionysus and Ariadne in the presence of *maenads* and satyrs. The two main figures are seated, and the nude Dionysus rests his right leg across Ariadne's left thigh, while she removes her veil.

In the remains of the funerary pyre above another contemporary tomb at Derveni, some 200 fragments of a papyrus roll were found which recorded a commentary on an archaic Orphic poem. This remarkable document, the earliest literary papyrus known and the earliest papyrus of any kind found in Greece, was recovered in 1962 during the same Greek excavations that resulted in the discovery of the Derveni krater. Authoritative transcriptions and studies of it have appeared recently, including an English translation. The papyrus provides details of rituals such as libations by *magoi* (magicians) of water and milk and the sacrifice of "innumerable and many-knobbed cakes" as well as references to *mystai*, and numerous verses from a theogony that may have served as a *hieros logos* or "sacred tale" in the Bacchic and Orphic mysteries.

Another major development is that archaeological discoveries since 1970 have swelled the number of small, inscribed gold sheets, some cut in the shape of leaves, from tombs in Greek cities in Italy, Crete, and mainland Greece whose cultic significance has been long debated. New texts, combining features of ones earlier scholars attributed to separate groups, now indicate that the entire corpus belongs to Bacchic and Orphic mysteries.

Archaeological context dates one of the most important new leaves, from Hipponion (ancient Vibo Valentia) in Italy, to the late fifth century B.C. It preserves the longest known text, and reads, in part, as if a master or mistress of ceremonies is advising the deceased on what to do and say in the realm of Hades, cautioning first against drinking from the first spring encountered, beside which there is a "white cypress" and where other souls are being cooled, but to go on to another spring where the deceased is advised to answer the questioning guardians with the words: "I am a son of Earth and Starry Sky; but I am desiccated with thirst and am perishing: therefore give me quickly cool water flowing from the lake of recollection." The text ends with the assurance that permission will be granted and that the deceased will continue on a "long, sacred way which also other mystai and bacchoi gloriously walk." In other texts, the closing lines assure the deceased that he or she may enter "the holy meadow, for the initiate is not liable for penalty," or even "shall be a god instead of mortal."

The assurances preserved in these texts occasionally include an enigmatic expression whose meaning is still debated. One example is on a leaf from a tomb at Thurii in southern Italy: "a kid [young goat] you fell into milk." The Greek word for kid, *eriphos*, also occurs as an epithet of Dionysus, and some scholars have suggested that the deceased was thus being identified with the god. On two gold sheets cut as ivy leaves from a late-fourth century B.C. tomb in Pelinna, Thessaly, however, instead of a kid, we find a ram and a bull "in the milk," showing that the formula has variants. It is clear from the context that the expression indicates that being in milk is good fortune for whichever animal is named, and for the deceased. At Thurii, the expression follows the declaration, "You have become a god from a human!" I wonder, too, if some suggestion of that formula is indicated in the pastoral scene near the east end of the north wall of the famous Bacchic mysteries fresco (late first century B.C.) in the Villa of the Mysteries at Pompeii. In that curious scene, a young satyr plays a syrinx (panpipes), while a young nymph, with pointed ears like her companion, suckles a kid. Could this be an allusion to the myth in which the child Dionysus, transformed into a kid by Zeus to hide him from Hera, was tended by nymphs on Mt. Nysa?

It is clear, in any case, that whatever benefits initiation into the Bacchic mysteries brought the living, initiates were also assured of a better afterlife in the Underworld. That feature of the cult had a long life, and is attested by gold leaves from the fifth century B.C. to at least the third century of the modern era. The gold leaf latest in date (A.D. 260) proclaims the dead girl it accompanied in her tomb, Caecilia Secundina of Rome, to have become a goddess.

Eternal life in some pleasant circumstance is no modest reward for initiation into a mystery cult, and the conclusion that it was offered to worshippers of Dionysus for perhaps over 1,000 years of history is no small contribution to the study of spiritual life in ancient Greece and Rome. To be sure, it has been achieved not by "unaided inference from material remains," as Hawkes expressed it, but by a combination of archaeological, textual, and iconographic evidence. The limitations we impose on archaeology might better be viewed as temporary; what once was thought impossible might yet become routine. Perhaps an interdisciplinary methodology, even in the absence of texts, will yet help define an approach to prehistoric religion. And there is much more still to be learned about mystery cults by this interdisciplinary approach.

18

WHEN GLUTTONY RULED!

Bones recovered from a Roman villa attest an age of culinary hedonism.

by Deborah Ruscillo

Alas and alack! What a nothing is man! We all shall be bones at the end of life's span, so let us be jolly for as long as we can.
—Gaius Pompeius Trimalchio

ROMAN DECADENCE IS VIVIDLY PORTRAYED IN ancient literary sources and in depictions on vessels, frescoes, and mosaics. But one of the most direct sources of information on the hedonistic ways of the upper classes of ancient Rome is their garbage. There is a mysterious magic about examining a simple rib fragment from a pork chop consumed almost 2,000 years ago, a magic that allows an animal bone analyst, or zooarchaeologist, to peek into the lives and appetites of ancient people.

Feasting was a significant part of Roman society, so much so that satires were written mocking the frivolity of such affairs. Augustus (r. 27 B.C.–A.D. 14) attempted to control public and private gluttony by enforcing severe laws against extravagant menus or exorbitant spending for such events. These laws were designed to protect the health and morals of citizens. Police were stationed in marketplaces to ensure modest purchases, informers were sent to dinners to oversee the affairs, menus were reviewed by state officials, and even dining rooms were constructed to have windows looking out on streets so that inspectors could check in without disturbing the gatherings. Hosting a sumptuous dinner that would have the neighbors buzzing and the uninvited envious became difficult for a time. But mere laws could not stifle the desire for delicacies and extravagant eating, especially among the elite of Roman society. The very people who established these laws were the first ones to break them! The love for good food or just the need to impress others was often too strong to be controlled by public code. In the days of the Empire, gluttony ruled and presenting your guests with high-quality and imaginatively prepared cuisine was considered a great virtue.

The best known Roman author on cuisine is Apicius, who lived during the reign of Tiberius (A.D. 14–37). Five-hundred recipes are preserved in writings ascribed to him (particularly the *De re coquinaria*), including some intriguing dishes such as camel heels, flamingo tongues, and roasted ostrich. The extravagance of the ingredients should not surprise us; Apicius, after all, was himself a member of high society and a reputable gourmet. His recipes were addressed only to those who could afford such luxuries—in other words, his own social peers. The emperor Elagabalus (r. A.D. 218–222) was said to have outperformed even Apicius in organizing banquets that would leave the palates of those invited tingling for days after. But the most famous Roman feast is the lavish banquet hosted by Trimalchio, an ex-slave accepted into high society because of his affluence and eccentricity, in Petronius' novel *Satyricon*.

Trimalchio's Feast

Petronius Arbiter lived during the reign of Nero (A.D. 54–68). According to Tacitus, a first-century A.D. historian, Petronius was a refined pleasure-seeker who was accepted into Nero's circle and was considered the arbiter of good taste (*arbiter elegantiae*). At one point he became the consul of Bithynia (in northwest Asia Minor), though he usually spent his days sleeping and his nights living the life of a hedonist. His *Satyricon* is praised as an amusing glimpse into the social life of Nero's favorite few, many of whom were ex-slaves like the character of Trimalchio himself. His mockery of specific personalities, like Tigellinus, head of the Praetorian Guard, resulted in his falling out of favor with Nero and a sentence of death. Despite Petronius' demise, however, we may join Trimalchio at his table whenever we open the *Satyricon*:

Spaced around a circular tray were the twelve signs of the zodiac, and over each sign the chef had put the most suitable food. Thus, over the sign of Aries were chickpeas, over Taurus a slice of beef, a pair of testicles and kidneys over Gemini, a wreath of flowers over Cancer, over Leo an African fig, virgin sowbelly on Virgo, over Libra a pair of scales with a tartlet in one pan and a cheesecake in the other, over Scorpio a crawfish, a lobster on Capricorn, on Aquarius a goose, and two mullets over the sign of Pisces. The centerpiece was a clod of turf with the grass still green on top and the whole thing surmounted by a fat honeycomb. With some reluctance we began to attack this wretched fare, but Trimalchio kept urging us, "Eat up gentlemen, eat up!

—*Satyricon*, 35

The extravagant feast included many courses involving such delicacies as dormice, sausages, peahen eggs, orioles, hares, capons, and fish. A continuous flow of wine accompanied the feast.

The guests were seated around a table on couches, as was typical during Roman banquets. The dining room was known as the *triclinium*, a term formed from the Greek word *triklinos* meaning "a bed for three." Each couch, accordingly, sat three reclining individuals supported by their left arm so that their left hand could hold their plate and their right hand was free to take food. Romans did not use forks, though they had spoons and knives. During the course of the dinner, slaves would serve the guests and cater to their comfort and enjoyment by providing perfumes and washing their feet. Entertainment would be provided by the likes of jugglers, musicians, acrobats, and actors.

The *triclinium* was lavishly decorated with inlaid furniture, mosaics, and frescoes. The dinnerware included plates, jugs and flatware in bronze, silver, gold, and electrum. Guests were required to have bathed and to be dressed in appropriate evening wear when entering the *triclinium*, taking care to enter with their right foot first (doing otherwise would bring bad luck). Men alone were guests; women ate with children and slaves.

Specifically chosen slaves prepared the meals (*coci*), while others were assigned specific tasks of pouring the wine (*cellarius*), carving the meat (*structor)*, and serving the guests (*ministratores*). Most households had at least one or two slaves; the richest had a full-time cook while others hired cooks just for their banquets. Usually dark and poorly ventilated, kitchens (*culinae*) had packed dirt floors and were unhygienic. Suitable for slaves only, they were not meant for public viewing.

The host, also known as the patron, was the organizer of the event, designing the menu, inviting the guests, orchestrating the slaves, and taking care of details. Hosting a successful banquet with impressive or unique foods, good company, lavish ambiance, and entertainment brought considerable prestige. The guest must want for nothing and a lasting impression was everything. The goal was to establish or maintain a reputable social position that would be achieved by inviting a selected group of influential people, or at least those who rubbed elbows with influential people. Through word of mouth, one's position could be elevated or lowered. Political positions, for example, were assigned to friends of the emperor. For this reason, a patron spared no expense in pleasing his guests, even providing a gift to take upon departing from his home. These gifts, called *apophoretae*, could include items such as food, pins, combs, vases, lamps, and games.

The Archaeology of Dining

Archaeological remains from Roman villas have confirmed the testimony of ancient authors concerning banquets. *Triclinia* and *culinae* have been excavated in Pompeii and many other Roman sites. Recent excavations at Epano Skala, in Mytilene on the Greek island of Lesbos, uncovered a Roman villa built in the Augustan era. The villa was rebuilt and expanded ca. A.D. 200, but a change in pottery types, including the introduction of numerous erotic lamps, suggests that around A.D. 300 the villa may have been converted into a tavern-brothel, in use until its abandonment some 50 years later. Close to the ancient harbor of Mytilene, the Epano Skala area is known from various sources, such as the late Roman novel *Apollonius of Tyre* and the writings of the Greek historian Xenophon (ca. 428–354 B.C.), to have been a well-established brothel district. The modern vicinity of the Epano Skala is still known for such establishments.

More than 35,000 animal bones were recovered from all periods at the site, almost half from the supposed fourth-century A.D. tavern-brothel. About 7,300 bones were recovered from the Roman villa levels. They represent a sample of the meals consumed over a course of 300 years and attest the wide variety of foods served at a Roman banquet, like that described by Petronius. The remains include wild boar, suckling pig, sheep, lamb, goat, kid, deer, hare, pheasant, goose, capon, and game birds such as thrush, starling, and woodcock. Bones of young cattle were also present. Romans used cattle primarily for plowing fields, and the meat of older cattle was considered too tough to be palatable. Of the recipes in Apicius' *De re coquinaria*, only four are dedicated to beef or veal (*bubula, vitellinam, vitulinam*). In contrast, there are over 90 recipes for roast pig (*porca, porcus*), or suckling pig (*porcellus, porcellinus*). Goose was typical in the Roman diet. It could be eaten boiled or roasted with a variety of sauces. Commonly attributed to French cuisine in modern times, goose liver paté was eaten with great zeal by the Romans. The first-century A.D. author Pliny credits the creation of goose liver paté to Apicius, who describes the force-feeding of figs to geese to enlarge their livers. We know, however, that the ancient Greeks also practiced this custom from Athenaeus of Naucratis' work *Deipnosophists* (*The Banquet of the Philosophers*), probably written just before A.D. 200.

Remains of lobster, crab, urchin, scallops, clams, mussels, sea snails, eel, red mullet, tuna, sea bream, sea bass, and scorpion fish were also recovered from the villa's dump. The assortment is not surprising considering the villa's proximity to the sea. Other sea creatures, such as octopus, squid, cuttlefish, and small fish, were undoubtedly consumed as well, though their remains do not preserve very well in the ground, especially after 2,000 years.

A contrast can be made with the bones from the later tavern-brothel, which are predominantly of pig, cattle, sheep, and goat, with almost no remains of birds or marine creatures. The two samples reflect the difference between a variety of gourmet meals associated with the earlier villa, resembling Trimalchio's feast, and simple cuts for feeding less scrutinizing clientele like those who may have frequented the later tavern-brothel.

The Economics of Hospitality

No doubt the meals from the villa, featuring a variety of meat, poultry, and fish were more costly than those of the tavern based on everyday cuts of meat. So how much would a banquet such as that hosted by Trimalchio cost? An edict of the emperor Diocletian from A.D. 301 gives the various prices of food in *denarii* (silver alloy coins). We can attempt to calculate the cost by converting *denarii* into *aurei* (gold pieces), and then figuring the cost in American dollars using the modern price of gold. Based on 15 guests and not including expenses for garnishes, perfume, the cost of the slaves, and dinnerware, all graciously offered by Trimalchio to his guests, the total comes to about 4,800 *denarii*. We know that 25 *denarii* equaled 1 *aureus*; accordingly, his dinner would have cost the equivalent of 192 *aurei*. We also know that 60 *aurei* were equivalent to one Roman pound of gold, 326 grams in modern measurements. Therefore, 192 aurei was equivalent to 1043.2 grams or 36.8 ounces of gold. At the time of writing this piece, the price of gold was $272.90 per ounce. So Trimalchio's banquet would cost about $10,042.00 in today's market! The cheapest items on the menu—chickpeas, African figs, and tartlet—each set Trimalchio back about $2.09. The 12 liters of Falernian wine would have drained $1,504.80 out of his wallet, while the costliest item, the wild sows, would have rooted out another $3,138.

More than $10,000 for one evening with 15 friends... imagine! Perhaps this figure is a bit contrived, but we get the picture of the cost of hospitality in high-society Rome. In truth, the guests of Trimalchio realized that he brought all these items from his own estates, so the cost to the host in this case was quite reduced!

A Way of Life

Seneca, the philosopher and tutor of Nero, tells us that Apicius, after falling heavily in debt with his frivolous life-style, drank poison and ended his life rather than go on without the extravagances he had enjoyed so often. Petronius, having been condemned to death by Nero, slit his own wrists and secretly bled to death during a last feast with his friends. These sad endings attest that eating well was not just a daily ritual, it was a philosophy and a way of life in Imperial Rome. Your reputation and acceptance in the upper echelons of society were often determined by your abilities as a generous host and as a connoisseur of ostentatious goods.

When you sit down to dinner with friends this holiday season, remember that you should always consider doing a little extra for the comfort and enjoyment of your guests. After all, your reputation can only improve with attention to details! Consider also that a zooarchaeologist may be wading through your garbage 2,000 years from now.

19

SAVORING THE GRAPE

For Romans, wine was the elixir of life, from cradle to grave.

by STUART J. FLEMING

There, when the wine is set, you will tell me many a tale—how your ship was all but engulfed in the midst of the waters; and how, while hastening home to me, you feared neither hours of unfriendly night nor headlong winds of the south....

—OVID, *The Amores* II.xi

ROME'S GREAT POETS AND PHILOSOPHERS extolled the virtues of relaxing with friends to enjoy good conversation and good wine. The more romantic writers, notably, the late-Republican poet Horace (65–8 B.C.), wrote of the finest of wines being savored in idyllic settings—by a quiet riverbank or under the shade of beautifully flowering trees. For most Romans, though, the family dinner table would have been the usual place for such relaxation. Everyone in the house had been up since dawn, and those who had gone into fields, or had business in the marketplace, sustained themselves through the day with little more than a light lunch of bread and fruit, and a beaker of well-diluted *vin ordinaire*. The slow rhythm of a late afternoon dinner at home was an opportunity to enjoy a slightly better quality wine, surely savored by those who could afford it.

If the Romans had any conventions similar to those of our Western world today—red wine with beef, white with poultry and fish, etc.—I don't know of them. But there was a reasonably well-established etiquette for wine's consumption during a Roman dinner of substance. A guest might expect first to be served some hors d'oeuvres, then a honeyed wine—a mulsum. Its sweetness would offset the taste of salted fish and pig's feet that, along with hard-boiled eggs and stuffed artichokes, were often included among the appetizers. Somewhat better wines would be offered after each of the subsequent two courses—mensa prima, which would be meat-, poultry-, or fish-based; and mensa secunda, which would be fresh fruit, a custard, or some honey-sweet dessert.

The comissatio was truly a Roman drinking party.

Roman taste, at least during the Republican and Early Imperial eras, leaned heavily toward sweeter wines which, because they were made from later season grapes, tended to be quite alcoholic. The Romans took their lead from long-standing Greek custom, adding at least some measure of water to the wine or, in elite circles, a few ladles of melting snow. The degree of dilution applied probably depended on the setting. While entertaining friends within the home, around quarter strength would be normal; among a raucous crowd in the city's tavern, perhaps dilution was forgotten altogether.

While etiquette may have been on shaky ground in a typical Roman wine bar, it was upheld during the convivium, a dining event structured around the family and a circle of friends. In Roman literature, the luxury usually associated with this kind of setting brings to mind the Greek symposion from which it derived some of its structure. But their common threads are somewhat superficial. While the Greeks went out of their way to ensure social equality among their invitees, a Roman patron would without hesitation host a convivium for his inferior amici and clientes—associates, longstanding or briefly met, who might be the means to business and political advantages. Unlike the symposion, which was in essence a drinking bout that followed a meal, the convivium was decidedly a banquet, with emphasis on richly prepared and novel food, the partaking of which was a pleasure—a conviviality—that would be accompanied by a generous flow of wines.

Two lengthy works of the second century A.D., Plutarch of Chaeronea's *Table Talk* and Athenaeus of Naucratis' *Banquet of the Philosophers*, provide us with detailed insight into the way that a *convivium* might proceed throughout the evening. The *convivium* was intended to be a joyous event. Italian alkanet (euphrosynum, "the plant that cheers") was added to the wine, and vervain (hiera botane, "sacred plant") was sprinkled with water on the dining couches because it was believed that such measures somehow contributed to the gaiety of the guests. Invariably there would be music, and at livelier gatherings there might be acrobats and mock gladiatorial battles.

The convivium also was a place to be philosophical about matters of substance, even if, in the sober light of morning, such matters shrank somewhat in consequence. In this setting guests might get caught up in a discussion of the fables of Aesop as parables for real Roman life and of how best not to give offense to a freedman guest whose memories of enslavement were scarcely a few years past. Amid all this chatter and banter would have been endless ponderings on the purpose and effects of wine in Roman society. The issue of the appropriate dilution of wine also was debated intensely, often with brilliant scholarly recourse to literature, past and near-forgotten. Athenaeus makes it clear that Greek custom was to mix three parts of water with one of wine—thus, in social shorthand, a "Triton"—and it looks likely that Roman wine connoisseurs generally went along with that ratio. But one of Plutarch's guests, Aristion, argued humorously in favor of a three-to-two mix, claiming that it would be in perfect harmony with the fifth concord of a lyre, to the tune of which so much drunken revelry took place.

The convivium, with its emphasis on food, simple entertainment, and fluid conversation was one thing; the comissatio was quite another. This was truly a Roman drinking party. It most likely took those guests who were still around at the end of a convivium far into the night hours and assuredly put them deep into their cups.

Did the Romans drink a lot? On the basis of quite flimsy evidence in ancient texts, apparently so, at least by modern standards. Unhealthy though such high consumption would have been, we should hesitate to censure such behavior too quickly. There seems little doubt that most Romans drank wine simply because the water being piped into their cities was none too pure and sometimes disease-ridden. And I would not be the first to suggest that general urban squalor—grim sanitary conditions, mold and mildew in shoddily built and poorly maintained apartments, etc.—drove many a poor Roman to drown his sorrows. Horace asked: "Who, after his wine, harps on the hardships of campaigns or poverty?" Another Roman author, Petronius, describing a banquet in his novel Satyricon, wrote,

Just then some glass jars carefully fastened with gypsum were brought on, with labels tied on their necks.... As we were poring over the tags, Trimalchio clapped his hands and cried, "Ah me, so wine lives longer than miserable man. So let us be merry. Wine is life."

20

ROME 2000

The Eternal City celebrates the jubilee in grand imperial fashion.

by ANDREW L. SLAYMAN

THE IDEA THAT ROME WOULD ENDURE FOREVER was born in antiquity. The poet Claudian, writing four centuries after the emperor Augustus, doubted that there would "ever be a limit to the empire of Rome, for luxury and its attendant vices, and pride with sequent hate have brought to ruin all kingdoms else."

The notion of Rome as an eternal city has persisted through time thanks to its abundance of durable ancient buildings and its equally durable reputation as the center of Western Christendom. The simple fact is that Rome has endured for so long and exerted such a powerful influence on history that it has become difficult to conceive of a world without it. "As long as the Colosseum stands, Rome also stands; when the Colosseum falls, Rome also will fall; when Rome falls, the world also will fall," wrote the Venerable Bede, an early eighth-century English Benedictine monk.

In the year 2000, Rome's city planners commemorated their ancient city by creating the grandest archaeological park in the world. Excavations that began in April of 1998 exposed 150,000 square feet of the forums built by the emperors Nerva, Trajan, and Augustus, formerly covered by the Via dell'Impero, built in 1932 as a parade ground for Mussolini's black-shirted legions. The newly exposed forums were the archaeological centerpiece of Rome's blockbuster celebration of the year 2000, which has been proclaimed a jubilee year by the pope. Celebrated every 50 years, jubilee years derive from an ancient Jewish custom of freeing slaves and forgiving debts. Over 24 million pilgrims and tourists flooded rome in 2000, which was three times the annual number of visitors in the preceding years.

In addition to the forums, archaeological projects included the restoration and reopening of a wing of the Domus Aurea (the emperor Nero's extravagant palace, closed since 1983) and the Museo Nazionale Romano (the national museum of Roman art, closed since 1985); the drilling of Rome's most deeply buried layers in search of traces of the earliest city; and the restoration of the Colosseum, the Round Temple in the Forum Boarium (the ancient cattle market near the Roman Forum), and the Ponte Fabricio (a Roman bridge spanning the Tiber still in use).

Exposing the Forums

The excavation of the forums of Nerva, Trajan, and Augustus, directed by Silvana Rizzo for the Sovrintendenza ai Beni Culturali (Superintendency for Cultural Treasures), was the largest of the jubilee projects, costing an estimated $10.5 million. It rejoined three great public spaces that were linked in antiquity: the Forum of Caesar, begun in 54 B.C. by Julius Caesar as an extension of the Roman Forum; the grounds of the Temple of Peace, dedicated in A.D. 75 by the emperor Vespasian and decorated with spoils from the Jewish War (A.D. 70–71); and the Forum of Trajan, built by the emperor between a.d. 106 and 112. The vaults supporting the Via dell'Impero, now known as the Via dei Fori Imperiali (Street of the Imperial Forums), which cross the Temple of Peace and the corners of Caesar's and Trajan's forums, were cleared of earth, turning the avenue into an aqueduct-like roadway elevated above the vast archaeological park. Visitors to the jubilee could wander through the vaults from forum to forum.

Rizzo and her team excavated the foundations of buildings that Mussolini demolished to make way for the Via dell'Impero, uncovering smooth, granite column drums from the Temple of Peace. Salvage archaeologists working in advance of Mussolini's bulldozers in the early 1930s did not have a chance to record the forums' stratigraphy. Rizzo's team, working at a more leisurely pace, were able to completely document the area from the late Republic (first century B.C.), when it was a residential quarter, through the Baroque period of the seventeenth and eighteenth centuries, when many imperial monuments were incorporated into contemporary buildings.

In the process, Rizzo made some startling discoveries. Four circular tombs were found in the southern part of the Forum of Caesar, dating to the end of the seventh or early sixth centuries B.C. Before Rizzo's excavations, much of what was known about the area in the Republican period came from descriptions of authors such as Cicero and Tacitus.

Rizzo and her team studied the remains of Republican residential structures razed to make room for the new monuments. Finally, near the porch of the Temple of Peace, a first-century A.D. bronze head of the Greek philosopher Chrysippus was unearthed. Chrysippus' stoic philosophy, which advocated living in harmony with reason, was popular among Rome's educated elite.

What was not adequately addressed by these projects was the problem of long-term preservation. The forums were another "big dig" in an era when such projects have become rare, and exposing so much ancient stone virtually guarantees damage from pollution while risking vandalism. Officials have lamented the inadequate funding for preservation of antiquities in Rome and spoken about enlisting volunteers and seeking private donations, but they have yet to make public a plan for minimizing the inevitable harm.

Shoring up the Domus Aurea

Second in size only to the forums project was the restoration of a portion of the Domus Aurea (Golden House), built by the mad emperor Nero on some 125 acres of prime downtown real estate conveniently cleared by the great fire of A.D. 64. The domus was regarded in antiquity as an obscene extravagance, encompassing three of Rome's seven hills. "Imagine, for the sake of analogy, a private palace in Manhattan covering all of Central Park, Riverside Park, and everything in between," says Larry F. Ball, an art historian at the University of Wisconsin-Stevens Point. The palace was largely demolished after Nero's death, but part of one pavilion was incorporated into the foundations of the public baths built by Trajan. Known today as the Esquiline Wing, 150 rooms of this pavilion are preserved underground in the Parco Oppio near the Colosseum. (It was within the baths' foundations, though outside the Domus Aurea, that the celebrated bird's-eye-view fresco of an ancient city was found in 1998 [see ARCHAEOLOGY, May/June 1998, p. 23]).

Discovered in the late fifteenth century and a tourist destination ever since, the pavilion was closed in 1983; the breath of thousands of visitors was causing its 320,000 square feet of frescoes (the largest concentration of ancient frescoes in Rome) to decay, and chunks of concrete were falling regularly from the ceiling. For 15 years inadequate funding prevented the superintendency from reopening it and carrying out anything beyond emergency work. Money made available by the jubilee committee has allowed for a systematic program of inventorying areas in danger, cleaning frescoes, stabilizing masonry, and installing new lighting. The pavilion has now reopened to groups of 25 visitors escorted by guides.

Cleaning the Colosseum

Restoration also took place at the Colosseum, built between A.D. 70 and 80 by the emperors Vespasian and Titus. The largest Roman amphitheater in the world, the Colosseum measures 620 by 512 feet and stands 157 feet tall. It was used for gladiatorial contests into the sixth century, when its brick and concrete vaults began to be appropriated for housing and workshops. Sometime in the

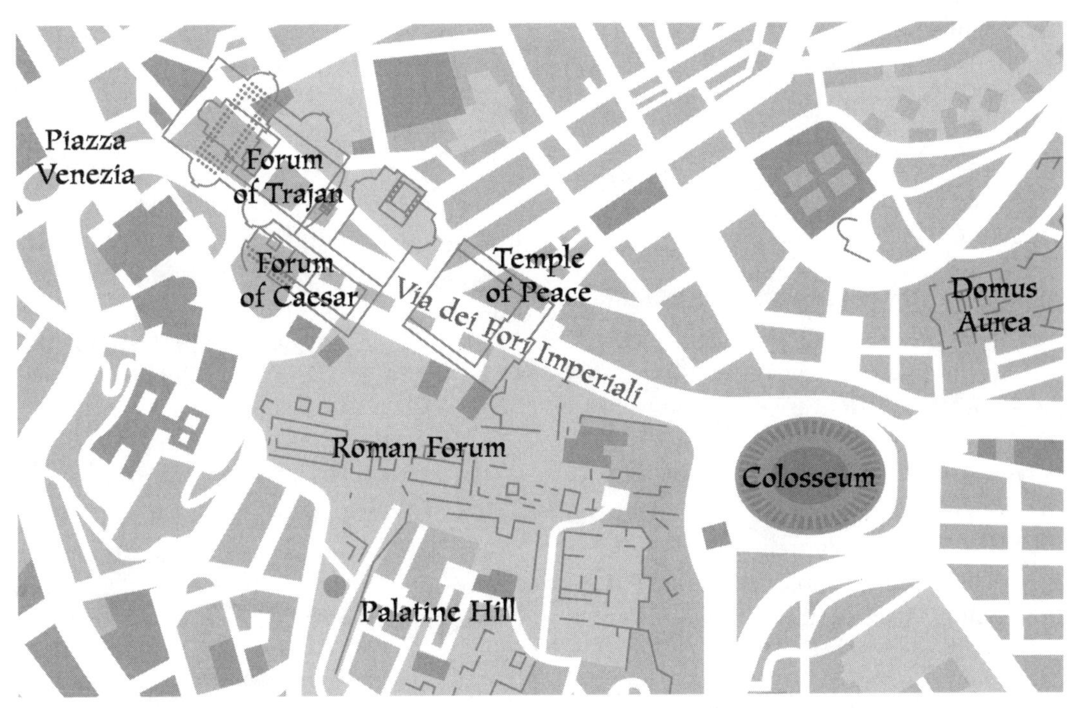

Excavation of the imperial forums, left, linked the forums of Caesar and Trajan with the grounds of the Temple of Peace to create the grandest archaeological park in the world. The vaults of the Via dei Fori Imperiali (Street of the Imperial Forums), pictured in the map above, will be cleared of earth, creating an aqueduct-like roadway elevated above the park.

first half of the fourteenth century, an earthquake destroyed the southern half of the outside wall, and the fallen blocks were used for construction elsewhere in the city.

The millennial conservation program, paid for by the jubilee committee and managed by the superintendency, entailed cleaning the stone, taking down remaining scaffolding, and stabilizing a number of vaults to enable visitors to see more of the structure. In addition, according to superintendent Adriano La Regina, part of the arena floor was rebuilt in oak, like the original, based on research by the superintendency and the German Archaeological Institute in Rome. The project allowed visitors to appreciate the Colosseum from the gladiator's point of view (minus the risk of death).

Fortifying an Ancient Bridge

The Ponte Fabricio, the best preserved Roman bridge in the city, was cleaned and restored for the jubilee (see Plate 11). Built in 62 B.C. by Lucius Fabricius, commissioner of roads, the bridge spans one branch of the Tiber where it divides around the Tiberine Island. It is more than 200 feet long, with two arches, and built of stone and concrete faced with travertine, now largely gone. Over the years the Tiber's current, particularly strong where it narrows passing the island, had damaged the bridge's piers, and the stone had accumulated its fair share of Rome's airborne soot.

Re-roofing a Famous Temple

Built in the late second or early first century B.C., the Round Temple is the oldest surviving marble building in Rome, owing its preservation at least in part to its conversion into a church during the Middle Ages. Long known as the Temple of Vesta simply because of its shape (her sanctuaries were often round), it is now commonly called the Temple of Hercules Olivarius, a monument mentioned both by ancient historians and in an inscription found nearby. It was designed in Greek style, probably by a Greek architect, and built of costly Pentelic marble imported from Greece; some of the columns were later replaced in Luna marble from Italy, presumably after being damaged.

Work on the Round Temple began in 1996 under the direction of Maria Grazia Filetici of the Archaeological Superintendency of Rome. The first stage of the project involved replacing the old roof with a new, wooden one to protect the Corinthian capitals of the portico from rain. Thanks to a $180,000 grant from the World Monuments Fund, restorers cleaned and repaired the stone walls of the cella (the chamber inside the portico), including a fifteenth-century fresco. The project then moved to the portico's columns. One capital was rebuilt almost from scratch, prompting objection from some archaeologists who said that the restorers were going too far. Other missing capitals have been replaced with simple octagonal blocks. The WMF also sponsored the cleaning of the podium on which the temple stands.

21

ROMAN LIFE ON THE DANUBE

A legionary town becomes an archaeological park.

by James Wiseman

Some 25 miles east of Vienna, on the right bank of the Danube, the ruins of Roman Carnuntum spread over an area of almost four square miles, from the little town of Petronell to the spa of Bad Deutsch-Altenburg. The ancient remains were recognized at least by the thirteenth century, when inhabitants of the region and visitors began uncovering Roman-period buildings and gathering up artifacts. By the nineteenth century it had come to be known as "the Pompeii before the Gates of Vienna," an exaggerated claim, but a description that conveys the romantic appeal of the site in those years. Some residents quarried ancient stones for building material and harvested artifacts on their property like cords of wood. Even into the twentieth century the region remained "a playground, a place to dig for finds, and a Duty-free Shop for hobby-archaeologists, collectors of antiquities, and art dealers," to follow the imagery of Werner Jobst, a long-time researcher of Carnuntum.

Although there were organized excavations beginning in the nineteenth century by architects, postal-service officers, soldiers, and teachers, it was only in the third decade of the last century that archaeologists began to direct work at Carnuntum. Since then, the change in the treatment of archaeological remains has been profound. Carefully documented excavation by professional archaeologists became standard, whether planned with a specific research focus or undertaken as part of a rescue-archaeology project necessitated by public works or other essential construction. Their research has greatly expanded our understanding of life on the middle Danube in Roman times both for civilians and for the military. Conservation of artifacts and site preservation have been emphasized, and the ancient remains are now being presented to the public in an informative, sometimes even entertaining manner.

Much of the credit for the transformation of activities at Carnuntum belongs to Jobst, professor of classical archaeology of the University of Vienna, who now heads the Archaeological Park of Carnuntum. The first phase of the project to create the park took place from 1988 to 1993, and included some activities that are now completed, like the renovation of the museum, and others that are still in progress, like the restoration of the great baths.

I had the good fortune to pay a leisurely visit to Carnuntum in 1990, and returned for another visit recently, so my direct acquaintance with the site spans most of the park's development period. It is an impressive achievement. Carnuntum is the largest archaeological preserve in Austria, and the Roman remains constitute a series of adjacent sites. On the east, on the outskirts of Bad Deutsch-Altenburg, is a large legionary fort surrounded by the *canabae* (Latin for a town of camp followers, traders, and wives of soldiers of a Roman legion), with an amphitheater located about 109 yards east of one of the principal gates of the fort.

A second fortified campsite to the west was occupied by a cavalry unit of auxiliaries; that is, not legionary soldiers, who were Roman citizens, but provincials who could earn Roman citizenship by providing 25 years of military service. To the west is an extensive civilian town, also fortified, with a second amphitheater whose seating capacity of about 13,000 far surpassed that of the legion's arena, which was about 8,000. Military exercises and parades were held in the latter, and spectacles at both amphitheaters included gladiatorial combat and wild animal fights. Cemeteries extended along the south side of the camps and the civilian town on both sides of the connecting roadways, and along the roads leading west toward Vindobona (Vienna), south toward Emona (Ljubljana, Slovenia), and east toward Aquincum (Budapest).

The first stone fort at Carnuntum was created late in the first century B.C. by Tiberius, who succeeded Augustus as emperor in A.D. 14, from which time a series of Roman legions occupied the fort until the loss of Pannonia to the Huns in 433. The civilian city, evolving from an earlier town of indigenous people, became the capital of Pannonia Superior in A.D. 103–107 during the reign of the emperor Trajan, with the legion's commander serving as provincial governor.

Carnuntum continued to grow in prestige and status over the next two centuries; its walls sheltered emperors and future emperors. Marcus Aurelius made his headquarters there for two years (A.D. 172–174) in his war against the Marcomanni and wrote the second book of his *Meditations* during that time. While serving at Carnuntum as governor of the province, Septimius Severus was promoted to emperor in 194 and raised the city to the level of colonia (colony), honoring it further with his own name, colonia Septimia Carnuntum. The most famous event at Carnuntum was the conference of the emperors in November 308, when the aged Diocletian was persuaded to leave his retirement palace on the Dalmatian Coast (in modern Split, Croatia) to meet Maximian and Galerius in an effort to make peace among the feuding successors of his original imperial Tetrarchy. The settlement that was reached was short-lived, and Constantine the Great soon became emperor of the Western Empire, and then (in 324) sole emperor. At Carnuntum, the imperial conference was commemorated with the dedication of an altar of the sun-god Mithras, a deity favored by Roman soldiers and known first in the East.

The eastern gods are particularly well-represented at Carnuntum.

Another monument that may have commemorated that event is the so-called Heidentor (or "Pagans Gate"), the only Roman edifice to survive above ground to the present day. It is a tetrapylon, that is, a four-gated building with a cross-vault and pyramidal roof, originally some 65½ feet high, located just south of the civilian city, about 1½ miles from the amphitheater. Two of the massive piers and a single arch are preserved to a height of about 41 feet and are visible from almost anywhere in the region. Its construction date is uncertain, however, and it may instead commemorate military victories of Constantius II (337–361), son of Constantine the Great. It seems particularly appropriate to me that this surviving remnant of centuries of plundering should have been adopted as the graphic symbol of the archaeological park.

Several shrines of Mithras have been found both in the civilian city and legionary town. The cult of the invincible sun-god, with its small, collegial gatherings of initiates in grotto-like shrines, was particularly attractive to soldiers of the first three centuries of the Empire, and Carnuntum was a major center for the spread of the cult in eastern Europe. One of the most spectacular groups of Mithraic sculpture known is now on display in the Museum of Carnuntum in Bad Deutsch-Altenburg, a monumental relief showing Mithras slaying a bull.

The eastern gods are particularly well represented at Carnuntum, in part because many of the soldiers stationed there originally came from the east; the legion that first occupied the fort, for example, was the Legio XV Apollinaris, which came from Commagene in Syria. There are statues, cult objects, and inscriptions honoring Cybele, Jupiter Heliopolitanus, and Jupiter Dolichenus (the strange deity with the double-ax who is often shown standing on a bull), among others.

The restoration of the museum, designed nearly a century ago by the architect Friedrich Ohman in imitation of a Roman villa, was one of the first tasks undertaken in 1988 by the park project. The building has been restored to its original handsome state, and, with some 3,300 artifacts and graphic displays, is the largest Roman museum in Austria. I was especially impressed by the diversity of objects from the daily lives of soldiers and the quality of their display: medals, decorative pieces for dress; paraphernalia for horses; tools, and other objects (weapons, of course, among them!).

A portion of the civilian town has been made into an open-air museum, so that visitors may stroll along paved streets and look into private houses, bathing establishments, a latrine, and even part of the great sewer system beneath the streets. In one area a portico bordering a street has been restored and gives access into a small, fully restored Temple of Diana and corridors leading to other structures. Nearby are exhibits of Roman games, pottery, and even Latin language instruction; visitors can also mint imitation Roman coins. The amphitheaters, too, have become centers for performances and events both for adults and for children.

Excavations continue in various parts of the ancient site, but the emphasis has clearly shifted from recovery to preservation. Carnuntum is an excellent example of what can successfully be accomplished in combining professional archaeological research, preservation, and interactive public education.

22

GALLIC BLOOD RITES

Excavations of sanctuaries in northern France support ancient accounts of violent Gallic rituals.

by JEAN-LOUIS BRUNAUX

When their enemies fall [the Gauls] cut off their heads and fasten them about the necks of their horses; and turning over to their attendants the arms of their opponents, all covered with blood, they carry [the heads] off as booty, singing a paean over them and striking up a song of victory, and these first-fruits of battle they fasten by nails upon their houses, just as men do, in certain kinds of hunting, with the heads of wild beasts they have mastered. The heads of their most distinguished enemies they embalm in cedar-oil and carefully preserve in a chest, and these they exhibit to strangers, gravely maintaining that in exchange for this head some one of their ancestors, or their father, or the man himself, refused the offer of a great sum of money. And some men among them, we are told, boast that they have not accepted an equal weight of gold for the head they show, displaying a barbarous sort of greatness of soul; for not to sell that which constitutes a witness and proof of one's valor is a noble thing. . . .

—DIODORUS SICULUS, Book V.29

MODERN HISTORIANS, RELYING on reports by Caesar and others, have characterized the religion of the Celts in Gaul as spontaneous rites, in contrast to the well-planned cultic practices of the Greeks and Romans. Archaeologists have now revealed that the Gauls did, in fact, build permanent ritual sites at places like Gournay-sur-Aronde and Ribemont-sur-Ancre in northern France. Dated to the end of the fourth or beginning of the third century B.C., these cult centers were the work of warlike tribes called the Belgae, thought to have arrived in northern Gaul from central Europe at the end of the great Celtic invasions of the fourth century B.C. The rituals performed at Gournay-sur-Aronde and Ribemont-sur-Ancre, however, went well beyond animal sacrifice, a commonplace rite among the Greeks and Romans, and included the triumphant display of the remains of enemies killed in battle or sacrificed to the gods of the underworld, from whom the Gauls believed they were descended.

Evidence from excavations at these sites suggests there are similarities between Gallic religion and Greek chthonic (underworld) cults. A sunken altar recovered at Gournay-sur-Aronde is similar to a Greek *escharon*, also consecrated to underworld deities. Although Greeks and Romans used stone while the Gauls used wood and mud brick, Gallic sanctuaries, like their Greco-Roman counterparts, were rectangular in plan, between 90 and 150 feet to a side.

Imposing wooden palisades enclosed the sacred inner precinct of these sanctuaries, accessible only by a monumental eastward-facing gateway. Access to the inner precinct would have been restricted to priests, initiates, and aristocratic dignitaries; the majority of congregants would have stood in the flat, open space outside the enclosed area. A structure within the enclosure housed and further protected the sunken altar.

Animal sacrifice was the most common ritual offering of the Gauls. Relying on ancient texts and Gallo-Roman sculpture, historians of religion have long believed the Gauls caught wild animals for this sacrifice. Excavations of the sanctuaries, however, have revealed that from the end of the fourth to the beginning of the second century B.C., the Gauls, like the Greeks, also sacrificed common domestic animals, principally cattle, pigs, and sheep. Priests would offer the divinity a skinned animal carcass, which remained on the altar until it had decomposed. The skulls were usually nailed to the gateway, probably to fend off evil spirits.

Corroborating the accounts of the first-century B.C. Roman historian Diodorus Siculus and other ancients, excavation clearly shows that human sacrifice was practiced as well. In the interior corners of the sacred inner precinct at Ribemont-sur-Ancre, human bones belonging to nearly 1,000 enemy warriors were burned as sacrificial offerings in open-topped ossuaries, square-shaped structures five feet to a side, adorned on the outside with crisscrossed bones. The priests first crushed the bones, probably to expose the marrow, where the Gauls, like the Greeks, located the soul on which underworld deities feasted. After breaking the bones, the priests dumped them into the hollow central chamber of the ossuaries where they were burned.

That the Gauls sacrificially burned their

enemies would surely have daunted anyone planning to wage war against them. Upon approaching a ritual site, a potential attacker might have seen smoke from burning bones rising from the sacred precinct. Or he might have seen the captured armor of conquered enemies fastened to tall poles or a tangled assemblage of headless corpses lying along the outer wall.

Two thousand iron weapons and pieces of armor found by archaeologists in a ditch adjacent to the sanctuary at Gournay-sur-Aronde were once displayed as intimidating war trophies. Examination showed that the swords and scabbards, war girdles, shields, and lances were originally arranged as some 500 individual suits of armor, either standing on the platform of the gateway or hung from poles around the sacred inner precinct. The number of suits of armor in the deposit indicates nearly a century of battles and of intensive use of the sanctuary as a depository for war trophies that both commemorated tribal victory and informed other tribes of the consequences of war with the Belgae, whom Julius Caesar, in his *Gallic War*, said were the bravest of the Gauls. The weapons, exposed for many years, fell to the ground when the wood and leather parts rotted; they were then ritually destroyed by the priests, a custom corresponding to a Roman practice described by the late-first-century A.D. historian Plutarch, and thrown into the ditch, where they were found more than 2,200 years later by archaeologists.

The sanctuaries seem to have served a double function, martial and cultic.

Evidence of human sacrifice was even more striking at Ribemont-sur-Ancre, where war trophies included headless human corpses and crushed, burned human bones. A particularly spectacular deposit of bones comprising some 80 skeletons was found outside the sacred area along the sanctuary's outer wall. All headless, the skeletons had been piled up and tangled together along with weapons, the bodies contorted into unnatural positions. Beheading is mentioned by Diodorus Siculus, recalling an account of the Greek historian and philosopher Posidonius, who traveled in Gaul at the end of the second century B.C. Posidonius related that Gallic warriors regularly cut off the heads of enemies conquered in battle to keep as personal trophies. Diodorus added that, after having cut off the head, the bodies and captured weapons were given over to servants. Since no skulls have been found at Ribemont, it is likely that warriors indeed kept the heads of their enemies, leaving servants to create the communal trophies of bodies and weapons found at the sanctuaries. A sanctuary may have also served as a communal trophy depository not only for victorious warriors of a particular tribe, but also for tribes allied in battle. Since different tribes often shared one or more gods, common trophies at cult sites may have facilitated treaties between them, secured by divine covenant.

The sanctuaries seem to have served a double function, martial and cultic. The Gauls designed them to celebrate victory in war and intimidate potential enemies while pleasing the gods of the underworld, whom they believed made them great warriors.

Considering the archaeological evidence from excavations at Gournay-sur-Aronde and Ribemont-sur-Ancre, it is time to reevaluate our understanding of the religion and cultic sites of the Gauls. Ancient sources offer a promising jumping-off point for archaeologists who, with each new excavation, are clarifying some of the vague or confusing descriptions offered by Greek and Roman historians. The human remains and weapons at Ribemont are examples of the dedicatory heaps of booty piled up in consecrated areas that Caesar mentions in his account of the Gallic War. The human bones nailed to what ancient historians thought were Gallic houses we now understand to be intimidating ornaments for the permanent cultic sites. Little by little, archaeology has added to our understanding of the warlike Belgae, whose brutality features so prominently in ancient literature.

23

SCOTLAND'S IRISH ORIGINS

Tracking the migration of Gaelic speakers who crossed the Irish Sea 1,700 years ago and became the Scots.

by DEAN R. SNOW

IRELAND IN THE EARLY CHRISTIAN PERIOD (A.D. 400–1177) was made up of at least 120 chiefdoms, usually described in surviving documents as petty kingdoms, typically having about 700 warriors. One of these petty kingdoms was Dál Riata, which occupied a corner of County Antrim, the island's northeasternmost part. Around A.D. 400, people from Dál Riata began to settle across the Irish Sea along the Scottish coast in County Argyll. Other Irish migrants were also establishing footholds along the coast farther south, as far as Wales and even Cornwall, but the migrants from Dál Riata were especially noteworthy because they were known to the Romans as "Scotti" and they would eventually give their Gaelic language and their name to all of what is now known as Scotland.

So far as we know, the only people already living in Scotland in A.D. 400 were the Picts, who were first mentioned by Roman writers in A.D. 297. This was in connection with an attack along Hadrian's Wall, in which the Picts had the help of Irish (Scotti) allies, so ties across the Irish Sea must have already been strong. Roman sources predictably describe their Pictish adversaries as barbarians and mention their use of blue paint, which some historians later interpreted perhaps too literally (Mel Gibson and his friends show up in the film *Braveheart* slathered with gallons of it). More likely the Picts were heavily tattooed.

The Picts lived mainly in eastern Scotland, north of modern Edinburgh. We know their homeland both from the distributions of Pictish place-names (which typically begin with "Pett" or "Pit") and the distribution of Pictish symbol stones, which were Pictish equivalents of a medieval coat of arms, each typically bearing the crest of a petty king and that of his father. The rugged west coast was only lightly occupied by Picts or some other Celtic-speaking people. Settlers from Dál Riata apparently established themselves along the west coast without much opposition. By A.D. 490 the population of Scotti was large enough that the head of the little kingdom moved the family seat across from Ireland. The Scotti alternately cooperated with and fought against the Picts for the next few centuries until the two were unified into a single kingdom under Cináed (Kenneth) mac Ailpín in A.D. 844. After that the Pictish language disappeared, along with the symbol stones and other archaeological traits that had distinguished them from the Scotti.

WHAT PROMPTED THE SCOTTI TO LEAVE Ireland? What attracted them to what is now Scotland? How did the two populations become one speaking Gaelic rather than Pictish? And what are the archaeological signatures of it all? Most archaeologists agree that Scottish Dál Riata was founded from Irish Dál Riata, not the other way around. Most agree that the archaeological evidence for the movement is almost invisible. Most agree that the spread of dominant Scottish society at the expense of the Picts in Scotland involved the movement of dominant warriors, a considerable amount of language switching to Gaelic from Pictish (which was related more closely to the language spoken by the Britons to the south), and only a modest amount of migration by individuals. Finally, most agree that the movement was accompanied, at least part of the time, by the spread of Christianity from Ireland to Scotland.

Small numbers of pioneering men and their families probably moved first, followed by others. The very first moves might have been nothing more than raids. There was probably some return migration, but a net positive flow from Ireland to Scotland over a period of decades or a couple centuries. Initial settlements were probably unopposed in this thinly populated part of northern Britain. Intermarriage with Picts followed and although we cannot yet specify the process, the Gaelic language of the immigrants proved to be dominant in the long run. Languages of dominant societies tend also to dominate, and I am assuming that this is what happened in the case of Scottish expansion. Political, economic, and linguistic supremacy must be considered separately, but in this case they appear to have traveled together.

If the origins of Dál Riata are to be found in the north of Ireland, then it makes sense to look there for clues as to why people moved across the Irish Sea. Finbar McCormick of Queens University, Belfast, who works with both archaeological evidence and the findings of palynologists, argues that there is clear evidence in the pollen record of a prolonged period of forest regeneration from about 100 B.C. to A.D. 340, just before the beginning of the Early Christian period. If the forests were coming back, farming and the human population must have been in decline. But the evidence shows that agriculture revived and human populations expanded again after the middle of the fourth century.

McCormick also observes that ringforts first appear in significant numbers after the beginning of the Early Christian period, sometime after A.D. 400. Ringforts—in Northern Ireland they are often called *raths* if they are earthen only, or *cashels* if clad in stone—are to some degree misnamed, for they were apparently used to contain and protect cattle and people around farmsteads. They were used for military purposes only if one regards protecting cattle against rustlers and people against slave raiders as such. Whether one built a *rath* or a *cashel* was probably determined in large part by the availability of stone.

We know from documents that cattle were the principal measure of a man's wealth in the Early Christian period, and that cattle rustling was widespread. But cattle had been part of farming in Ireland since the Neolithic. Why did they take on such significance as indicators of wealth and prompt the construction of hundreds of *raths* and *cashels* after A.D. 400? McCormick concludes that while previously cattle were used mainly for meat, the advent of enclosures marks the beginning of serious dairying. The energy yield of dairy cattle is about four times that of beef cattle. The population of dairy farmers grew rapidly, leading to competition for pasturage and increased cattle raiding, especially in northeasternmost Ireland. A check of a data base of sites in Northern Ireland, made possible by Queens University's Michael Avery, was revealing. Of 5,459 sites classified as *raths*, *cashels*, or other enclosures, nearly one-half (2,516) are of the Early Christian period. Moreover, almost one-quarter (564) of the Early Christian cases are in County Antrim, home of Dál Riata.

The Scots and the Picts are generally thought to have practiced very similar economies, but if McCormick is right about the importance of dairying among the Scots, they could have had a significant adaptive advantage. If cattle were important and at least partially explain the dominance of Dál Riatan migrants, perhaps we should expect to find large numbers of *raths* and *cashels* in Scottish Dál Riata. Alas, they are not there. But there is fortunately at least one plausible ecological explanation for this as well. McCormick argues that the land in western Scotland is so unproductive that the potential densities of human and cattle populations were too low to make the concentration of herds in enclosures practical. Whatever the reason, we know that Gaelic speech and Irish society spread into Scotland, but we cannot use *raths* and *cashels* as archaeological signatures of that spread. Nor did *souterrains*, underground structures used by the Irish for storage and refuge, move with them to Scotland. On the other hand, some of the poorly dated structures referred to as *duns* in Scottish Argyll look more than a little like Irish *cashels*, and the late ones could easily have been built by Dál Riata immigrants. Dunadd, a fortress in Argyll, was used, if not founded, as the capital of Scottish Dál Riata after A.D. 490 (see Plate 13).

Neither can archaeologists use characteristic portable artifacts to track the Dál Riata incursion. A bronze brooch, Irish in style, was found in the crannog at Loch Glashan, and molds to produce the same kinds of brooches have turned up at Dunadd (see Plate 14). Artificial islands, crannogs are typically Irish sites, and there are a few examples in Scotland. But for the most part neither the kinds of archaeological sites that are common on the Irish side of the sea nor portable artifacts like brooches are frequent enough in western Scotland to provide a convincing archaeological signature of the migration. Souterrain ware, typical of northeastern Ireland during the Early Christian period, was apparently also made by a few specialists in Scotland from the end of the eighth until the twelfth century. But this was after the Scotti were already established in Dál Riata, and this early commercial ware remained mostly restricted to the Irish side. In Scotland archaeologists find instead imported food storage vessels (known as French E-ware) that might have been valued more for their contents than themselves. More of these have been found at Dunadd than anywhere else in Britain. Clearly, none of this marks Scottish expansion as neatly as archaeologists would like.

Christianity also moved across the Irish Sea. St. Patrick reputedly began his mission in A.D. 432, decades before the Dál Riatan center of gravity moved from Ireland to Scotland. Irish monasticism flourished between A.D. 520 and 620. Colum Cille, the monk also known as St. Columba, established his new monastery on the Scottish island of Iona in 563. From then on the Christian cross was carried increasingly by the people of Dál Riata. We should not be surprised that cattle dominate the animal remains recovered by archaeologists working at Iona. While Colum Cille had some success converting the Picts to Christianity, the Scots were the principal beneficiaries of his work. Offering solace in this life and salvation in the next to anyone that wanted it, the religion was very popular. For chieftains, the Celtic church of Colum Cille offered legitimization that traditional belief systems did not. It was the beginning of the symbiotic relationship between clergy and secular leaders that culminated in feudalism across much of Europe.

ALL OF THIS MAKES IT CLEAR THAT THE Scots were doing what most migrants have usually done throughout human history. They were reinventing themselves as part of the process of expansion. The difficulty, of course, is tracking the movements of people who are changing, sometimes dramatically, at the same time as they are moving. In this case Christianity left a clear archaeological signature. The first Christian carvings in Ireland were crosses on pillars and slabs. Tall, ringed crosses like that near what is, according to legend, the common grave of St. Patrick, Colum Cille, and St. Brigid in Downpatrick, Northern Ireland, appeared by the eighth century. In Scotland the stone expressions of Christianity gradually spread

Take Your Pict

From A.D. 400 to 1000, northern Great Britain saw the withdrawal of Roman forces, arrival of the Scotti from northeastern Ireland, disappearance of the Picts, formation of a united kingdom of Scotland, and colonization by the Norse.

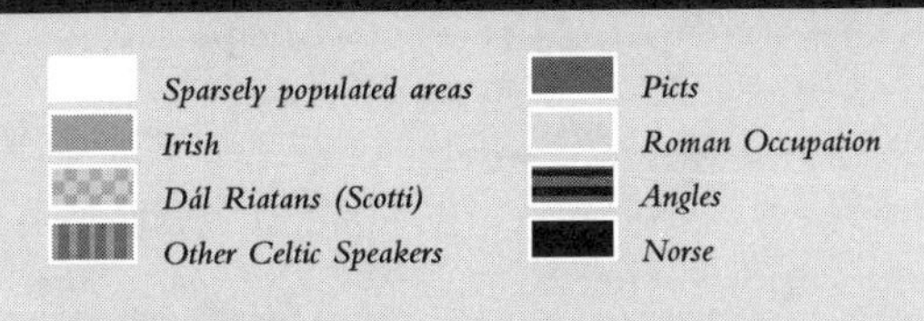

Settlers from the Irish petty kingdom of Dál Riata were beginning to establish themselves in what would later be called Scotland. Picts were well established north of other Celtic speakers except perhaps on the west coast and in the Hebrides.

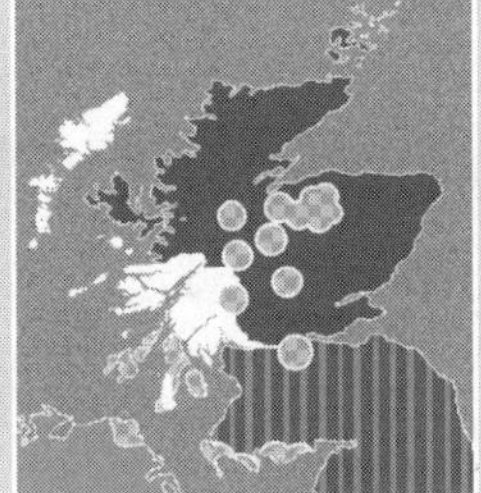

Departure of Roman legions in A.D. 407 left Britain to Picts, other Celtic speakers, and growing numbers of Irish settlers. Enough Scotti were in place by A.D. 490 to allow them to move the seat of Dál Riata from across the Irish Sea.

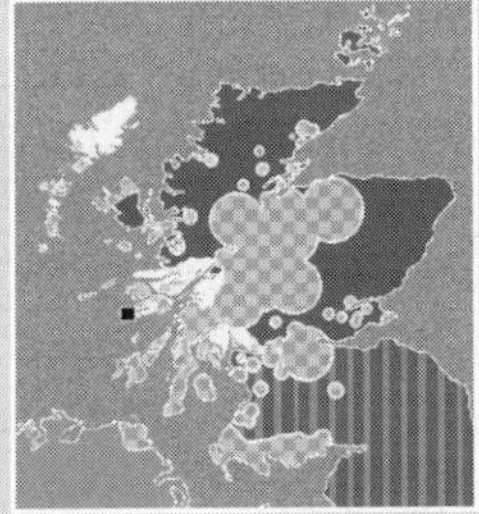

Colum Cille left Ireland and established a monastery on Iona in 563 (dark box). From this time on expansion of the Irish Scotti was assisted in part by the spread of Christianity.

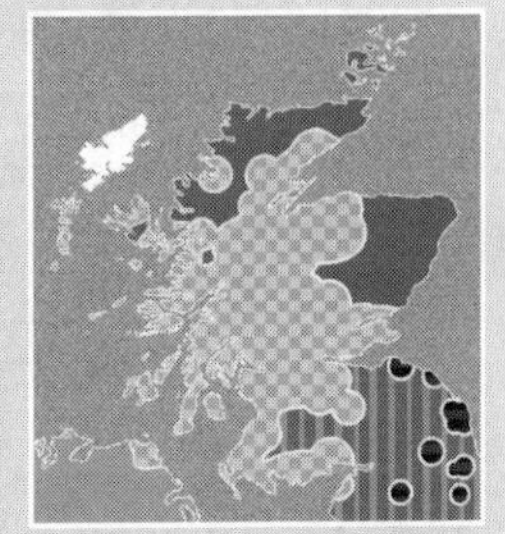

As the Scottish presence in Britain grew, so did that of the Angles and Saxons, many the descendants of Roman mercenaries. Angle settlements expanded south and east of Scottish territory.

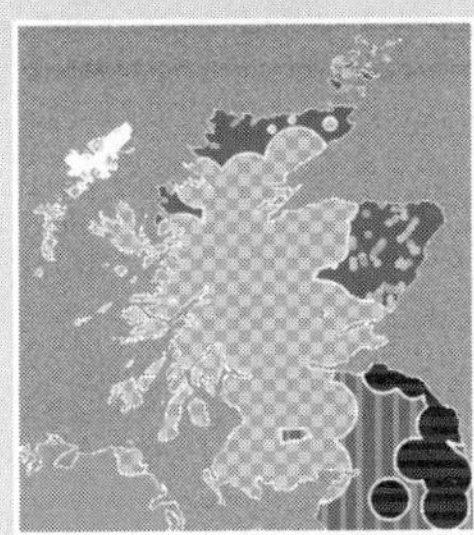

As both Angle and Scottish communities grew, small Norse settlements began to appear in the islands of Orkney and the Outer Hebrides.

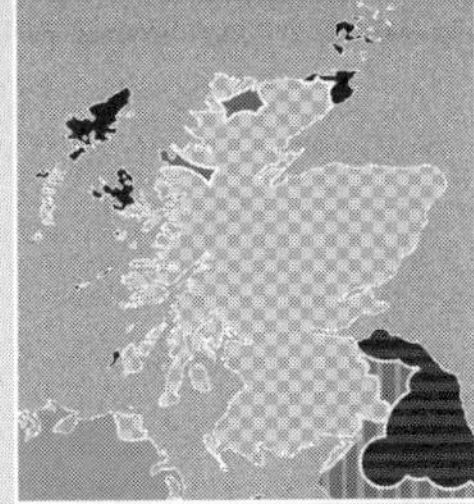

Competition from the Norse and Angles probably contributed to the unification of Scots and Picts into a single kingdom in 844. Pictish language and culture disappeared. Norse raids forced the abandonment of Iona by 878.

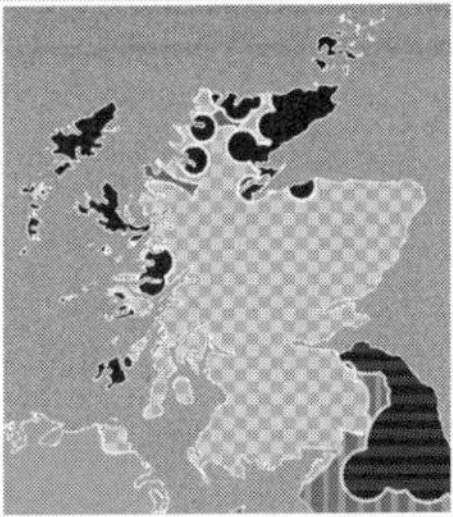

By 1,000 years ago, the Picts were a memory and the united kingdom of Scotland was caught between Germanic Norse and Angle settlers.

to the Picts as well. As part of this process, crudely shaped Pictish symbol stones bearing only what were probably the crests of local kings were replaced by more elaborate dressed and ornamented stones that also sometimes bore Christian symbols.

The changes were not painless. Scottish power and influence began to threaten the Picts and the Roman Catholic church threatened the Celtic church of Colum Cille. In the first half of the eighth century the Dál Riata Scots defeated the Britons, Iona accepted the Roman Easter, Columban monastic communities were expelled from Pictish lands, and the Picts temporarily defeated the Scots, all in quick succession.

Around the end of the century, a new threat changed everything. The Vikings began raiding Ireland in 795. Rich monasteries were favored targets, and they carried out their first raid on Iona in 802. They returned and killed 68 of the monastic community in 804. For the next 50 years the Vikings raided, established trading colonies, and began settling portions of both Ireland and Scotland. The Picts and Scots were able seafarers, but they were no match for the Vikings. Beleaguered monks packed up the shrine of Colum Cille, abandoned Iona, and moved back to safer quarters in Kells, Ireland, in 878. By this time Viking raiders were even besieging Paris.

The Norse threat may have accelerated the merger of Scots and Picts. The process was already advanced, facilitated by the patrilineal principle of Scottish descent and the matrilineal principle of Pictish descent. Politically expedient marriages were commonly arranged. Ambitious males could often claim descent through both prominent Scottish fathers and prominent Pictish mothers, as did four early ninth-century Pictish kings. Males tend to dominate in such arrangements, and the Pictish practice of reckoning descent from a man to his sister's son could not survive in the face of the Scottish preference for descent to pass directly from father to son. By 844, the Picts and the Scots, linked by countless intermarriages and under constant pressure from the Norse, were ready to merge into a single kingdom. With that the process of Irish (Scottish) migration to northern Britain was complete, and from this time until the end of the eleventh century most Scottish kings were buried at Iona.

So far so good, but what of the observation of James Mallory of Queen's University, Belfast, and many others that we have no archaeological evidence whatsoever for actual population movement from Ireland to Scotland? Artifacts and even architecture can move through trade and exchange even if people do not. But logically it seems less likely that people could migrate without also carrying along artifacts and building habits that archaeologists might later use to track their movements. The solution probably lies in the scale of analysis and logic of the expectations. If archaeologists insist that Scottish migration must be marked by a convenient trail of *raths* and *cashels* containing deposits of Irish-style brooches they will surely be disappointed. On a more general scale, however, it is clear from archaeology alone that the trappings of Christianity—crosses, churches, and monasteries—spread into Scotland and that Pictish symbol stones disappeared. Gaelic speech clearly replaced Pictish and we can track the process through the place-names of Scotland.

We can reasonably expect more evidence to emerge as archaeological research progresses. Dominant societies often retain traditional burial practices while taking on many of the domestic attributes of subordinate populations, so we may expect to find diagnostic Scottish burials in what otherwise may look like Pictish sites. Perhaps patterns of key differences in clothing or grave offerings will emerge as archaeologists uncover more Scottish and Pictish burials.

Recent research by James Wilson of University College, London, and his colleagues has shown little detectable genetic contrast between Irish and Pictish populations, so the Irish migration to Scotland in the first millennium A.D. left no clear DNA trail. The two source populations were already too close to allow the geneticists to distinguish them. The Norse and Anglo-Saxon migrations were another matter, and the male descendants of these populations are clearly distinct from Celtic ones. The contrast is particularly striking in the Orkneys, where the genes of migrating Norsemen are still easily identified in their modern descendants.

INVESTIGATING THE ARRIVAL OF IRISH settlers in Scotland and the disappearance of the Picts in the first millennium A.D. may seem an odd switch for somebody who has spent decades studying the archaeology of the northeastern United States, but this recent undertaking of mine was not without reason. Fifty years ago, archaeologists generally agreed that the Northern Iroquoians had developed in place over a millennium or more, and that no migrations were required to explain their long-term cultural development. This theory was a reaction against the excesses of earlier scholars who believed they could explain everything prehistoric by elaborate but unrealistic migration scenarios. By the 1990s, however, enough contradictory evidence had accumulated to suggest that this explanation was too simple. I wrote a series of articles arguing that an expansion of Iroquoian-speaking communities from the Pennsylvania Appalachians into what are now New York and southern Ontario better explained the archaeological, linguistic, biological, and ethnographic facts. The Iroquoian expansion probably involved the displacement, absorption, and occasionally the destruction of former residents of the region. The ensuing debate convinced me that we cannot understand cultural evolution without a realistic understanding of human demography, and that we cannot understand human demography without allowing for migration. People are born and die, and along the way they form and dissolve social groups of vastly variable sizes, construct things, trade with one another, and engage in warfare. They also move about while doing all of this, sometimes covering great distances and often coupling their movements with social reinvention. If we cannot identify the archaeological signatures of historically known cases of migration and language spread by dominant societies, we have no hope of spotting them in the prehistoric record.

What the Scottish case and others like it tells us is that migrations by relatively small dominant societies are much more common in human history than many archaeologists have been willing to admit (much less assume), particularly in North America. Typically, the signatures of it have been explained away too easily as evolutionary change in place. There are so many good examples of change associated with the migration of whole societies or dominant subsets of them, that any major change over time that can be observed archaeologically is likely to have involved migration in one of its many forms, however minor. We should be assuming population movement as a first principle rather than denying it.

PART VI:

SOUTH & CENTRAL AMERICA

24

FROM PARLOURS TO PYRAMIDS

Fleeing the "gilded cage of English civilization," artist and adventurer Adela Breton became a skilled copier of Maya murals and reliefs in the early 1900s.

by MARY MCVICKER

AT THE AGE OF 50, WHEN MANY OF HER CONtemporaries were beginning to think of a comfortable retirement, Adela Breton was entering the most productive years of her career. It was 1900, the place Chichén Itzá, the Late Classic and Postclassic (ca. A.D. 800–1200) Maya ruin in Yucatán, Mexico. Adela had come to verify the accuracy of drawings of the renowned British Mayanist Alfred P. Maudslay. Although she'd already traveled throughout Mexico, nothing could have prepared her for the challenge of working at Chichén.

She had spent the first 37 years of her life in Bath, England. Her schooling included the usual subjects entertained by a Victorian gentlewoman, particularly the study of art. Her mother, who died when Adela was 24, is a shadowy figure, but her father, a retired naval officer with strong interests in archaeology, travel, and exotic places, must have been an important influence. Adela had similar interests, but she bided her time, taking care of her parents, particularly her father. Years later she would refer to this period as "wasting time at Bath."

When her father died in 1887, she inherited sufficient money to give her financial independence. Released from her obligations, she left almost immediately for the Canadian Rockies. The opening of the Canadian Pacific Railroad in 1885 had provided ready access to the area, and women in particular were attracted by opportunities to camp and explore and enjoy a less fettered existence. Some even rode astride—never Adela, however! "The Rocky Mountains were so good, everything perfect except the American women who would ride astride, a sight to make gods & men weep. In all my wild rides it never occurred to me as being possible or necessary," she wrote to Miss Mead, a secretary at Harvard's Peabody Museum, on July 29, 1904.

Adela made her way through the western part of the United States down to Mexico, spending the next 12 years painting and drawing everywhere she went. When she asked Maudslay if there was work she could do while she was in Mexico, he asked her to verify the accuracy of his drawings from Chichén, which he wanted to include in the archaeology section of his great eight-volume work, Biología Centralia America. He told her there would be nothing more valuable than a record of the murals at Chichén Itzá.

Her first season at the ruins got off to a bad start. Edward H. Thompson, the United States Consul at Merida, owned a hacienda and the land on which Chichén Itzá was located, and, in a manner of speaking, she was his guest. Excerpts from Thompson's letters reveal irritation and admiration. "Miss Breton is here and I gather from what the tourists say who went with her to Uxmal she's a...Tartar. They say she complained all the way out all the time while she was there and all the way back....," Thompson wrote Frederick Ward Putnam at the Peabody Museum on March 3, 1900.

In the months that followed, matters didn't improve. In an April letter, also to Putnam, Thompson wrote, "Miss Breton returned from Chichén today, I understand. To tell the honest truth she's a nuisance. She is a ladylike person but full of whims, complaints and prejudices.... To my horror I found out the day I left Chichén that she proposes to return to Chichén shortly for another period of time. She certainly is an artist as regards landscapes at least, and she has made one painting in the intervals of her work for Maudslay that is really very nice."

Adela, in her turn, found Thompson irritating, but she was determined. In a May 9, 1903, letter to Alfred M. Tozzer of Harvard University, she wrote that, "It was rather amusing, & very annoying, to stay on by main force as it were, against their will [Thompsons']. But my work became more important as I went on, & I could not be driven away."

Adela's work at Chichén marked her entry into the professional world of archaeology and anthropology. When Zelia Nuttall, the American archaeologist and ethnohistorian, visited Chichén in 1902, she asked Adela if she could send some of her sketches to Putnam. Impressed by her work, Putnam immediately commissioned Adela to make copies of the site's frescoes.

Adela became good friends with Tozzer, who was also working at Chichén and who wrote his mother regularly, offering the following sketch of "the eccentric Miss Breton" in a February 5, 1902, letter:

She is an English maiden lady of much means.... Her appearance is typical of an independent, unmarried spinster of fully 60 [Adela was 52], tall, thin, and with a long face, grey hair...extremely near sighted, but straight as an arrow. She wore a short skirt, a dark blue shirtwaist with straight collar attached, and brimmed straw hat covered with flowers and planted perfectly square upon her head, but the surprise comes when she starts to talk. She is English...to the very bone and her speech is as exaggerated as any affected English you ever heard upon the stage. She is an artist and a very good one too. She seems to have a special gift of drawing the carvings of the ruins. She has spent many years in Mexico and Yucatán doing this work of copying and drawing the glyphs and sculptures of the ruins. She travels with her inseparable and wonderful servant, Pablo, who cuts paths for her, cooks for her, and makes himself generally useful by tending to her numerous wants....Her hobby among all the others is this servant.

You look at Miss Breton and set her down as a weak, frail and delicate person who goes into convulsions at the sight of the slightest inconventionality in the way of living. But I assure you, her appearance is utterly at variance with her real self. She seems to court discomfort at any cost....

–Letters to his mother, Letter 12, Tozzer Library.

Archaelogists discover a saga of ecological exploitation, change, adaptation, and defeat.

LIVING AND WORKING AT Chichén was difficult; the bugs and the heat, even during the cooler season, added to the strenuous nature of the close, precise work Adela was doing. Light was a problem as well. Details were either exposed to natural light—which visibly hastened their deterioration—or, if they were in an enclosed area, they were badly lit. Recognizing the fragility of the murals and reliefs, she began to copy them inch by careful inch—all the while continuing her work for Maudslay.

Accurate color reproductions required hand copying by someone who combined artistic ability, an exacting attention to detail, and a comprehensive knowledge of the culture that had originally produced the images. Adela's talent made her work highly sought after. Her original tracings and her copies of those tracings, sometimes to scale, were commissioned by museums and archaeologists. "The drawing to 1/4 scale gets on very slowly in these twilight days...." she wrote to

Mead in 1906. "Drawing to 1/32 of an inch and correcting to 1/64 is very trying to brain and nerves as well as to eyes and hand...."

These commissions kept her from pursuing her own copying. In a 1913 letter to Professor Bowditch at Harvard, she wrote, "I want very much to get on with my own work & see about publishing my fresco copies & the Acanceh reliefs, & then do some more fieldwork before I am too old." She was 63.

Adela never lost her taste for travel as a release from "the gilded cage of English civilization," as she told Tozzer, a comment strikingly resonant with one made by Gertrude Bell, the Victorian traveler known for her explorations of the Middle East and Arabia: "To those bred under an elaborate social order few such moments of exhilaration can come as that which stands at the threshold of wild travel."

Although she didn't return to Mexico after 1908, Adela continued to study, copy, write articles, and give papers. She was active in the International Congress of Americanists, co-editing the 1912 proceedings with Franz Boas, who would shape the course of American anthropology. In her later years she worked extensively with Maya languages, studying and copying old manuscripts. Although World War I and poor health slowed her down, she worked and traveled until her death in 1923—when she was returning home from a conference in Río de Janeiro.

Her travels and work in Mexico were a source of much reflection in her later years. In a June 5, 1918, letter to George Byron Gordon, director of the University of Pennsylvania Museum, she wrote, "The mornings here [Moncton, New Brunswick] are so like tierra caliente that I often sigh and think of Chichén, and of the wide green ways between the forests of Northern Vera Cruz, with the big blue butterflies and morning glories like bits of sky fallen here and there. I, too, have been in Arcadia."

Aim, Fire, Thwok! Atlatl devotees show off their stuff

Quick: what lethal, mammoth-piercing weapon is displayed in museums around the globe and can be made in your garage for less than 50 bucks? Ask any of the dozens of devotees who have traveled from across the country to southeastern Ohio for the 14th annual meeting of the World Atlatl Association (WAA), an organization that promotes knowledge of this powerful prehistoric weapon and its use as a modern sporting device.

"The atlatl is a cumbersome weapon system, but it's so powerful," says past WAA president Charlie Brown, striding across the throw site at Flint Ridge State Memorial park on a rainy Saturday morning in June. He stops about 60 feet before a foam target, hefting a dart, which looks like a six-foot-long arrow, in his left hand. In his right is the atlatl, a wooden device almost as long as his forearm and a bit wider than a ruler, with a spur angled upward at one end. It resembles, for lack of a better analogy, an oversized crochet hook. Brown fits the concave end of the dart against the spur, grasping the atlatl at its opposite end, then pulls his right arm back beyond his shoulder, keeping the weapon and its accompanying dart parallel to the ground.

With a quick overhand motion, he propels the atlatl toward the target. The flexible dart compresses for a brief second, then springs forward as it is released from the atlatl spur. The dart hits its mark with a satisfying thwock and burrows deep into the foam target backing. "It's a weapon that has been used almost all over the world," says Brown, admiring the atlatl still gripped in his hand. "It has amazing speed and force."

Speed—the darts can fly at more than 100 miles per hour—and force were the qualities that made the atlatl the weapon of choice for Pleistocene hunters in Europe, Asia, and the Americas, who at least 20,000 years ago discovered that increasing the length of the throwing arm through the use of an atlatl dramatically increased the power and range of a projectile. For vulnerable Homo erectus, this meant that thick-skinned food sources such as mammoths could be more effectively pursued from a safer distance; many scientists now believe that it was atlatl-armed hunters, and not climatic changes, that were primarily responsible for the extinction of Ice Age megafauna.

Archaeological evidence for atlatl use has been found everywhere in the world except for Africa, from antler and bone components of Upper Palaeolithic atlatls in the caves of southern France to wooden weapons preserved for thousands of years in the rock-shelters of the American West. Although the atlatl was generally replaced in the Americas by its stealthier, more accurate cousin—the bow and arrow—about 2,000 years ago, it is still used today by some Inuit tribes and in parts of Mexico to hunt birds and fish, as well as by Australian aborigines, who call it the woomera. American fans prefer to call it by its Nahuatl name, which is how the Aztecs referred to their spear-throwers, feared by the Conquistadors for their armor-piercing capabilities.

For fans of a weapon responsible for the extinction of the woolly mammoth, featuring enormous darts that can be discharged with the force of a .357 Magnum and travel the length of a football field, WAA members are remarkably low-key. "This is just really a nice group of folks," says Leni Clubb, a founder of the WAA, surveying the rainy scene from a tent where she collects scorecards from accuracy competitions and dispenses oatmeal cookies. For Clubb, a member of the Colorado Archaeological Society (CAS) and an avocational archaeologist for over 40 years, the atlatl was "just another interesting artifact" until 1983, when she signed up for a throwing contest in Wyoming. Sixty-eight at the time, Clubb was the first woman to enter an atlatl competition.

Clubb and fellow CAS members formed the WAA in 1987. It presently has 436 members, 35 of whom live outside the U.S. The association publishes a newsletter, The Atlatl (European fans have recently published a Francophone version, Le Propulseur), coordinates competitions ("throws"), and tracks the results of International Standard Accuracy Contests, designed to enable atlatlists everywhere to compete for the title of "Best in the World." Many WAA members compete in both primitive (atlatl, spear, and point must be constructed of material available to prehistoric man, with the exception of artificial glue and sinew) and open (anything goes) classes.

The annual WAA meeting is not a place to sample mastodon burgers and wax nostalgic over the good old palaeo-days. Here at Flint Ridge, regulars on the atlatl circuit and new friends made over internet atlatl discussion groups compete and, more important, trade performance tips. Most members fashion their own atlatls from various types of wood, bone, or synthetic material, and take the opportunity to test-drive each other's creations. Banner stones, small, crescent- or butterfly-shaped stones with a hole drilled through the center, often associated with atlatl finds in North America, are a source of endless controversy. Were they good luck charms? Silencers to dampen the hissing noise some atlatls make when thrown? Weights to balance and improve the flexibility of an atlatl? (After many experimental projects involving atlatl performance, archaeologists are still out on this one.) Darts are also a hot topic: they have to be flexible enough to spring off the atlatl, but not so flexible that they sacrifice accuracy. River reed makes a great dart shaft, but Martha Stewart-brand reed garden stakes are a very acceptable substitute. The world-record atlatl throw, 848.56 feet, was achieved with a carbon-fiber atlatl and aluminum dart. "Guy modeled it on his computer," sniffs a purist.

Throwing an atlatl is addictive. The moment before the dart releases, you can feel the energy of its spring curl all the way to your throwing shoulder, then back up to the tip of the atlatl as the dart zips away with breathtaking force. WAA members love this rush. They compete throughout the rainy day, even while a debate ensues as to whether distant sirens are a tornado warning, or simply summoning volunteers for some other weather- related disaster. They're also happy to spread the atlatl gospel, coaxing visitors—a considerable number despite the weather—to take a try at one of the supervised practice targets. Atlatl vanity plates and "Ask Me About My Atlatl" bumper stickers accessorize cars in the nearby parking lot.

Early Sunday morning, the rain is still coming down and a dozen or so atlatlists are back on the throwing field. Throws are scheduled until the afternoon, when awards will be presented to the most accurate atlatlists at the meet, from novice to master class. Ray Strischek, Best in the World in 1997, spots a lackluster performance and shouts cheerily to the soaked atlatlist, "To hell with that rotator cuff! Put your shoulder in it!" The next dart streaks into the center of the target, and is followed by a congratulatory slap on the back, in acknowledgement of the WAA's motto: "Too long have I hunted mammoth alone."

–Kristin M. Romey

25

ON THE HEALER'S PATH

A journey through the Maya rain forest.

by ANGELA M.H. SCHUSTER

There is in this land a great quantity of medicinal plants of various properties; and if there were any person here who possessed a knowledge of them, it would be most useful and effective, for there is no disease to which the native Indians do not apply the plants.
—DIEGO DE LANDA, *Relación de las Cosas de Yucatán*, 1566

WHACK-ACK-ACK-ACK. EACH STRIKE OF THE machete echoes through the rain forest, setting off a cacaphonous response from all manner of birds and monkeys. A clean cut in a tree trunk begins to ooze a blood-red sap. "*K'ik'-te*, the blood tree," explains our guide Leopoldo "Polo" Romero. "We use it to treat open sores and chronic skin conditions." For Polo, a 56-year-old Yucatec Maya, the bewildering tangle of vines and trees through which we have been hiking for the past several hours is a jungle pharmacy rich in prescriptions for every known human affliction. Polo is a bush doctor and treater of snake bites. He is also one of a handful of *curanderos*, traditional Maya healers, who has come to the 6,000-acre Terra Nova Medicinal Reserve in western Belize to share his knowledge of the rain forest and the curative properties of its plants with scientists from the New York Botanical Garden and the National Cancer Institute. Established in 1993, Terra Nova is the world's first ethnobiomedical forest reserve and the brainchild of Rosita Arvigo, a Chicago native and Maya-trained healer.

For nearly three millennia the Maya flourished in the rain forests of Guatemala, Mexico, and Belize, harvesting roots, fruits, and foliage for food, fuel, fiber, construction materials, and, perhaps most important, medicine. Even with the advent of European medical practices following the Spanish conquest of the region in the sixteenth century, traditional ways survived and, in some areas, continue to be the sole source of healthcare. "As my mentor, Don Elijio Panti, would tell me," says Arvigo, "for every ailment on Earth, the spirits have provided a cure—one just has to find it."

A professional herbal healer, Arvigo, 60, of Italian-Syrian descent with deep-set eyes and narrow features, spent seven years among traditional Nahuatl healers in Mexico's Sierra Madre Mountains. She came to western Belize in 1976, believing that, with its rich heritage in traditional medicine, it would be an ideal place to both practice and learn. "I also had two small children and I wanted to bring them up in a fresh, natural environment rather than in the hustle and bustle of Chicago."

With her then husband, fellow healer Greg Shropshire, Arvigo purchased a small plot on the bank of the Macal River just outside San Ignacio and set up a clinic in town.

"It was a warm June day in 1983, and this elderly man, his slight, sinewy frame bent by time, came and sat on our clinic porch," says Arvigo, recounting her first meeting with Don Elijio. "I invited him in and we began to talk. The old man asked me what was in the glass jars on the clinic shelves and I began to explain their contents and the principles of herbal healing. Greg and I had brought a large supply of healing herbs from the States, but found that they were beginning to mold and rot in the humid tropical environment. Don Elijio was quick to notice the poor condition of the plants and immediately began telling me how to care for natural pharmaceuticals in a tropical environment. When he told me his name I suddenly realized that I had been giving a lecture on herbs to one of Central America's most revered *h'men* [doctor-priests]."

"Great and terrible stories had circulated about this old Mopan Maya," she continues. "Some people spoke of near miraculous healings, cured diseases, and numerous lives clutched from death's bony hand. Others, however, claimed he was nothing more than a lecherous old drunk and a witch who cast evil spells on innocent people." Rumors had circulated that Panti was from a family of sorcerers, his father a hechisero, a practitioner of black magic who enchanted women and was believed to have been responsible for a number of unexplained deaths.

Little did Arvigo know that her meeting with Don Elijio would lead to an apprenticeship lasting until his death at the age of

103 in 1996. During more than a decade of study, the Maya *h'men* taught her about the curative properties of the rain forest and the spiritual tools needed to use it. "Don Elijio's knowledge of the plants was staggering. He regularly used nearly 200 of them to treat patients from as far away as the northern Yucatán," she says. "I cannot tell you how often I wondered whether, as a non-Maya, I even had the capacity to learn it all. In time, the dark, mysterious forest of trees and lianas suddenly became a familiar place of knowledge and healing."

Like traditional healers worldwide, Maya *curanderos* operate by what is known as a doctrine of signatures—that is, many plants tell you how they should be used. Those that are red or bear red fruit or flowers are for blood-related conditions or burns and rashes; yellow plants—the color of pus and bile—are for infections and ailments of the liver and spleen; blue plants tend to contain sedatives and are used to treat the nervous system; white plants signal death and are often poisonous.

THERE ARE A VARIETY OF TRADITIONAL healers in Belize, each with their own specialty or level of learning. A granny healer, for example, is a man or woman who has raised a sizable brood of children, grandchildren, and even great-grandchildren, using only home remedies to treat common household ailments such as diarrhea, cramps, skin diseases, and nervousness. Granny healers are well versed in rain forest medicine, but tend to care for only their immediate families. A village healer is essentially a granny healer whose practice has grown beyond his or her immediate family to include an entire village. Aiding granny and village healers are midwives, often trained by a parent or grandparent to deliver babies in rural areas and to treat children using an array of herbal teas, poultices, and powders. The massage therapist, or *sobadera*, treats muscle spasms, backaches, sprains, stress from overworked muscles, and general aches and pains using herbal baths, poultices, teas, and oils to massage painful areas. "This knowledge," says Arvigo, "is passed down from generation to generation and is often considered a divine gift."

The bone setter, *kax-bac* or *guesero*, specializes in sprains, fractures, broken bones, and pulled ligaments, using manipulation techniques along with a type of acupuncture known as pinchar, in which stingray spines are used to relieve pain. Snake doctors treat venomous or infectious bites caused by snakes, spiders, scorpions, bats, rats, and rabid dogs, as well as puncture wounds from rusty implements. In areas infested with poisonous snakes and insects, these doctors are often a patient's only hope since most hospitals are far away and many do not have the proper antivenin. Treatment often consists of puncturing a patient's skin in the affected area with stingray spines or thorns. The snake doctor's practice and formulas are secret and usually passed on to only one person in a generation, but according to Polo, one must chew tobacco while sucking out toxins in order to avoid being poisoned himself.

The most experienced healers, however, are the *h'men* (literally, "he or she who knows"), doctor-priests who have the experience, power, and mandate to deal with both physical and spiritual ailments. They are believed to have the ability to contact the spirit world and ask for assistance in the diagnosis and treatment of ailments. A traditional healer would never embark on a course of action for a patient without first attempting to determine whether an ailment was of physical or supernatural origin.

"IN WESTERN MEDICINE," SAYS ARVIGO, "we separate the physical from the mental or spiritual, seeing M.D.s for sickness; psychiatrists for mental problems. For the Maya, there is no such separation between the physical and mental or spiritual. Stress, grief, or other mental ailments bring on disease and vice versa." It is the shaman's job, she says, to heal the mind, body, and soul by physical and spiritual means—the physical with plants, the spiritual with incantations and prayers.

The incantations and prayers that accompany treatment are invocations of both ancient deities—the Nine Benevolent Maya gods, especially Ixchel, goddess of healing and weaving—and Christian saints. Use of such invocations is well known from antiquity, having been documented in one of the earliest surviving treatises on New World medicine. Written in Yucatec Maya using European script, the manuscript, which is known as the Ritual of the Bacabs, contains 46 medicinal incantations and prescriptions. Though it dates to the late eighteenth century, it is clear from the archaic nature of the language used in the manuscript, which is currently in the collection of the Princeton University Library, that it was copied from a much earlier document.

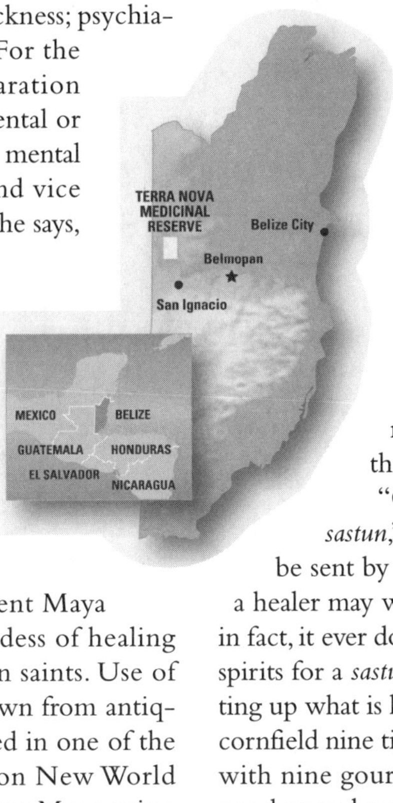

In Maya medicine, says Arvigo, diseases are regarded as semipersonified beings that can be controlled or ordered about by a shaman. Medicinal plants provide the cure, she says, but healers often rely on supernatural forces for guidance in determining precisely which plants or parts of plants to harvest and how to prepare them. Crossing the divide between the physical and spiritual worlds, however, requires a *sastun* (*sas* means "light" or "mirror"; *tun*, "stone"), usually a small, glistening, translucent stone. By peering into it, a shaman can determine the source of an illness or divine answers to questions, communing with the spirits as if they were close friends.

"One can not simply acquire a *sastun*," she explains. "A *sastun* must be sent by the Maya spirits. Sometimes, a healer may wait years for one to arrive, if, in fact, it ever does." Don Elijio had asked the spirits for a *sastun* for two years, she says, setting up what is known as a *primicia* altar in his cornfield nine times a year. The altar, adorned with nine gourds filled with *atole* (a sweetened corn beverage), one for each of the Maya gods, is used on feast days to conduct a ceremony in which one can commune with spirits and ancestors. One day, having just completed a *primicia* ceremony, Don Elijio was suddenly overtaken by a feeling of joy and happiness and found himself skipping back home like a young boy. When he arrived, his wife presented him with a luminous green stone, saying, "Look what I found on the floor today. A child must have left it here. Isn't it pretty?" And that was how he received his *sastun*. Arvigo now possesses Don Elijio's *sastun*, which he gave to her shortly before his death.

Realizing the richness of Maya traditional medicine and the importance of recording practices that had been handed down for generations before they disappeared, Arvigo founded the Ixchel Tropical Research Foundation in 1986. "I knew that the ways of traditional healers like Don Elijio were being eclipsed by Western medicinal practices, and that, like other fragile vestiges of Prehispanic culture, they would soon disappear without a trace. People, especially in developing countries like Belize, don't want to appear backward by associating with traditional healers. They would rather see Western doctors in starched white lab coats who dole out synthetic drugs. Some drugs, such as cortisone, which comes from dioscorea, and vincristine, which is used to treat Hodgkins disease and comes from the rosy periwinkle, are extracted from the very plants growing in a patient's backyard."

The dynamic between researchers and traditional healers has changed in recent years.

In an effort to preserve what remains of traditional Maya medicine, Arvigo embarked on a campaign to interest the scientific community in its extraordinary potential. "Can you imagine, here I am, witnessing what may be the last traces of Prehispanic medicinal knowledge in one of the last contiguous stands of old-growth rain forest in Central America, which is gradually being destroyed for farming and development, and I'm wondering whether Don Elijio's profession is going to die with him and the rain forest. Had any of his plants been studied by modern science? Was he all that was left of the medical system of the ancient Maya, the last thread dangling from a once glorious tapestry of healers who were revered, perhaps even deified by their society?"

"I began a vigorous letter-writing campaign to scientists around the world. One day, a friend passed along a newspaper article about a worldwide search for medicinal plants bearing anti-cancer and anti-AIDS compounds. The scientist in charge of collecting Central American specimens was ethnobotanist Michael Balick of the New York Botanical Garden."

"We get numerous requests for research support," says Balick, 48, whom I visited in his New York Botanical Garden office, "but we are only able to pursue a few of them. When I received Rosita's letter back in '86, I thought this would be an ideal project for us. We had just received a grant from the National Cancer Institute to screen Central American plants that had the potential for providing cures for two diseases for which modern medicine has only limited therapies—cancer and AIDS."

"Less than $1/2$ of one percent of the planet's 265,000 species of higher plants has been exhaustively analyzed for their chemical composition and medicinal properties," he says. "From that 1/2 of one percent comes some 25 percent of all prescription pharmaceuticals that have been developed to date, drugs such as the heart medication digitalin from foxglove and the anti-inflammatory cortisone from dioscorea. As you can see, we have a long way to go."

"Given the number of plants out there, we simply do not have the resources to study them all. So, as scientists, how do we go about narrowing our research and increasing our chances of collecting the plants with the greatest curing potential? One way is to talk to the people who use them. We call this technique ethno-directed screening."

Balick and his team took to the field with Arvigo and Panti, collecting more than 3,000 specimens for testing and interviewing local healers about their use. After being properly pressed and dried, duplicate sets of specimens—stems, leaves, fruits, flowers—were sent to herbaria in both Belize and the United States, the latter being studied at the New York Botanical Garden.

IN ADDITION TO ITS COLLECTION OF rare medicinal trees, vines, and herbs, Terra Nova is home to seedlings rescued from tracts of rain forest that have given way to development, guaranteeing that future generations of healers and scientists will have plants to harvest. In addition to Terra Nova, Arvigo founded the Rainforest Medicine Trail at her farm just outside San Ignacio. The trail, which is open to the public, exhibits 50 of the most commonly used medicinal plants in the Maya world. Her farm also functions as a research station and a base of operations for a commercial enterprise that produces and sells a variety of tinctures made from Maya medicinal plants.

Arvigo and Balick note that the dynamic between researchers and traditional healers has changed in recent years. "We no longer simply go and observe," says Balick, "we form research partnerships. Most traditional healers with whom we have worked are elated that science is incorporating their knowledge rather than ignoring it. Should any drug come as the result of their traditional knowledge, the traditional healers will profit from it." Both the Botanical Garden and the National Cancer Institute have an agreement with the Traditional Healers Foundation, established to ensure the curanderos share the proceeds from any drug development.

Whether the plants will ultimately yield treatments for diseases such as cancer and AIDS remains to be seen as it will be some years before the Belize botanical collection has been exhaustively analyzed. "Our goal," says Arvigo, "has been simply to document the remnants of what once existed and to make it freely available to all who wish it."

The author would like to thank the Traditional Healers Foundation of Belize, The New York Botanical Garden, and the Department for Middle American Research, Tulane University, for their assistance in the preparation of this article.

PART VII:

NORTH AMERICA

26

FLIGHT OF THE ANASAZI

Where did they go after abandoning Mesa Verde? A site in southern New Mexico provides intriguing clues.

by STEPHEN H. LEKSON

IN 1988, MY COLLEAGUE KARL LAUMBACH AND I were surveying the lower end of a three-mile-long gorge of the Rio Alamosa for the National Park Service. There we found the remains of a 150-room pueblo atop an isolated, 100-foot-tall butte. Aptly named the Pinnacle Ruin, it is the most spectacular of the many Alamosa sites (see Plate 15). As we looked out over the landscape, the site's attractions to the ancient inhabitants of the region were obvious: the river offered a permanent water supply, the site overlooked several hundred acres of fine bottom farmland, and the nearby mountains had abundant fuel wood and big game. Today, we are excavating here in hopes of solving the mystery of the Anasazi disappearance.

When nineteenth-century European explorers first came upon the Southwest's magnificent ancient buildings—like

Cliff Palace at Mesa Verde and Pueblo Bonito at Chaco Canyon—those ruins had long been deserted. We know from tree-ring dating that they were abandoned by A.D. 1300, but the totality of the abandonment defies easy explanation. Rarely in human history do populations as large as 15,000 to 20,000 people completely desert an area as rich in resources as the Four Corners where they had lived for centuries.

Who built the Mesa Verde and Chaco Canyon sites, why did they leave, and where did they go? We know who built them. After initial speculations by explorers and journalists that Cliff Palace and Pueblo Bonito were built by the Lost Tribes of Israel or Phoenicians or Aztecs, anthropologists at the turn of the last century proved what Native Americans knew all along: the ancient ruins of the Four Corners were built by the ancestors of the modern Pueblo peoples who live today at Hopi, Zuni, Acoma, and the many Rio Grande Pueblo towns of New Mexico (see ARCHAEOLOGY, September/October 1995). The name we commonly use for these ancestral Pueblo people is Anasazi, which means "enemy ancestors" in Navajo—it is not a Pueblo word.

With that issue resolved, archaeology in the Four Corners focused on the "why" question: Why did they leave? Tree-rings tell us that there was a drought from about A.D. 1275 to about 1300, but Carla Van West, formerly with the Crow Canyon Archaeological Center, believes from her research on crop productivity, precipitation, and population that it was only the last in a series of droughts the Four Corners peoples had survived, some of which were comparable or worse. By Van West's calculations, many thousands of people who lived in the Four Corners in 1275 could have remained and thrived, but between 1275 and 1300 everyone left.

Steven LeBlanc of the Peabody Museum and Christy Turner of Arizona State University have both argued there were increased levels of violence in the final decades, hastening the departure (see ARCHAEOLOGY, May/June 1999). Intense violence would be a good reason to leave, but violence itself was probably a symptom of larger problems. Perhaps there were weather complications that compounded the effects of the drought. Matthew Salzer of the Laboratory of Tree-ring Research at the University of Arizona suggests a huge volcanic eruption, somewhere far beyond the Anasazi world, that caused a "nuclear winter" in 1259, shortening an already short growing season. Jeffrey S. Dean of the University of Arizona, again looking at the tree-ring data, sees the onset, about 1250, of a prolonged era of climatic chaos: not only was there less precipitation, but it fell in unpredictable seasonal patterns. The combination of circumstances would be catastrophic for farmers relying on rainfall to water their crops. Bad weather might have "pushed" Four Corners peoples from their ancestral homes.

To these "push" explanations, some archaeologists now add "pulls"—attractions from the areas to which the Anasazi moved. Images of kachina (spiritual beings in Pueblo religion) appear first in the areas of the modern Pueblos during the fourteenth century. William Lipe of Washington State University believes that the newly emerging kachina religion, in which participants wearing sacred masks dance to insure rain and prosperity, drew people away from the Four

Corners. Others studying the origins of kachina religion, such as Charles Adams of the Arizona State Museum, argue that it emerged in those areas as a response to the huge influx of strangers from the Four Corners. But we can't have it both ways: kachina ceremony can't be both the cause and the effect of the Four Corners migrations.

Where did the Anasazi go? We know from archaeology and Pueblo traditional histories that many of them went to areas of the modern Pueblos of Arizona and New Mexico, but traditions also suggest that the migrations were long and convoluted. A clue comes from ceramics derived from the characteristic Mesa Verde black-on-white pottery (see Plates 16 and 17). Some Mesa Verde people went beyond the Rio Grande to the edge of the Great Plains, around Santa Fe, New Mexico, where Galisteo black-on-white pottery, clearly a post-Mesa Verde type, is found. Population in the Santa Fe region increased in the fourteenth century after the abandonment of Mesa Verde and the Four Corners, but the increase appears to be far less than the numbers that left Mesa Verde in the late thirteenth century.

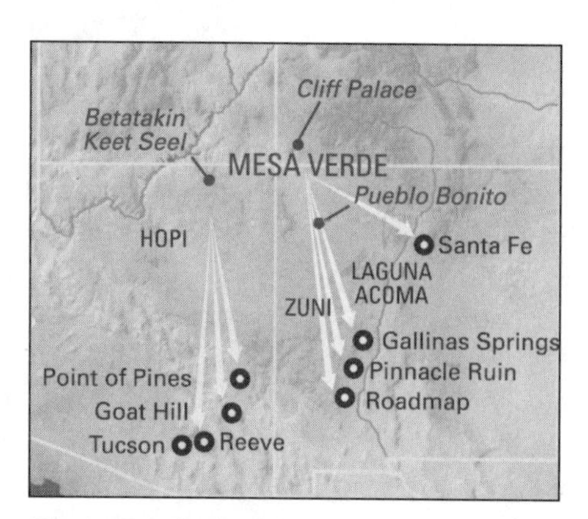

The Anasazi abandoned the Four Corners region by A.D. 1300. Evidence now suggests they moved long distances to new homes.

Many Mesa Verde people, it seems, went much farther south from the Four Corners, down to the Rio Alamosa and beyond. Pinnacle Ruin is one of several very large sites in the area that has ceramics that look very much like Mesa Verde black-on-white pottery types. The walls of these far-south post-Mesa Verde sites are built of well-coursed masonry. While not built of the fine sandstone masonry characteristic of the Mesa Verde country, the ruins are unlike earlier, local sites, that share more with the Mimbres culture than with the peoples of the north (see ARCHAEOLOGY, November/December 1990). They have multistoried room blocks, T-shaped doorways (conspicuous at Mesa Verde and other Four Corners sites), enclosed plazas, deeply stratified middens, and kivas—all of which are Four Corners features, and absent from earlier local sites. Far-south post-Mesa Verde sites like Pinnacle Ruin and the nearby Gallinas Springs and Roadmap sites stick out like the proverbial sore thumb.

Together, these sites have more than 800 rooms—too few to accommodate all of the people who left the Mesa Verde region, but still the largest known post-Mesa Verde communities. At a distance of 260 miles, the Pinnacle Ruin and the Roadmap sites are almost twice as far from Mesa Verde as the modern Pueblos where most Four Corners descendants now live. It isn't just the distance that's important. It is that these southern Mesa Verde sites housed large groups—scores of families, probably entire clans—that moved and resettled as organized towns. That is not how archaeologists had imagined the abandonment of Mesa Verde and the Four Corners area. The conventional view was of trickles and spurts: a family here, two families there, drifting off to join cousins in distant villages, where the Pueblos now live. It now appears that the Mesa Verde area was rapidly and completely abandoned, with thousands of people leaving in only a few decades. The scale of the abandonment suggests that decisions were made not by families but at a

The Case for Mass Emigration

Our goals at Pinnacle Ruin during the first year's work were simple: to determine depth of fill within rooms and recover datable materials, to obtain a ceramic sample from midden areas (if any), and to produce an accurate site plan. The room excavations, directed by Brian Yunker, a University of Colorado graduate student, were set next to a wall partially exposed by a shallow, old looter's pit. The wall face turned out to be well plastered and the wall itself impressively massive—over a foot thick. While only a few inches of the wall were above the ground surface before our excavation, it proved to be over five feet tall, but no higher. At least in this part of the ruin, structures were only one story. A large pine post, presumably a roof support, was found set at the base of the wall, but it was too decayed to yield a tree-ring date. Excavations elsewhere on the site, directed by Curtis Nepstad-Thornberry (another University of Colorado student), exposed a deep, stratified midden whose richness and layering was remarkable. None of the archaeologists who visited the site had seen a midden like that in southern New Mexico, but it does look like those at Mesa Verde, where richly stratified trash deposits are typical.

The pottery offers more evidence for the identity of Pinnacle Ruin's inhabitants. Toni S. Laumbach of the New Mexico Farm and Ranch Museum, who is analyzing the pottery, has found that more than 60 percent of it is a post-Mesa Verde type, which we call Magdalena black on white. El Paso polychrome, a local pottery, is the next most frequent painted type, followed by smaller amounts of polychrome pottery from the Zuni and northern Rio Grande areas. Based on dates of these types elsewhere in the Southwest, the Pinnacle ceramics date to the early to mid-1300s, or shortly after the abandonment of the Four Corners (ca. 1275–1300), but occupation of the site may have begun earlier, in the 1200s, when waves of people began to leave the Mesa Verde region. We obtained two radiocarbon dates that precisely bracket 1300, strongly suggesting that the Pinnacle Ruin was occupied at that critical time of migrations and resettlements.

Two small test pits, even as intriguing as those at Pinnacle Ruin, are a thin framework on which to build a new model of Anasazi history, but two other post-Mesa Verde sites complement the Pinnacle Ruin. The first, Gallinas Springs, is very large, with 500 rooms, six kivas, and an extensive midden. Emma Lou Davis, working for the National Park Service in the 1960s, interpreted Gallinas Springs as a southern post-Mesa Verde site. Three small field projects were undertaken there by three different groups in 1974, 1977, and 1987. Draft reports describe ceramics identical to those at Pinnacle. Joseph Tainter, a U.S. Forest Service archaeologist who directed the 1977 fieldwork, suggested that Gallinas Springs was settled by a large post-Mesa Verde population moving into an "empty niche" in southern New Mexico. The Roadmap site, even farther south than Pinnacle Ruin, has never been excavated. I discovered the site in 1983, while working on a project directed by Margaret C. Nelson, now of Arizona State University. From surface observations, Roadmap appears to be about 100 rooms with two enclosed plazas. There are no obvious depressions indicating kivas and no visible midden. The shards found were of the same telltale Mesa Verde-like pottery style found at Pinnacle Ruin.

–Stephen H. Lekson

higher, perhaps regional political level, spurred by crop failures, food shortages, and a deteriorating social climate marked by incidents of violence (see ARCHAEOLOGY, January/February 1997).

Village- or town-sized migrations are also known from the western half of the Four Corners, away from Mesa Verde. At the same time people were leaving Mesa Verde, they were also leaving Betatakin and Keet Seel, cliff dwellings at Navajo National Monument, and many other large towns of the Kayenta Anasazi region of northeastern Arizona. Several small village sites with Kayenta pottery and architecture have been found in the mountains and deserts of southeastern Arizona, from Tucson east to the New Mexico state line. Fieldwork in the 1950s at a huge pueblo site called Point of Pines in southeastern Arizona revealed a migration similar to Pinnacle Ruin's. Emil Haury of the University of Arizona excavated a late thirteenth-century "neighborhood" that stood out in contrast to the rest of the 800-room pueblo. The architecture and pottery of this foreign neighborhood closely resembled those of the Kayenta region. Haury concluded that 50 or 60 families—"a large enough group to maintain religious practices and to function as a social unit"—had migrated 200 miles from the Kayenta region and joined indigenous peoples of the Point of Pines region. This migration ended unhappily: most of the rooms in the Kayenta neighborhood were intentionally burned, with all of their contents in place. Haury noted that after that conflagration no trace of the Kayenta people or their pottery remained at Point of Pines.

More recently, other Kayenta villages were discovered and excavated in the San Pedro River Valley, just east of Tucson, such as the Reeve site, and at Goat Hill, near Safford, Arizona, excavated by Kyle Woodson, then a graduate student at the University of Texas at Austin. These are unmistakable Anasazi settlements at distances even greater than Pinnacle Ruin's from their original homeland. They show that the situation at Pinnacle Ruin was not unique. Village-scale migrations, moving hundreds of miles from the Four Corners area, which includes both Kayenta and Mesa Verde, to the deserts of the southern Southwest were not common, but neither were they rare.

We will continue to work at Pinnacle Ruin. This year, the project will utilize Earthwatch volunteers in excavations, testing for the presence of kivas—a Four Corners feature absent from the Mimbres tradition. We will learn much about the abandonment of the Four Corners by looking at sites like Pinnacle Ruin because they give us new insights into where the Anasazi went and how they got there. Many of them, we now know, went hundreds of miles, well beyond the regions of the modern Pueblos. And they went as large groups, as entire villages. Ironically, Pueblo tribal officials reading about Pinnacle Ruin in the local papers told me this wasn't news to them; in their traditional histories it is clans, villages, and whole peoples that move.

27

CLOSING THE IGNORANCE GAP

Florida's once neglected history and prehistory now get top billing in K–12 textbooks statewide.

BY JERALD T. MILANICH

IT WAS PARENTS' NIGHT IN GAINESVILLE, FLORIDA, the year 1987. Squeezed into an undersized desk and leafing through my daughter's eighth-grade social science textbook, my emotions went from disbelief to dismay. The missions of Spanish colonial Florida were not mentioned, nor were the early French settlements in Florida and South Carolina. The history of the United States began with Jamestown and the Pilgrims. Worse, the 12,000 or more years in which Indians had lived in Florida, from the time of the Paleoindians to the present, were also ignored.

The experience came flooding back the other day when I was clicking through my morning e-mail. One message from a school in St. Petersburg caught my attention: "Our fourth-grade class is doing a project on famous Floridians," it read. "One girl has selected Cacique María. I am having a very rough time even finding a mention of her. Could you help us find information? Anything would be greatly appreciated." I put the teacher in touch with one of my graduate students who is writing a book about female chiefs in the southeastern United States.

I was impressed that a fourth grader knew the term *cacique*, originally a Caribbean Arawak word for chief. I was even more impressed that the student had even heard of María, a Timucua Indian woman who was chief of the Spanish Franciscan mission town of Nombre de Dios in 1600. Six years later she inherited the position of chief of San Pedro de Mocama on Cumberland Island, Georgia, where she took up residence. Doña María, as the Spaniards called her, is not exactly a household name. In 1970 when I surface collected the site of San Pedro on the south end of Cumberland Island, an integral part of Spanish Florida in the colonial period, I had never heard of her.

This case is not an isolated one. My e-mail regularly brings queries from students for information about Precolumbian and colonial Florida. Their questions often stem from something they have read in one or another of the popular books my colleagues and I wrote in the mid-1990s: How did Indians store corn? What wood was used to make dugout canoes? Did Indians use cast nets?

The hunger for information has not gone unnoticed by Florida education officials or book publishers. The Department of Education mandates that social studies courses emphasize Florida history in the fourth and eighth grades. State-wide standards require student understanding of "early Spanish settlements," "early Spanish missions" and "loss of Native American homelands." It is no wonder fourth graders have heard of Cacique María. They are required to know "people and events related to the early exploration of Florida" and "significant events in the colonial period." They also are expected to know "aspects of the cultural, social, and political features of Native American tribes in the history of Florida."

Educators in the state take this charge seriously and classroom teachers work hard to find appropriate materials they can pass on to their students. Some have collaborated with archaeologists to prepare curricula and lesson plans. See, for example, web pages for the E. Dale Joyner Nature Preserve at Pelotes Island, Florida at pelotes.jea.com and the Florida Division of Historical Resources at dhr.dos.state.fl.us/bhp/fhep/.

Just how much archaeologists are influencing what is taught in Florida's schools hit home two years ago, when I began working with editors from Harcourt School Publishers to develop a Florida social-science text for fourth graders. I was pleasantly surprised to discover that they wanted to use the latest information on the Indians of Florida and Spanish colonization. That information comes from popular books that recount the results of both Precolumbian and historical archaeological investigations. In the 1990s, Kathleen Deagan and Darcie MacMahon, both colleagues at the Florida Museum of Natural History, collaborated on *Fort Mose: Colonial America's Black Fortress of Freedom* and Robin C. Brown, an author and avocational archaeologist, wrote a beautifully produced book: *Florida's First People.* My word processor and I wrote *Florida Indians from Ancient Times to the Present*, along with books on the Timucua Indians and the Spanish missions. Other archaeologists contributed popular books about the Apalachee and Seminole Indians and on the archaeology of South Florida.

In March of this year, when I received a copy of the Harcourt textbook on which I had worked, I sat down and read chapters 2 through 4. Fourth grade in Florida was never like this; for that matter, neither was my daughter's eighth grade. "The Earliest Floridians" is followed by "Exploration and Early Settlement" and "Colonial Florida." Changing climatic conditions at the end of the Ice Age are there along with the state's first inhabitants, the Paleoindians. Windover, the famed Early Archaic period peat bog site with preserved 7000-year-old human tissue near Cocoa, is also covered, as are shell middens, Timucua Indians, and native chiefs like Doña María. This was the first K–12 textbook that incorporated information on many Florida Indians, especially groups in south and central Florida. Centuries before the Seminoles there were the Tocobaga, Uzita, Jororo, and Matecumbe Indians, as well as the Calusa and Tequesta. The Spanish missions, many of which I excavated in the 1990s, also received their due.

During my own public school years (1950–1963) in Orlando, nobody even talked about the Spanish period in the Southeast. On the classroom wall, there would be a giant map showing important Colonial locations, and the whole southern part of the United States would be blank! Precolumbian inhabitants of the state and the Spanish missions merited but a few sentences. Twenty-four years later, my daughter would read of De Soto the Conquistador but little of the fact that for some 300 years Spain made a major effort to settle, conquer, and hold the Southeast. In some texts, there was more about the horses the Spaniards brought to America than the Spaniards who brought them.

But times have changed and archaeologists have woken up. Textbook writing has convinced me that archaeology has gone from being an insular discipline appealing to a small but ardent group of supporters to being mainstream. Teachers, publishers, and archaeologists all are working successfully to bring the past to the present by incorporating information gleaned from archaeology into school coursework.

Florida's experience is not unique. The Society for American Archaeology, an organization that has lobbied hard for curricular reform, reports a growing awareness among educators nationwide of the need to incorporate such information in the standard curricula. Knowing about our Native American heritage is now as important as being able to name the U.S. presidents.

I'll bet when King Juan Carlos and Queen Sophia of Spain walked through the streets of St. Augustine this past April the students lining their route knew a lot more about their colonial city and the Spanish colonization of Florida than their predecessors did a decade and a half ago. Imagine the questions they'll be e-mailing next year.

28

REMEMBERING AFRICA UNDER THE EAVES

A forgotten room in a Brooklyn farmhouse bears witness to the spiritual lives of slaves.

by H. ARTHUR BANKOFF, CHRISTOPHER RICCIARDI, *and* ALYSSA LOORYA

AS KIDS, WE RODE OUR BIKES THROUGH THE QUIET streets of the Marine Park section of Brooklyn, New York. We didn't know each other then, but we each recall pedaling past the Hendrick I. Lott house, whose gracious porch, peeling white paint, and ample grounds overgrown with tall weeds set it apart from the street's cookie-cutter houses (see Plate 18). The roads and homes surrounding it, we later learned, stood on land that was once the Lott farm. Years later, as archaeologists, we finally understood the importance of this place. Occupied across three centuries by the same family, the Lott House is a microcosm of New York's evolution from the 1720s to 1989, when its last occupant died. With a team from the Brooklyn College Archaeological Research Center, we came back to explore the house that had fascinated us as children.

For three years, we have investigated the ways in which the Lotts responded to their changing landscape, excavating around the house, examining the structure itself, perusing archives, and tracking down Lott descendants. The site, which the city is in the process of acquiring, has been designated an official Save America's Treasures project and a federal and local landmark. We have chronicled our work on ARCHAEOLOGY's website, reassembling jumbled stratigraphy to better understand the construction sequence at the house. A privy revealed dolls, pipes, a gold pocket watch, and the upper plate of a woman's false teeth. We recovered endless quantities of clam and oyster shells and ceramics. Through it all, one question haunted us. During the eighteenth century, according to census data, the Lotts owned more slaves than most other families in the town of Flatlands, now Marine Park. We had found no direct evidence of where—or how—those slaves might have lived.

Finally, this past winter, we found it: a forgotten room that would reveal key evidence of the persistence of African religious rituals among slaves in New York—the only evidence for it, in fact, beyond the eighteenth-century African Burial Ground in Lower Manhattan (see ARCHAEOLOGY, March/April 1993, pp. 28–38), where some graves reflected continued adherence to such ritual symbols and traditions. It is unusual to uncover in New York City undisturbed archaeological deposits that date prior to the turn of the nineteenth century. The urbanization that has changed the face of this metropolis since the mid-nineteenth century has obliterated evidence of slave life, whereas on the large plantations in the rural South, slaves were typically housed in separate quarters whose archaeological remains still exist today.

Recently, archaeologist Diana Wall of City College of the City University of New York reexamined artifacts from many eighteenth-century sites excavated in New York City from the late 1970s through the 1980s. By looking more closely at these material remains in light of new information based on recent work done in the South, the Caribbean, and on the West Coast of Africa, she hopes to identify artifacts that enslaved Africans used or owned. Among her discoveries is a pewter serving spoon, recovered in 1984 from a Lower Manhattan landfill and inscribed inside its bowl with three "X"s. When first excavated, the "X"s were overlooked, but Wall believes the marks—reminiscent of those found on ceramic objects excavated outside New York—were made by African slaves to mark it as theirs.

FROM THE EARLY 1790S, DEBATE OVER abolition raged in New York's legislature. While slavery wasn't officially abolished in New York until 1827, by the turn of the nineteenth century, its end was in sight. Census records reveal that, in the early 1800s, the Lott family owned at least 12 slaves. But within the first ten years of that century, during the construction of the main portion of the present-day Lott House and two decades before New York abolished slavery,

Hendrick I. Lott freed all but one of his slaves, an elderly woman. Perhaps he knew what was coming. Or perhaps, as family oral tradition recalls, he did it to demonstrate his support of the abolition movement. The Lotts were members of the Flatlands Reformed Dutch Church, which, beginning in the late eighteenth century, preached that all people should be free. Federal census records seem to indicate that, after freeing his enslaved laborers, Lott hired them back as paid workers; the number and ages of free blacks corresponds to the register of slaves ten years earlier.

By 1800, the Lotts had outgrown the small, salt-box-style house with attached lean-to the family had lived in for almost a century. In 1800, they moved their house from an unknown spot elsewhere on the property to its current location and joined it to a grand, new house. We had always thought of the lean-to as a single room tacked on to the original house to provide extra kitchen or work space, but in late 1999, while surveying the interior architecture of the lean-to, we noticed a small trap door in the ceiling of a closet. Rounding up a ladder and a couple of flashlights, we climbed up through the door. When our eyes adjusted to the dark, we saw we were facing three tread-worn steps leading to a boarded-up door. To each side of the steps we saw a doorway leading to a windowless, cramped garret room roughly ten feet square. We were standing in a forgotten second story of the lean-to. We noted that the steps had likely once

Yankee Slavery

Most people do not think of New England as a "massive landscape of slavery," but that's what archaeologist Gerald Sawyer sees when he looks at documentary and archaeological evidence from the site of an eighteenth-century plantation in southeastern Connecticut. The 30-square-mile plantation, called New Salem by its owner, Colonel Samuel Browne, operated from 1718 until 1780.

A team led by Sawyer, an instructor at Central Connecticut State University, has found evidence of African burial customs on the plantation, including cairns surrounding a Christian burial ground and in groupings on a hillside below it, some of which resemble those used to mark burials in Ghana and Jamaica. The burial ground contains nine poorly carved headstones engraved with now indecipherable initials. Pieces of quartz were placed next to many of the headstones, a known African-American ritual practice.

New Salem was one of many New England plantations that were part of the so-called triangle trade, in which rum was shipped to Africa and exchanged for slaves, who were brought to the West Indies and exchanged for molasses, which was shipped back to Rhode Island to produce more rum. Some ten percent of slaves brought to the New World ended up in the North.

"Our written history suggests that there was no such thing as slavery in the North," says Sawyer. "But our Connecticut site was not working in isolation—enslavement there could not work without a global colonial political system behind it."

Sawyer believes that freed and escaped slaves lived on the periphery of the New Salem plantation and intermarried with Native Americans and poorer whites. He has found remnants of hillside rock structures on the edge of the plantation that resemble dwellings of African-Jamaicans.

–Sydney Schwartz

continued down to where we had positioned our ladder.

We stooped to explore the four-foot-high space. Re-used boards, some with bits of wallpaper from a former incarnation, make up the floor, secured in place by rose-headed square-cut nails, suggesting pre- or early-nineteenth-century construction. Candle drippings speckle the floorboards by the stairs.

The room to the left has a chimney slathered with mortar to seal a hole—apparently once a beehive-shaped oven to heat the room or warm food. Dark soot stains are still visible on the brick. On the floor we found a door—a perfect fit to the doorway—with a rectangle cut out, most likely for ventilation. The room to the right of the stairs is slightly smaller, with no source of heat; its door also now lies within the room, a perfect match to the room's doorway. This second door has no cut rectangle. Perhaps without a chimney, this room had no need of ventilation. The third, boarded-up door would have led to a Lott-family bedroom in the adjoining salt-box.

We had finally found the living quarters for at least one of the Lotts' slaves. It would have been an inhospitable place to live, close and dark without natural light or fresh air; in short, hardly the sort of place in which one would expect liberal-minded abolitionists to house anybody.

IN BOTH THE NORTH AND THE SOUTH, slaves assigned domestic responsibilities often lived within the household. Diaries, letters, and contemporary histories indicate that in the North, even field workers frequently lived in the main house. It is doubtful that all 12 of the Lotts' slaves lived in these small rooms. Judging from the proximity of the garret rooms to the family bedroom on the other side of the now boarded-up door, it seems likely that the slaves residing in these rooms were assigned domestic responsibilities. Perhaps, in accordance with the southern model, the Lotts' farmhands lived in separate quarters.

We are left wondering what it might have meant for the enslaved Africans who did call the garret rooms home to live in the lap of the family. Archaeologists have argued that the layout of the typical plantation—with the big house high on a hill overlooking a cluster of shabby slave quarters—served to cow slaves into intimidated submission, hammer home a stratified social vision, and deter mingling. On the flip side, that separation may have fostered the development of a community of slaves with its own cultural tradition. Perhaps slaves living within the household would have felt doubly isolated, cut off not only from the family with whom they shared a roof, but also from the community of slaves. The forgotten room under the eaves makes it difficult to argue that any moral opposition to slavery the Lotts felt translated into exceptional treatment of their slaves.

As surprised as we were to discover the rooms, nothing prepared us for what we uncovered beneath the floorboards. In the southwestern corner of the larger room were four intact corncobs and a fifth apparently gnawed into three parts by rodents. The five full corncobs may have comprised a geometric figure when laid down, possibly a five-pointed star. There may have been a similar arrangement of the dozens of cobs in the northern room as well, but rodents have disturbed any pattern beyond recognition.

Corncobs were also present under the floorboards near the chimney. Corncobs were used as kindling in colonial times, but these cobs were not burned. Stripped cobs were used as bedding, but kernels were intact on these, suggesting that they were placed beneath the floorboards whole. Ritual placement is the most likely explanation.

Yet another exciting find came from beneath the floorboards of the smaller room: a cloth pouch—its contents, if there were any, disintegrated beyond recognition—tied with hemp string, half the pelvis of a sheep or goat, and an oyster shell.

Ritual items have been uncovered beneath floorboards at several sites in the South and relate to the Hoodoo or Voodoo practices that derive from West African cosmology, in which objects were buried beneath the floor as protective talismans. The Lotts' slaves themselves most likely came from West Africa, whose population was depleted as captives were taken to northeastern America as slaves. And although no direct parallel to our corncobs has been found, we feel certain that these items may have had some ritual use for the slaves living at the Lott House. Shells, bones, and pouches have been found under floors and in walls of rooms where slaves lived or worked in Maryland and farther south, as well as in South America and the Caribbean, clearly suggesting the continuation of African practices beyond African soil (see ARCHAEOLOGY, May/June 2000, p. 21). As in this case, caches were typically clustered around doorways and fireplaces where spirits were thought to enter and exit.

Ritual items have been uncovered beneath floorboards at several sites in the South.

The placement of ritual items under floorboards does not necessarily indicate that enslaved Africans were practicing their beliefs covertly. In some West African cultures, objects were secreted under entrances to buildings to keep evil out. On the other hand, we cannot rule out the possibility that religious activity took place only out of sight of slave owners.

Debris from above the floorboards in the garret rooms, including a scrap of newspaper dating to the time of the Spanish American War (1898–99), suggests reuse of the space at the turn of the twentieth century, perhaps for storage. Wooden latches still in place would have held the door to each room shut from the outside.

OUR EXCAVATIONS HAVE also turned up an item offering another link to enslaved Africans. Recovered outside the foundation of an old, detached stone kitchen on the property—in a deposit dating to between 1775 and 1850—were shards of a decorated red slipware plate made of locally mined clay. The bottom of this plate, which we have almost completely reconstructed, exhibits an incised "X"—carved sometime after firing—similar to that on the Manhattan spoon Wall examined.

Common slipware plates, readily available

among European colonists during the eighteenth century, went out of fashion soon after the Revolutionary War. Such an ordinary item is an unlikely Lott-family heirloom. Why then was this plate—manufactured between 1730 and 1770—found in an early nineteenth-century deposit? Perhaps it was discarded by the family, then claimed and marked by the newly freed Africans. Inscriptions like this, sometimes accompanied by a circle or rectangle, have been found marking artifacts elsewhere, including at several South Carolina plantation sites. For the Bakongo, a group living along the lower Congo River, the "X" is a cosmogram representing the boundary between the living world and the world of the dead, with water lying in between. One study in South Carolina found a number of "X"-inscribed objects under water. In our context, is the "X" simply a mark of ownership, or do objects so inscribed carry a ritual meaning?

THERE IS STILL ANOTHER THREAD IN this story of enslaved Africans, and it comes from the Lotts themselves. Two Lott descendants, Catherine Lott-Divis and Carol Lott McNamara, who did not know each other as children, grew up hearing stories about a second-floor room in the main section of the house with a door leading to a storage space in the eaves of a gambrel roof. The space, more a discreet nook than a room, is accessible only through a bedroom closet. Catherine and Carol separately recalled a family legend that the room was used as part of the Underground Railroad in the 1840s.

Archaeologists around here joke that every pre-Civil War House in New York City claims to have been part of the Underground Railroad. Yet when one takes into account that the Lott family freed its slaves almost 25 years prior to the abolition of slavery in New York State, and, in turn, hired them as paid workers, it is possible the house really was used as a stop on the Railroad. It is known that the Underground Railroad did run through Staten Island, Brooklyn, Queens, and the Bronx to circumvent Manhattan, where strong economic and social ties to the South made it less hospitable to runaway slaves.

Today, the huge basement of the Lott House is piled high with paint cans, beautiful old lamps, bottles, an enormous old washtub, and even a cast-iron stove. Recently, poking around, we found a pitchfork branded with the initials JHL—Johannes H. Lott, Hendrick's son. There's an early-twentieth-century photograph showing a Lott woman gaily picking beans in the sun with field hands, black and white (see Plate 19). We try to imagine a young Johannes, pitchfork in hand, sweating happily alongside his father's soon-to-be-freed slaves, but the picture painted by our discovery under the eaves is more ambiguous.

29

BIRTHPLACE OF AMERICAN BOOZE

Celebrating Washington's own whiskey distillery.

by ERIC A. POWELL

IT'S A GRAY MORNING AT MOUNT VERNON, GEORGE Washington's grand estate overlooking the Potomac River. As a thin drizzle falls, the general's field hands grumble and stomp their feet, shivering despite their heavy homespun breeches. The men stand ready to grab barrels of liquor floated ashore from a barge moored just off the plantation's wharf. It's an important delivery—the general likes his whiskey (and the Caribbean rum in Martha's punch).

As the barrels hit the water, the men wade into the frigid Potomac and drag the liquor up to waiting carts. Washington himself gravely supervises, issuing orders that his workers mostly ignore.

Martha is also there. So are representatives of the national media, on hand to record the event, as well as executives from 11 major American liquor companies who congratulate Washington (actually actor William A. Sommerfield) on a job well done. Once the barrels are loaded onto carts, and the media are herded onto buses, all embark on a three-mile pilgrimage to one of the birthplaces of American booze—Washington's distillery.

The historical reenactment of a routine whiskey and rum delivery celebrates renewed attention to the first president's least known business venture. In 1797, a Scottish farm manager named John Anderson convinced Washington that distilling whiskey would be a great way for the former president to make a fast buck. Washington admitted in a letter to Anderson that liquor was "a business I am entirely unacquainted with," but the Scot's enthusiasm for the distillery persuaded him to give it a shot.

Distilling whiskey was our first president's least-known venture.

After a successful trial run with one still, Washington and Anderson broke into the big-time liquor business with the purchase of three additional copper stills (one of which now resides in the Smithsonian). By 1798, Mount Vernon was the site of the second largest distillery in the mid-Atlantic region, churning out 11,000 gallons of corn and rye mash whiskey and earning Washington $7,500 dollars in one year.

The distillery continued operating after Washington's death until at least 1808, when an advertisement for Mount Vernon whiskey appeared in a local Alexandria paper. Recent excavations at the site by Esther White, director of archaeology at Historic Mount Vernon, indicate that the distillery was carefully dismantled sometime in the early nineteenth century, probably to provide building materials for neighboring houses.

Now thanks to White's efforts, one of Mount Vernon's most profitable enterprises (along with fishing and growing wheat) is poised to make a comeback. Using archaeological evidence, Mount Vernon Estates and Gardens, the nonprofit foundation that runs the historic plantation, plans to rebuild the stillhouse as a museum to educate visitors about the role of liquor in early America.

A faithful reconstruction of the distillery will be no small task. The 75- by 30-foot building was solidly constructed of local sandstone. At its peak, the stillhouse was packed with five copper stills, five worm tubes (copper tubes that collected condensed distillate), a boiler, and 50 mash tubs.

Eager to play up their industry's links to the first president, the Distilled Spirits Council of the United States, which represents the manufacturers and distributors of spirits, has ponied up $1.5 million for the project. Plaques from liquor companies sponsoring the reconstruction will be prominently displayed; literature given out at the site will also credit corporate donors.

The barrels of rum and whiskey that arrived most recently at the Mount Vernon wharf represent Big Liquor's largess—every big distillery in the country had a barrel floated down the Potomac for the occasion. Once reconstruction is complete, the barrels will be opened and sampled. Remaining liquor will be bottled as Mount Vernon commemoratives: Mount Vernon Bacardi Rum and Mount Vernon Maker's Mark, to take just two examples. Mercifully the liquor is restricted to beverages Washington would have imbibed in his own time, limiting the prospect of say, Mount Vernon Kahlúa, or even worse, Mount Vernon Beefeater.

The celebration continues with a lavish luncheon. Washington offers a simple toast punctuated by a hearty "huzzah!" The dignitaries then dutifully down Martha's famed rum punch, a trifle on the weak side.

Bureau of Alcohol, Tobacco, and Firearms director Brad Buckles presents James Rees, executive director of Mount Vernon, with a federal permit authorizing production of spirits at the plantation. Buoyed by the excitement (and maybe the punch), Rees says he relishes the thought of Mount Vernon competing with the assembled distillers. The whiskey magnates roar their approval, welcoming George Washington back to the business after a 200-year absence.

30

FIRE FIGHT AT HEMBRILLO BASIN

Buffalo Soldiers hold their ground in a nighttime skirmish with the Apache.

by KARL W. LAUMBACH

ON APRIL 6, 1880, JUST FOUR YEARS AFTER custer's defeat on the Little Big Horn, Captain Henry Carroll of the Ninth Cavalry cautiously led 71 cavalrymen toward an Apache camp in the Hembrillo Basin of south-central New Mexico. Suddenly, volleys of gunfire rang out from the surrounding ridgetops and puffs of smoke marked the discharge of black-powder cartridges. Rushing to the top of a low ridge, the troops dismounted, every fourth man holding horses. Forming skirmish lines, they returned fire until the sun went down. Then they held their ground and waited for reinforcements.

The Ninth was one of six black regiments formed after the Civil War to help keep the peace on the frontier (see

Plate 20). Its members were called Buffalo Soldiers by the Cheyenne because their curly hair reminded the Native Americans of buffalo hides. At Hembrillo, two companies of the Ninth Cavalry pursuing the Apache war chief Victorio had been surrounded by a superior force of 150 Chiricahua and Mescalero Apache. Unlike the Battle of the Little Big Horn, the Buffalo Soldiers' nightlong battle against two-to-one odds was largely forgotten. Until recently, the record of the fight was based on reports of white Sixth Cavalry officers who credited themselves with saving Carroll's soldiers from "a condition of helplessness." Recent battlefield archaeology and historical research tell a different story, one of bravery in the face of a highly organized Apache force.

In 1987, an archaeological crew from Human Systems Research, Inc. (HSR), returned from a field survey in the White Sands Missile Range with stories of amazing panels of Apache rock art. The crew had found the art near a spring in the Hembrillo Canyon, which drains the high walled Hembrillo Basin of the San Andres Mountains. On a follow-up trip, White Sands Missile Range archaeologist Robert Burton and I visited the painted images of mounted warriors and miniature depictions of cougar, javelina, deer, and dragonflies. The rock art indicated the area had long been a sacred Native American site.

In reviewing the literature on the local Apache, we discovered General Thomas Cruse's Indian War memoir, *Apache Days and After*, which noted that a major battle of the Victorio War had taken place in the canyon. The two-year war began when Victorio's Chiricahua Apache band lost their promised reservation and were forced by the Indian Bureau to share land with several other Apache bands (see Plate 21). In his account of the ensuing war, Cruse described a desperate battle around a spring, with troopers surrounded by Apache positioned on a semicircle of higher ridges and rock breastworks where there was no natural cover. Excited by the prospect of finding the battleground, we surveyed around the Hembrillo Canyon spring for evidence, only to come up empty-handed. Oddly enough, it would ultimately take a treasure hunt to find the battlefield.

The best known feature of Hembrillo Basin is Victorio Peak, a 400-foot-high hill named after the Apache chief and allegedly the site of a fabulous treasure. An itinerant foot doctor named Milton "Doc" Noss is said to have discovered stacks of gold bars in a crevice there in 1937; the gold was subsequently lost in a cave-in. Stories about the treasure's origins attribute the cache to the Aztecs, Spanish bandits, or Victorio's Apache. Descendants of Doc Noss' wife made an attempt to retrieve the treasure. Hoping to find evidence of the battle, Burton accompanied them and found a couple of cartridges ejected from Springfield .45 caliber carbines on a low ridge well within the basin. Then Harold Mounce, a volunteer who had been a 16-year-old participant in a 1949 hunt for Noss' gold, led us to more cartridges and one of the rock breastworks mentioned in military reports.

The interior ridges of the basin are formed by a series of limestone uplifts, each capped with gray outcroppings that provided cover for the combatants. We found our first cartridges in a pack rat nest below an impressive breastwork that looked down on a series of lower uplifts. On one of these we found clusters of cartridges fired from the .45-55 caliber carbines used by the Buffalo Soldiers; those with head stamps (numbers and letters on the head of the cartridges) had been manufactured in 1877 and 1878.

Since we assumed that the clusters of cartridges marked the defensive position of Carroll's besieged soldiers, volunteers with metal detectors swept the area, paying particular attention to positions that could have provided cover for the attacking Apache. As we moved farther up the ridge, we found clusters of .44 caliber Henry cartridges mixed with other non-military ones (Apache used whatever arms they could buy or capture), suggesting that the Apache had fired from this protected position. More Apache breastworks were discovered, some along the edges of arroyos, others on the limestone outcroppings of adjacent ridges.

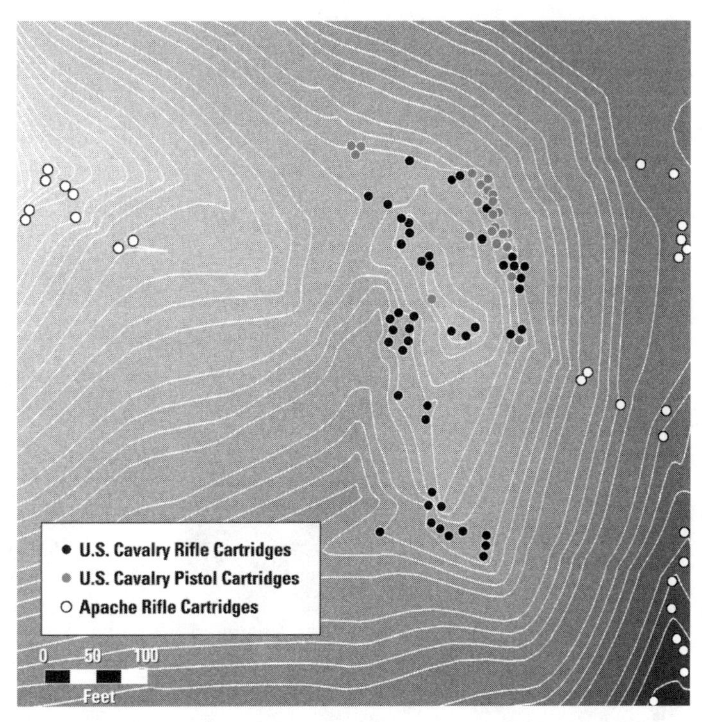

Carroll's two skirmish lines were marked by .45 caliber carbine and .45 caliber Colt pistol cartridges (the Colt was the standard Army issue sidearm). The distribution of pistol cartridges shows that during the night one of the two companies was forced to drop its carbines and defend itself with sidearms. Pistols were typically used only when fighting in close quarters, suggesting Apache came close to the lines.

The metal-detector reconnaissance took more than two years, and with the help of 59 volunteers we covered 900 acres of the battlefield. Each artifact, including every cartridge, was carefully mapped and replaced in the ground by a numbered tag. Jim Wakeman, then an associate professor of surveying at New Mexico State University, used a global positioning system and sophisticated software to produce a map that faithfully reflected the undulating topography. Wakeman's high resolution map and the artifact data base were then entered into a Geographic Information Systems (GIS) program, that plotted each artifact on the computerized map.

Douglas Scott, an archaeologist for the National Park Service's Midwest Archaeological Center in Lincoln, Nebraska, helped us analyze our finds. In the mid-1980s, Scott pioneered the use of police-style forensic analysis of artifacts recovered from the Custer Battlefield. His analysis resulted in a significant reinterpretation of Custer's tactics during the battle (see ARCHAEOLOGY, March/April 1990). After comparing firing

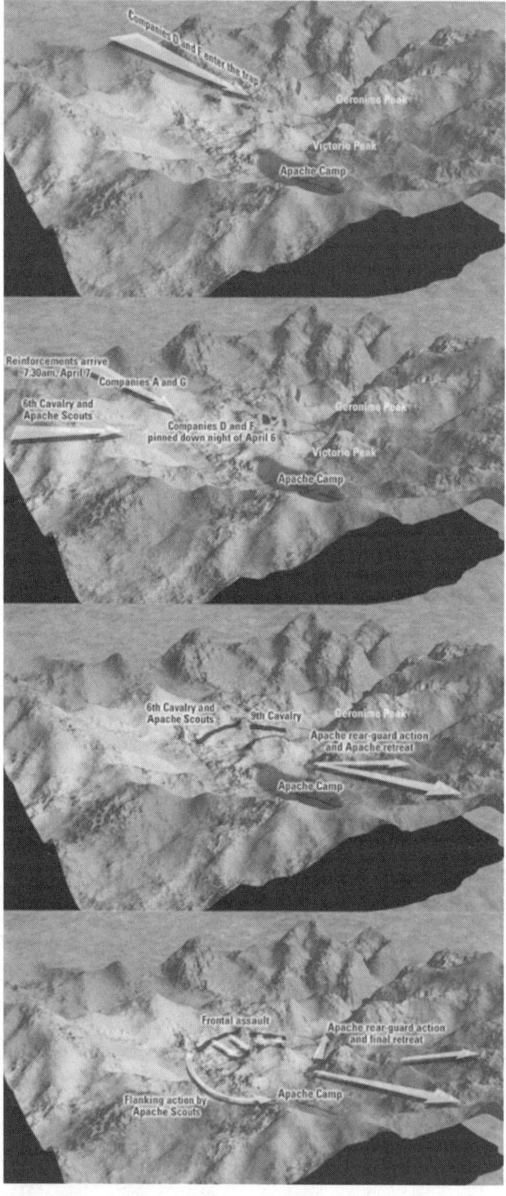

The Ninth Cavalry's D and F companies entered the Hembrillo Basin in the late afternoon of April 6. Surrounded by Apache, the troopers held their ground until the next morning, when they were reinforced by companies A and G, the Sixth cavalry, and 100 White Mountain Apache scouts. The combined force then drove the Apache chief Victorio and his followers out of the basin.

pin and ejector marks on the cartridges under a microscope, Scott reported that the 800 cartridges collected from Hembrillo were fired from 145 different rifles or carbines and 39 different pistols. Because marks on the cartridges vary with the ejector mechanism of the weapon, he could even identify the make and model of the guns that fired them. When this analysis was added to the GIS program, we could track individual weapons across the landscape and watch the battle unfold on the computer screen.

As the archaeological information became more complete, the historical record began to expand as well. The oft-quoted Sixth Cavalry accounts portrayed the Buffalo Soldiers as incompetents who, sick on bad water from nearby Malpais Springs, had wandered helplessly into Hembrillo looking for good water, only to find the springs guarded by Victorio's Apache.

There are no Ninth Cavalry accounts of the battle of Hembrillo in the published literature, and for 115 years history provided the Buffalo Soldiers no defense against the bigoted reports of the Sixth Cavalry. In 1995, Charles Kenner, noted Buffalo Soldier historian, drew attention to an unusual 1903 article on the Victorio War published in an obscure military pamphlet *The Order of Palestine Bulletin*. The article was written by John Conline, a First Lieutenant who had commanded Company A of Carroll's Ninth Cavalry during the army's pursuit of Victorio.

Conline's report tells of watering with the Ninth's other three companies at Malpais Springs on April 4, 1880. The next morning he led two scouts and 29 troopers south to Hembrillo Canyon, where he found tracks of Apache driving cattle up the canyon. Cautiously following the tracks, Conline soon found himself embroiled in a two-hour skirmish with about 50 Apache. One of Conline's scouts, fluent in Apache, heard Victorio shouting orders. Withdrawing after dark, Conline rejoined Carroll's command, bivouacking on the old Salt Trail, a wagon path used by southern New Mexico communities to access salt beds in the Tularosa Basin.

Now that Victorio was aware of their presence, it was imperative for the Ninth to act quickly lest the Apache melt away in front of them. The next morning, according to Conline, Carroll took Companies D and F into the San Andres by a northern route, sending Companies A and G south to find an alternate route into the mountains. The Ninth was moving aggressively to engage Victorio until help could arrive. But once in the mountain canyons, Carroll had second thoughts about his strategy. A courier was sent to Companies A and G with instructions to follow Carroll's trail into the mountains.

Carroll entered the Hembrillo Basin sometime between 4:30 and 6:00 P.M. on April 6. He did it with the knowledge that Victorio was in front of him and that he had two companies following his trail into Hembrillo. These were hardly soldiers sick on bad water, stumbling blindly into Victorio's camp, as portrayed in Sixth Cavalry accounts. Furthermore, the Ninth had been carrying their own water, according to a previously overlooked letter from one of the Ninth's officers to his mother.

To avoid an ambush, the Ninth approached Victorio's camp across the mountains from the north rather than the more obvious eastern route through Hembrillo Canyon. The distribution of Apache cartridges on the western side of the basin, previously unexplained, suddenly made sense to us. Victorio recognized the tactical advantage of occupying the combined ridgelines on the north side of his camp. When Carroll's Buffalo Soldiers came down the northern rim of the basin, those ridges became Victorio's first line of defense.

The Apache waited as Carroll's command moved deep into a V formed by two ridgelines on the north side of Hembrillo Basin. When they opened fire, the range was still several hundred yards, too far for an effective ambush. Carroll took the prescribed action for dealing with an attack on both flanks and the front. He led his troops forward, driving some Apache from the central uplift of what is now called Carroll's Ridge. Cartridges from those Apache guns were found along the U.S. skirmish lines.

The Apache encircled the Buffalo Soldiers, but nightfall came to the troopers' rescue. Records indicate that the moon did not rise until 4:30 A.M. and was then only a thin sliver. Despite the dark, some Apache managed to creep close. At least three of them, firing either 1866 Winchester or Henry rifles, reached a low uplift just 150 yards from the skirmish line. Their rifles, utilizing a double firing pin, easily jammed. The cartridges often did not fire when first struck and had to be carefully rotated in the chamber and re-struck. Scott's analysis showed some had been struck as many as 23 times. It was obvious that the Apache riflemen had spent some time in one location, patiently forcing each precious cartridge to fire.

The distribution of the cartridges across the battlefield reflects Victorio's superb control over his fighters. Just as the Henry ammunition was found together, cartridges from 15 .44-40 caliber 1873 Winchesters were clustered by a nearby spring. Victorio probably concentrated those short-ranged repeating rifles to keep soldiers from reaching water during the night. Cartridges from certain .45-70 and .50-70 caliber Springfields were also consistently associated, suggesting that the Apache were fighting as highly organized units.

Unaware their comrades were pinned down, Companies A and G camped north of Hembrillo Basin, waiting until morning to join Carroll. From the west came one company of the white Sixth Cavalry, together with 100 White Mountain Apache scouts, the Chiricahuas' bitter enemies. After stumbling toward Hembrillo through the brush and the rocks of the Jornada del Muerto (Dead Man's Journey, a desert basin aptly named for the many travelers who had perished there), they arrived early the next morning. At the same time Companies A and G also descended into the Hembrillo Basin.

A trail of cartridges marks the Apache route as they fought their way out of the Hembrillo Basin.

Victorio was quickly aware of both groups of reinforcements. His Apache withdrew from their tightening circle around Carroll and took positions on Victorio Ridge, a natural fortress formed by a group of four consecutive limestone uplifts overlooking the troopers from the south. From that vantage, Victorio's rearguard stymied the cavalry for several hours as Apache women and children fled the basin. At this point, the battle involved 300 U.S. troops and 150 Apache, the largest number of combatants of any battle during the Victorio War.

The Apache guns on Victorio Ridge were not the short-ranged Winchesters, but rather long-range .50 or .45 caliber Springfields, Remingtons, and Sharps, all capable of keeping the attackers at bay some 600 yards away. Cartridges indicate that when the frontal assault on Victorio Ridge finally began, the Apache moved to the west to meet the attack on the westernmost uplift. When flanked by the White Mountain Apache scouts, Victorio abandoned the ridge, moving south to confront the scouts.

Victorio's Apache were doing what they did best, fighting a defensive battle with a mountain at their backs. A trail of cartridges marks the Apache route and their successive defensive positions as they fought their way out of the Hembrillo Basin, always keeping the pursuing troops below and in front of them. According to Conline, the Apache front was as much as two miles wide at this point.

Once the Apache disengaged from their final position on Victorio Peak, the Battle of Hembrillo was over. Scouts reported the bodies of three Apache in the vicinity of the Apache camp. Carroll had been hit twice and seven Buffalo Soldiers were wounded. Two would later die at nearby Fort Stanton, an army outpost near the Mescalero Reservation.

That night 400 U.S. troops and more than 300 horses and mules tried to make do with the limited spring water available in the basin. The next morning, a combined force of Buffalo Soldiers and White Mountain Apache Scouts reconnoitered the south rim only to find a rear guard of Apache waiting to see what would happen next. A brief skirmish ensued and again the Apache rear guard retreated. Late in the evening of April 8, the troops marched east across the White Sands desert to meet the 10th Cavalry (also Buffalo Soldiers) at the Mescalero Reservation, where Apache sympathetic to Victorio were disarmed and a significant part of Victorio's support base was lost to him.

The battle in Hembrillo was the largest confrontation of the Victorio War. The pressure broke up Victorio's large camp, forcing him west to the Black Range and finally into Mexico. In October 1880, his band was surrounded by Mexican troops at Tres Castillos, an isolated range of low desert mountains in northeastern Chihuahua. In an ensuing massacre (the Apache were out of ammunition), Victorio was killed and his men almost totally wiped out. The few who remained joined the rest of the Chiricahuas in their exile in Oklahoma after the surrender of Geronimo in 1886.

The archaeology of the Hembrillo Battlefield has given us new insight into Victorio's tactical abilities, particularly his control and disposition of available firepower. Archaeology has also stripped the veil from Carroll's long night, revealing an aggressive strategy and defensive positioning in the face of an attack from established positions. It is now possible to walk the ground the Buffalo Soldiers held, and look out on the basin from the ridges Victorio defended. Standing behind the stacked rock breastworks, visitors can grasp the tactical situation and understand the Apache style of defensive warfare and mobility that became a standard lesson plan for future West Point officers. Today, the U.S. Army uses the battlefield as a "walk around," a place where junior officers can study and analyze the U.S. and Apache battlefield strategies.

31

HAM HOCKS IN YOUR CORNFLAKES

Examining the role of food in African-American identity.

by Mark Warner

We have rocked generations of babies to sleep crooning "Shortenin' Bread," laughed to the comedy of "Pigmeat" Markham and "Butterbeans" and Susie, and danced the cakewalk, tapped our feet to the rhythms of "Jelly Roll" Morton, shimmied with wild abandon to gutbucket music in juke joints or sat down with friends and "chewed the fat." We've had the blues over the "Kitchen Man," longed to be loved like "Lilac Wine," and celebrated with "A Pigfoot and a Bottle of Beer." In short, we've created our own culinary universe...it's the warmth of the kitchen tempered by the formality of the dining room and the love of a family that extends over generations and across blood lines.

—Jessica Harris, *The Welcome Table: African-American Heritage Cooking*

OUR STORY TAKES US INTO THE kitchen of a now-empty two-story frame house in Annapolis, Maryland. The house was built in the 1850s, and over 120 years, two African-American families lived here. Today, the kitchen is cold, and those families, the Maynards and Burgesses, are all but forgotten in this weekender's paradise full of sunny shops, sailboats, and scenic cobbled streets. In 1991, with the Archaeology in Annapolis Project, Paul Mullins and I excavated the former Maynard-Burgess home. One thing we found in abundance was food remains. Could the sawn, burned, gnawed animal bones unearthed on the property tell tales that would warm the kitchen once again?

As patterns in the bones began to emerge that set this house apart from those of white Annapolitans, I was faced with questions of how food acquires cultural meaning. Maryland, of course, counted itself a Southern state, and in the middle 1800s Annapolis was an amalgam of free blacks, slaves, and whites. With free blacks under the constant threat of being sold into slavery, identity lived in limbo. Under such circumstances, mundane choices such as what to put on the kitchen table may be surprisingly revealing.

John Maynard, black and born free in 1810, worked as a waiter. In or about 1834, he married a slave named Maria Spencer and purchased the freedom of her three-year-old daughter, Phebe Ann. In 1838 he purchased his wife's freedom, and in 1848, he bought the lot on predominantly white Duke of Gloucester Street that would become the site of his family's home. Maria, who worked as a laundress, continued to live in the house for several years after John's death in 1875. We don't know when Maria died, but between 1880 and 1914 the house passed through the hands of several family members before it was purchased by Willis Burgess, a domestic at the U.S. Naval Academy. The Burgess family, related to the Maynards through marriage, was financially comfortable and active in African-American social circles; several newspaper accounts of community events such as church functions and dances mention Burgess women. In short, the Maynards and Burgesses were part of a stable middle-class community of African Americans.

Our excavations uncovered the usual assortment of historical materials such as broken bottles, plates, and remains of what the families ate. It was the animal bones that particularly interested me. We recovered approximately 7,500 bones from a post-1905 privy, a post-1889 cellar, late nineteenth-century yard scatter, and an area below the floorboards of an 1874 addition to the house. At first glance, they seemed typical of the urban Chesapeake region: lots of pork and beef, some fowl and fish. It was after all the bones were weighed and counted and the remains summarized that an interesting and complex pattern of food consumption emerged. While the two families were acting like white consumers, purchasing the same standardized cuts of meat as everybody else, they were also making choices that unequivocally set themselves apart from whites, as seen in the pig and fish remains.

The Maynard and Burgess families, it seems, ate significantly larger amounts of pork than beef. This may not seem like the stuff of headlines, except that it is historically well established, and archaeologically corroborated, that white Victorian society forsook pork in favor of beef. This preference was entrenched by the mid-1880s. Technological innovations such as the refrigerated railroad car played a part, but so did shifting consumer demands. As historian Harvey Levenstein observes of Victorian America in his 1988 book *Revolution at the Table*, "the middle class followed their social superiors, who shunned fresh and salted pork and deigned only to eat an occasional slice of smoked ham...in middle class eyes pork ranked far below not just beef, but lamb, poultry, and game as well."

'In middle class eyes pork ranked far below not just beef, but lamb, poultry, and game as well.

Was this preference for pork specific to the Maynards and Burgesses, or part of a broader pattern of behavior? To answer this I looked at the animal remains from 13 other sites in the Chesapeake region—six black-occupied, seven white-occupied—that were economically similar to the Maynard-Burgess site and roughly contemporary with it. Overall, the patterns at African-American sites matched the Maynard-Burgess house, while cow remains predominated at white-occupied sites.

During the late nineteenth and early twentieth centuries, the United States government sponsored an array of studies on consumer behavior, five of which, all dating to roughly the turn of the century, were detailed accounts of meat consumption by African Americans. All of them document a significantly higher percentage of pork consumption in comparison to beef. Still more revealing was a 1926 study of several thousand people of different ethnic backgrounds that explored consumer preferences in meat purchases and consumption, asking questions such as: "What kinds of meat are preferred by the individual members of your household?" On that survey, African Americans named pork more frequently than any other group questioned. In a recent comparative study of white and African-American foodways in the Carolinas, cultural anthropologist Tony Whitehead documented the same contrasts. Clearly, whites in the late nineteenth century turned to beef, while blacks did not.

The fish remains, too, were quite revealing about the Maynard and Burgess families. We recovered more than 1,000 fish scales from a very small sample of soil right next to the back door, leading us to believe that they were cleaning fish in their backyard. Almost all of the fish represented were shallow-water species that could have been caught from shore or with a very small boat in the waters surrounding Annapolis. By contrast, those advertised in city newspapers and recovered from a fish market site in Wilmington, Delaware, included larger numbers of deep-water species such as cod and fewer shallow-water ones, like perch and catfish.

The remains illustrate a discriminative consumerism, with the Burgesses and Maynards selectively operating in the marketplace in a different manner from whites and opting out of the marketplace altogether through participation in private economies outside the scope of whites. Ultimately, the question remains, why are the private catching of fish and the preference for pork important? To simply say that something is archaeologically significant does not automatically mean that it was culturally significant as well. The challenge is to infer the meanings these materials had for the people who lived there.

The answer lies at the intersection of two big issues—the symbolism of food and racism toward blacks. To start with the symbolism of food and the idea that food choices are culturally meaningful I turn to contemporary anthropology. The cultural anthropologist Sidney Mintz provides an important foundation for investigating what the food choices may have meant to the Maynards and the Burgesses:

For many people, eating particular foods serves not only as a fulfilling experience, but also as a liberating one—an added way of making some kind of declaration. Consumption, then, is at the same time a form of self-identification and of communication. The employment of food to achieve a feeling of well-being or freedom is widely felt and understood. Much of the symbolic overloading of food rests particularly in its utility for this purpose. The satisfactions seem modest; the meal one eats in confirming that "you deserve a break today" may be neither expensive nor unusual. And yet this act of choosing to consume apparently can provide a temporary, even if mostly spurious sense of choice, of self, and thereby of freedom.

–(Tasting Food, Tasting Freedom 1996:13)

Mintz argues broadly that food is part of self-identity, but what about pork and African Americans specifically? Let's face it: people do not generally enter a store thinking, "hmmm, I think I will make a statement about who I am and buy pork today." Still, foods undeniably evoke culture; think of chicken noodle soup, or a hot dog at a baseball game. Although it works subtly, food can be an important aspect of individual and group identity.

In exploring the values and beliefs of people, historical archaeologists have multiple sources available to connect with the archaeological data. Some sources are conventional, such as the government and anthropological studies mentioned above; others are unexpected, in this case, music and cookbooks. My survey of blues lyrics revealed only about 100 songs with specific meat references in them. Yet of that total, pork is most frequently mentioned. One of the lengthiest examples is from a song by blues artist Rube Lacy, which goes in part:

I don't want no hogheads,
Don't eat no chittlins
Don't want no spareribs,
Don't eat no backbone
Mama, got a hambone,
I wonder can I get it boiled
'Cause these Chicago women
Are about to let my hambone spoil.

–Eric Sackheim, *The Blues Line.*
(Hopewell, NJ: The Ecco Press, 1993)

Clearly this song is not directly about food, but rather about sex, where "hambone" is a euphemism for the penis, but what can be inferred is that the pig and pork have some additional symbolic meaning here. Perhaps the most unequivocal statement on the symbolic significance of pork comes from a 1970 song by George Clinton, the "father of funk." Clinton asks "What is soul?" and responds by answering "Soul is a ham hock on your cornflakes." His lyrics place pork in winking opposition to what is stereotypically white America's breakfast of choice. His message is clear: we are going to make our own choices about what we eat—and by implication who we are. When I looked at cookbooks from the period, I found a similar pattern. In African-American cookbooks the numbers of pork and beef recipes were similar, with only one cookbook showing a strong preference for pork. In the white cookbooks, however, there were far more beef than pork recipes.

Finally, why might food be so particularly important to African Americans? In the words of Ruth Gaskins, quoted by Evan Jones in the 1990 book *American Food*:

For over two hundred years we were told where to live and where to work. We were given husbands, and we made children, and all these things could be taken away from us. The only real comfort came at the end of the day, when we took either the food that we were given, or the food that we raised, or the food we caught, and we put it in the pot, and we sat with our own kind and talked and sang and ate.

Consider the Annapolis in which the Maynards and Burgesses lived. They were part of a stable, socially and economically heterogeneous African-American community, but it was a world clouded by many forms of racism. Overt avenues of expression of African-American identity would have been potentially risky endeavors, so people like the Maynards and Burgesses were left to employ more subtle strategies such as food.

The experience of these two families, reflected in the excavated remains of their food, matches a broader pattern, one described by Sheila Ferguson in her 1989 book *Soul Food: Classic Cuisine from the Deep South*:

But soul food is much more than a clever name penned by some unknown author. It is a legacy clearly steeped in tradition; a way of life that has been handed down from generation to generation, from one black family to another, by word of mouth and sleight of hand. It is rich in both history and variety of flavor.... [Food] *is, like the blues or jazz an inextricable part of the African-Americans' struggle to survive and to express themselves.*

By choosing pork and by avoiding city markets through fishing, the Maynards and Burgesses were quietly affirming their identities as African Americans.

32

DIVING ON THE TITANIC

An archaeologist explores the famous wreck.

by James P. Delgado

PEERING THROUGH THE TINY PORTHOLE, I GAZE into the darkness. The minisub's external lights illuminate a small patch of the seabed's yellow-white silt and clay as a large rattail fish undulates across my field of vision. Suddenly a massive wall of steel looms out of the darkness. Thick orange, red, and bright yellow "rustsicles" (icicle-like formations of rust) streak down the black metal plates and onto the seafloor. The abrupt encounter with the corroded steel almost takes my breath away. But, it's not the suddenness of the moment that grips me; it's the fact that I'm two and one-half miles below the North Atlantic at the bow of RMS *Titanic.*

Despite years of shipwreck exploration as a maritime archaeologist and a decade as director of a maritime museum, *Titanic* was never high on my list of lost ships to visit. I'd never considered it an archaeological site, but rather an underwater museum and memorial. Until recently, my interest in the vessel, discovered in 1985, was confined to the world of archaeological and museum politics. I've helped author a proposed *Titanic* treaty between Canada, France, the United Kingdom, and the United States. As a board member of the International Congress of Maritime Museums and the Council of American Maritime Museums, I've had exhaustive discussions with the former management of Atlanta-based RMS Titanic, Inc.—the salvage company awarded rights to *Titanic* by a U.S. District Court in Norfolk, Virginia, in 1988—as we grappled with the ethics of some museums' decision to display artifacts recovered from the wreck site. I have also pressed the company to adopt an archaeological approach to its work and guarantee that the artifacts from the wreck not be privately sold. As part of an independent team of archaeologists and museum professionals, I traveled to the Toulon headquarters of the Institute of France for Research and Exploration of the Sea (IFREMER), co-discoverers of the wreck with Robert Ballard. There we reviewed hundreds of hours of video, numerous photos, and dozens of dive logs from the joint IFREMER/RMS Titanic, Inc., salvage effort. As a member of the International Council on Monuments and Sites, I've also tackled the issue of shipwrecks as heritage sites and am in the midst of preparing to nominate *Titanic* to UNESCO's list of World Heritage Sites.

LAST SUMMER I RECEIVED AN INVITATION from Seattle-based Zegrahm Expeditions to join a group of adventure travelers from the United States, Australia, and Britain who had paid $35,500 each to look at but not touch the wreck. I had read or heard of a number of alarming accounts of encounters with *Titanic*—tales of subs colliding with the wreck, remotely operated vehicle inspections deep inside the ship, conflicts within the ranks of the salvagers over what should be brought up, and rapid deterioration that would cause *Titanic* to collapse within a few years. Rather than read or hear more about it, I decided to go and see for myself. I would also be the first archaeologist not affiliated with salvagers to dive on the wreck.

After a three-day, 368-nautical-mile voyage from St. John's, Newfoundland, our research vessel *Akademik Msistlav Keldysh* arrived at the wreck site literally days after RMS Titanic, Inc., concluded its year 2000 salvage operation. Because the Russian crew and scientists aboard *Keldysh* must scramble to find money for their ship and its global research program, the vessel and its two Mir submersibles have been among the principal participants in the salvage dives. They know the site well.

The participants in the Zegrahm Expeditions dives received daily briefings on submersible operations, shipwreck archaeology, and, of course, *Titanic*. Weather permitting, the ship's submersibles would each take two adventurers per day down to the wreck to observe and photograph the ship and the debris field. RMS Titanic, Inc., had fought a long, hard court battle to keep others away from the wreck, arguing that tourism or filming dives infringed on their proprietary rights. The final judicial decision limited their rights to filming and artifact recovery. While I believe that the public should have the right to visit historic and archaeological sites whenever it is safe for them and the site, I also realize that free access effectively limits RMS Titanic's commercial options and could encourage the company to focus solely on profits from artifact recovery. There are no simple answers to the questions posed by this wreck.

AFTER DEBRIEFING EACH DIVE GROUP ON their return, reviewing their videos, and assembling a site map, it's now my turn. Scott Fitzsimmons, president of Zegrahm Expeditions, and pilot Evgeny Chernaiev are to be my companions in Mir 2. The 18.6-ton Mir 1 and Mir 2 submersibles, built in 1985–1987 at a cost of $25 million each, are capable of diving to depths of up to 3.73 miles (19,700 feet). The heart of each sub is a nickel-steel pressure sphere within which three persons—a pilot and two observers, as well as life-support equipment, imaging sonar, and the sub's controls—have to fit. It's a tight, cramped workspace. A fiberglass skin covers the sphere, leaving three viewing ports (one forward and one on each side), video and still cameras, thrusters, and two manipulating arms exposed, as well as landing skids on the sub's bottom.

Climbing into the Mir 2, Fitzsimmons and I take up positions beside Chernaiev as he prepares for launch. We lie, half-flexed, on narrow, padded benches along the side of the sphere. As the hatch is secured and the life support system starts up, a huge crane hoists us off the deck and over the side of the ship. We hit the water and the sub tips and rolls for a few minutes as Chernaiev checks systems and reaches overhead to power up the ballast pump. As 3,300 pounds of water flood into the ballast spheres, we start to spiral down into the darkness at a rate of 106 feet a minute.

After a long fall, the sonar begins tracking the seafloor beneath us. Chernaiev starts Mir 2's thrusters, and we slow our descent and lightly touch down. We're at 12,675 feet—the average depth of the world's oceans—and the pressure outside the sphere is more than 6,000 pounds per square inch. In the darkness 1,650 feet away, the sonar clearly shows the sharp angle of *Titanic*'s bow, which plowed the seafloor when the ship hit bottom. Within a few minutes, we're at the bow. Rising up along it, we pass the ship's two eight-ton anchors resting inside their hawse pipes. Just behind the tip of the bow, a 50-ton spare anchor is still stowed on the deck; its size is stunning. Bigger than our sub, it is a powerful reminder of the scale of this ship. From the bow, we maneuver over rows of anchor chain, capstans, windlass, winches, and the no. 1 cargo hold, reaching the base of the foremast, now sheared from the hull and resting against the winches.

Climbing along the mast, we pass an oval hatch marking the location of the crow's-nest. Clearly visible in photographs of the wreck taken in 1985 and 1986, immediately after its discovery, the crow's-nest is now gone. There are conflicting claims over who has bumped into and damaged the ship. RMS Titanic says the Russians have; the Russians say it was IFREMER. While this feature had no archaeological value, its loss diminishes one's sense of being at the place where the drama of April 14, 1912, began, when lookout Frederick Fleet picked up his telephone to the bridge and shouted, "Iceberg, right ahead!"

From the broken mast tip we drift toward the starboard side, passing the bridge, much of which is gone, either smashed by a falling funnel or swept away by the sea as Titanic sank. All that remains is the brass telemotor, or steering gear, the wooden sill of the bridge's bulkheads, and a tangle of electrical wires. Five brass memorial plaques, placed here by earlier expeditions, and a bundle of plastic red roses are silent reminders that this is a gravesite (see Plate 22).

There are other, equally powerful reminders of the "night to remember": empty davits from which lifeboats hung, gaping doorways and windows of the officers' quarters, and a huge hole where the ornately carved first class staircase led below. At the edge of one deck, two chandeliers are visible, hanging from their wiring. We follow the sloping deck to a break in the hull and fall to the seabed again, turning forward to look into the severed bow section's boiler room. Here, torn, crumpled steel and crushed and twisted water and steam pipes are a testament to the forces that ripped *Titanic* apart.

The area around the stern is thick with debris... off to one side, we spot a pair of boots.

We head for the stern section, 1,800 feet away. The seabed is marked with skid marks and scoops from the salvage dives; very few artifacts are visible, but soon we encounter ceramics and now unidentifiable, corroded objects of copper, brass, and steel. Despite claims by salvagers that their work is archaeologically based, it becomes obvious that they have been highly selective in what they retrieve. We see unmarked and third-class ceramics, and a few broken or badly chipped second-class pieces—no first-class china. We see scoop marks that show where selected pieces have been plucked from clusters of artifacts—no grids, no scientific sampling—simply for their display or monetary value. What is happening here, two and one-half miles down and out of sight of much of the world, is not archaeology.

The area around the stern is thick with debris, suggesting that even after more than 100 salvage dives vast portions of the wreck site remain unknown and untouched. I see large items—a cargo crane, a broken engine cylinder, and a propeller—along with torn, curled, and warped pieces of the hull. There are also smaller items, including champagne bottles, the ornate bronze end of a deck bench, plates, a small bronze ship's bell, and a lantern that I'm amazed to still see here, given the numerous "clean" patches of bottom we've passed over elsewhere. Off to one side, we spot a pair of boots. Small, flat-heeled, and calf-length, they are the shoes of a working-class woman, perhaps a steerage passenger. They lie side-by-side and are still laced tight. The body is long gone, consumed by the sea.

Chernaiev believes we are in an area of the wreck he has not seen before, although he is not certain. This highlights a troubling aspect of the salvage dives. Before each year's dive operations, by IFREMER's *Nautile* or Russian Mirs, crews deploy three navigational transponders on the bottom, which should allow the sub and the surface vessel to plot their position relative to the transponders and the wreck. But every year each dive operation has used different positioning points. Even so, sub tracks and artifact positions could be plotted on an overall site plan. But the last time I saw IFREMER's dive plots, none had been collated and assembled onto an overall plan of the site. And that's just *their* data. The Russians have been diving on *Titanic* since 1991 for the IMAX film *Titanica*, filmmaker James Cameron, Zegrahm Expeditions, and RMS Titanic. I doubt that their dive plots and artifact positions have been merged with previous years' information. In short, other than the well-known intact bow section and the stern and the sub pilots' recollections, no detailed "road map," let alone a highly detailed archaeological site plan, exists.

AS WE PREPARE TO SURFACE AFTER nearly eight hours, six of them inspecting the wreck, I pause to reflect on the ship's condition. Some lighter plating is rapidly vanishing, but heavier metal remains solid. Paint still adheres to some surfaces, wood is present on railings and in sections of the deck, and rope lies on the decks and hangs from lifeboat davits. The rivers of rust that bleed from the hull and the rustsicles that hang like stalactites show that the bacteria that consume the steel are at work. But will they consume *Titanic* within a few years, or even a decade, as RMS Titanic, Inc., has claimed? I posed the question to corrosion specialist Dale Buckley of the Bedford Institute in Dartmouth, Nova Scotia. Buckley and his colleague, Patricia Stoffyn-Egli, were the first scientists to analyze samples of rusticles recovered during the 1991 IMAX filming expedition. Their assessment is that the rates of decay vary depending on the composition of the metal; that the bacteria are not consistently present (I saw sections of hull with no visible corrosion); and that *Titanic* will be around, and visibly identifiable, for centuries.

The conclusion that the ship is in no imminent danger of disintegration won't please the folks at RMS Titanic, Inc. They maintain that artifacts must be recovered from within the wreck before it collapses. As we debate the wreck's future and the proposed treaty, however, it appears that we do have some time in which to make decisions. As one of only 100 or so people to have dived on *Titanic*, I feel that I certainly know more about the wreck now—and yet I know very little after just six hours on the site. More dives, by other archaeologists—and by museum professionals and policy makers—are needed, as well as more dives for the public. If we are to debate what to do with the wreck and what value it possesses, then we need as much information as possible, unfettered by proprietary considerations.

After years of studying *Titanic*, reading the history books, and watching hours of video of other dives, this visit brought the past to life in that special way that archaeological discovery often does. It also gave me a better sense of the ship and the disaster that befell it, her passengers and crew. Isolated images, black-and-white photos from 1912, and modern color video clips now meld seamlessly into a rerun of my dive. I close my eyes and even now see *Titanic*.

33

TITANIC IN THE COURTS

A chronology of the tangled legal interests surrounding the RMS *Titanic.*

by RICARDO J. ELIA

1912 ON APRIL 15, THE WHITE STAR ocean liner RMS *Titanic* sinks on her maiden voyage after striking an iceberg in international waters 400 miles off the coast of Newfoundland. More than 1,500 passengers and crew perish. Claimants in the United Kingdom and United States seek compensation for personal injury, loss of life, and loss of property.

1916 *Titanic*'s owner, Oceanic Steam Navigation Company, pays a total of $664,000 to settle all legal claims.

1985 *Titanic* is discovered on September 1 by a joint expedition of the Woods Hole Oceanographic Institution and the Institute of France for the Research and Exploration of the Sea (IFREMER). American co-leader Robert Ballard makes several dives to the wreck site in the submersible *Alvin*. The team decides not to salvage artifacts from it.

1986 In July, during a second season of exploring the site, Ballard places a plaque on *Titanic*, urging that the site be left undisturbed as a memorial. Congress passes the RMS Titanic Maritime Memorial Act, which directs the United States to enter into negotiations with other interested nations to establish guidelines to protect the "scientific, cultural, and historical significance of RMS *Titanic*." The act also expresses the sense of Congress that, pending such an agreement, "no person should physically alter, disturb, or salvage the RMS *Titanic*." The Department of State contacts the United Kingdom, France, and Canada but finds little interest in an agreement.

1987 IFREMER contracts with Titanic Ventures, a limited partnership, to salvage artifacts from the site. Titanic Ventures makes 32 dives to the site and recovers some 1,800 artifacts. The operation draws protests; *Titanic* survivor Eva Hart decries the "insensitivity and greed" and labels the salvors "fortune hunters, vultures, pirates." Titanic Ventures sells its salvage interests and artifacts to RMS Titanic, Inc. (RMST). In October, Telly Savalas hosts a live television program featuring the opening of a suitcase recovered from *Titanic*'s debris field. Instead of riches, the valise holds a small amount of coins, jewelry, and banknotes, including Italian lire.

1992 Rival salvage company Marex Titanic Inc., which says it found the ship, sues in the Eastern District of Virginia for salvage rights and ownership of the 1,800 artifacts recovered by Titanic Ventures. The court, asserting jurisdiction over a non-U.S. ship in international waters in the interest of furthering international order, rejects Marex's claim in favor of Titanic Ventures. The decision is reversed on appeal because of a procedural technicality, and Marex, which never recovered artifacts from the site and thus establish "possession," fades from the scene.

1993 In July, RMST recovers 800 artifacts. It files an action to seek exclusive salvage rights; on August 27, the Norfolk court issues a temporary warrant appointing RMST custodian of the wreck, site, and artifacts, pending possible claims from other parties. RMST settles with the Liverpool and London Steamship Protection and Indemnity Association, one of *Titanic*'s original insurers.

1994 On June 7, the court names RMST salvor-in-possession of the *Titanic* and sole owner of any items recovered from the site. RMST's status as exclusive salvor is valid so long as it remains "in possession," a condition that effectively compels it to mount salvage expeditions every year or two. In July, more than 1,000 objects are recovered from the wreck site. In October, an exhibit of *Titanic* artifacts recovered by RMST opens at the National Maritime Museum in Greenwich, England.

1995 After learning about RMST's salvage efforts, the United States, United Kingdom, France, and Canada initiate discussions on a *Titanic* agreement.

1996 In February, John A. Josyln, an independent salvor, files a motion challenging RMST's standing as exclusive salvor of *Titanic* and declares his intention to visit and photograph the site. The court issues a preliminary injunction preventing him from searching, surveying, salvaging, or photographing the site. In August, the court enjoins third parties from entering the site to photograph it. The 1996 RMST expedition, in cooperation with The Discovery Channel and accompanied by a tourist cruise chartered to observe the recovery, nets 74 objects, but a highly publicized effort to raise a 20-ton piece of the hull fails. The company that arranged for the cruise—and provided funding and equipment for the expedition—later sues RMST, claiming co-salvor status and seeking $8 million for breach of contract, fraud, and other damages.

1997 *Titanic* exhibitions open in Memphis, St. Petersburg, Long Beach, Norfolk, and Hamburg, Germany. In April, The Discovery Channel airs *Titanic: Anatomy of A Disaster*. Negotiations on a *Titanic* agreement take place between 1997 and 2000 by the United States, United Kingdom, Canada, and France. In December, Paramount Pictures releases the film *Titanic*, including footage made during 12 dives to the site by director James Cameron.

For $32,500, individuals are promised they will be able to visit and photograph the site.

1998 Deep Ocean Expeditions advertises "Operation Titanic." For $32,500, individuals are promised they will be able to visit and photograph the site in Russian deep-sea submersibles. RMST requests a preliminary injunction, and, in an order dated June 23, the court declares that RMST, as salvor-in-possession, has the right to exclude others from visiting the site in order to photograph it. In August, RMST completes another salvage expedition, again in conjunction with The Discovery Channel, and recovers 70 artifacts, including the piece of the hull it attempted to raise in 1996. Despite the court injunction, Operation Titanic visits the wreck site in September. Exhibitions are held in Boston and Japan.

1999 On March 24, the Fourth Circuit court reverses the earlier ruling, stating that RMST cannot exclude others from visiting, viewing, or photographing the *Titanic* site. RMST appeals to the Supreme Court; in October, the high court declines to review the case, leaving RMST without exclusive photographic rights. Exhibitions are held in St. Paul and Atlantic City. In November, shareholders vote to remove RMST president George Tulloch and the company's attorney, Allan Carlin. The new president, Arnie Geller, promises to accelerate the pace of artifact recovery. Tulloch and Carlin sue RMST seeking to reverse their removal.

2000 In January, RMST settles with Tulloch and Carlin, paying the former executives $2.5 million in return for their promise not to meddle in company management for 18 months. Also in January, the United States, United Kingdom, Canada, and France develop a draft agreement concerning *Titanic*. The agreement sets forth rules for the management of the site, establishing in situ preservation as the preferred policy for the site. In April, RMST sues to prevent the U.S. from seeking an international agreement, arguing that such efforts are unconstitutional. In June, the National Oceanic and

Atmospheric Administration (NOAA) requests public comments on proposed site-management guidelines.

RMST announces plans for the summer's expedition; for the first time, the company intends to enter the ship to search for "high profile targets," including a $300-million diamond shipment. Also for the first time since salvage began in 1987, RMST hires a "project archaeologist." But the primary goals of the salvage—to maintain the project's salvor-in-possession status and recover "desirable objects" for display—remain decidedly non-archaeological.

On July 28, U.S. District Judge J. Calvitt Clarke issues an order forbidding RMST from penetrating or cutting into *Titanic* or from selling artifacts. The salvage expedition, conducted in August under the direction of CEO G. Michael Harris, is plagued by bad weather and equipment failures. Harris is fired at its conclusion. Following RMST's salvage operations, Zegrahm Expeditions, a Seattle-based company, takes a small group of adventure tourists to the *Titanic* site.

On September 15, Judge Clarke dismisses RMST's case against NOAA and the Department of State, which had been negotiating an international agreement on the *Titanic*. The judge notes that RMST's claims were premature, but that RMST could renew its motion if and when an agreement was signed and implemented.

ABOUT THE AUTHORS

MATTHEW ADAMS is a research scholar with the Institute of Fine Arts and the University of Pennsylvania Museum.

MARK ALDENDERFER is professor of anthropology at the University of California, Santa Barbara.

BERNADETTE ARNAUD is an archaeologist based in Paris.

NIXOS AXARLIS is a journalist based in Athens.

BRENDA BAKER is assistant professor of anthropology at Arizona State University.

H. ARTHUR BANKOFF is chairman and professor of anthropology and archaeology at Brooklyn College, City University of New York (CUNY), director of the Brooklyn College Archaeological Research Center, and archaeological advisor to the New York City Landmarks Preservation Commission.

MICHEL BRENT, a former regular contributor to the Belgian news magazine *Le Vif-L'Express*, has specialized in cultural heritage issues in West Africa.

BOB BRIER is a professor of philosophy at the C.W. Post Campus of Long Island University, Brookville, New York. His most recent book, *The Murder of Tutankhamun: A True Story*, was published in 1999.

JEAN-LOUIS BRUNAUX directed excavations at Ribemont-sur-Ancre and is the author of *Les Religions Galoises* (Paris: Éditions Errance, 1996).

SUE D'AURIA is assistant curator at the Huntington Museum of Art in West Virginia and an expert on mummification.

JAMES P. DELGADO is executive director of the Vancouver Maritime Museum and president of the Council of American Maritime Museums.

NANCY HATCH DUPREE is a senior consultant at the Agency Coordinating Body for Afghan Relief in Peshawar, Pakistan, and is vice-chairperson of the Society for the Preservation of Afghanistan's Cultural Heritage. From 1966 to 1974 she participated in prehistoric excavations in Afghanistan conducted by her late husband Louis Dupree.

RICARDO J. ELIA is a professor of archaeology at Boston University and vice president for professional responsibilities of the Archaeological Institute of America.

STUART J. FLEMING is scientific director for the Museum Applied Science Center for Archaeology at the University of Pennsylvania. He is author of *VINUM: The Story of Roman Wine* (Glen Mills, PA: Art Flair, 2001).

NORMAN HAMMOND is a professor of archaeology specializing in the Maya at Boston University.

CHRIS HELLIER is a freelance writer based in France.

ELIZABETH HIMELFARB is a former associate editor of *ARCHAEOLOGY*.

PETER LACOVARA is curator of ancient Egyptian, Nubian, and Near Eastern art at the Michael C. Carlos Museum.

KARL W. LAUMBACH is an archaeologist with the nonprofit Human Systems Research, Inc. A native New Mexican, he has spent the last 27 years pursuing a variety of research projects in New Mexico.

STEPHEN H. LEKSON, an assistant professor of anthropology at the University of Colorado in Boulder, is co-director of the Pinnacle Ruin fieldwork with Karl Laumbach of Human Systems Research in Las Cruces, New Mexico.

ALYSSA LOORYA is a Ph.D. candidate at CUNY's Graduate Center.

MARY MCVICKER, an independent scholar, writes about the history of archaeology in Mesoamerica. She has co-edited catalogs for two exhibitions of Precolumbian art, and is the author of a biographical sketch of Adela Breton for *The Art of Ruins*. She is also completing a full biography of Breton.

JERALD T. MILANICH is curator in archaeology at the Florida Museum of Natural History.

DAVID O'CONNOR is Lila Acheson Wallace Professor of Egyptian Art and Archaeology at the Institute of Fine Arts, New York University; Professor Emeritus of the University of Pennsylvania; and Curator Emeritus of the Egyptian Section, University of Pennsylvania Museum. He is currently completing a book, *The Sacred Landscape of Abydos*, to be published by Thames and Hudson.

THÉRÈSE O'GORMAN is head of conservation at the Michael C. Carlos Museum.

A. G. PASTRON is an archaeologist working in the San Franciso area.

DIANA CRAIG PATCH is a researcher in the Department of Egyptian Art at the Metropolitan Museum of Art.

ERIC A. POWELL is associate editor of ARCHAEOLOGY.

CHRISTOPHER RICCIARDI received his Ph.D. in archaeology from Syracuse University.

JANET RICHARDS is assistant professor at the University of Michigan, and directs the Abydos Middle Cemetery Project.

KRISTIN M. ROMEY is managing editor of ARCHAEOLOGY.

MARK ROSE is executive editor of ARCHAEOLOGY.

DEBORAH RUSCILLO, a lecturer in the department of anthropology at the University of Winnipeg, has analyzed faunal remains from the Athenian Agora, Kommos, Mytilene, and other Greek sites. Excavation of the Epano Skala site was a joint effort directed by professor Hector Williams of the University of British Columbia and A. Archontidhou-Argyri of the 20th Ephory of Prehistoric and Classical Antiquities.

SANDRA SCHAM is an archaeologist who has been living and working in Israel since 1996. A former curator of the Pontifical Biblical Institute Museum in Jerusalem, she is currently affiliated with the department of anthropology at the University of Maryland at College Park.

ANGELA M.H. SCHUSTER, formerly senior editor of ARCHAEOLOGY, is now with the World Monuments Fund.

SYDNEY SCHWARTZ is an editorial intern at ARCHAEOLOGY.

ELIZABETH SIMPSON is a professor of ancient art and archaeology at the Bard Graduate Center in New York City; she is director of the Gordion Furniture Project and a research associate at the University of Pennsylvania Museum of Archaeology and Anthropology in Philadelphia.

WILLIAM KELLY SIMPSON is professor of Egyptology at Yale University.

ANDREW L. SLAYMAN is a former senior editor of ARCHAEOLOGY.

DEAN R. SNOW, a professor of anthropology at the Pennsylvania State University, has studied Iroquoian archaeology since 1969. His work in Northern Ireland and Scotland was supported by the British Council.

CAROLYN SWAN is a former editorial intern at ARCHAEOLOGY.

MEG TURVILLE-HEITZ is a freelance writer in Cambridge, Wisconsin.

MARK WARNER is an assistant professor in the department of sociology, anthropology, and justice studies at the University of Idaho.

HAIM WATZMAN is a freelance science and academic affairs writer in Jerusalem.

JAMES WISEMAN is a contributing editor to ARCHAEOLOGY and is professor of archaeology, art history, and classics at Boston University.

INDEX

A

Abkhazia, burials in, 117
Abusir, German expedition at, 10
Abydos, tombs and temples of ancient, 47–52
Abydos Middle Cemetery Project, 54
Achaemenids, 97, 115
Actium, Battle of, 10–11
Adams, Charles, 180
Adjara, 121
Aeetes, king of the Colchians, 113–123
Afghan culture, preservation of, 96–104
Afghanistan, rule of Democratic Republic, 96–97
Africa
 African-American identity, influence of food, 202–206
 Kenyan fossil excavation, 33–35
 Religious rituals of slaves, 186–191
 Reproductions of West African terra-cotta sculptures, 36–43
African Burial Ground, 187
Agassiz, Louis, 57
Agua Fria, 14
Ägyptisches Museum und Papyrussammlung, 11
Ahab, King, 83
Ahmose, Dynasty XVIII king, 50–51
Al-Aqsa Mosque, 87, 89

Al-Marwani Mosque, 89
Alamosa sites, 178
Albans, St., 14
Alcock, Nat, 15
Alexander the Great, 132
Amadou, 37–39, 43
Amaksu, Ken, 8
Amanullah, King, 97
Ameny, 48
American Antiquities Act, 1906, 14–15
Amir Abdur Rahman, 97
Amun, temple of God, 60
Anasazi, disappearance of the, 178–182
Animal mummification, 63–64
Animal sacrifice, 152
Antelava, Ilya, 119
Apache Days and After, 196
Apalachee Indians, 185
Aphrodite, dedications to, 17
Apicius, 135, 137, 138
Apollonius of Tyre, 137
Apophoretae, 136
Appion, 11
Apsaros, 122
Aq Kupruk, 103
Arad site, 84
Aramis, Ethiopia, 35
Archaeological Park of Carnuntum, 148
Archaeological Resources Protection Act, 1979, 9
Archangel Cathedral, 20
Arctic Circle, inhabitants in the, 27
Arctic National Wildlife Refuge, 15
Arden, Agnes, 15
Arden, Mary, 15–16
Ardipithecus ramidus, 35
Ardipithecus ramidus kadabba, 24
Argonautica, 113, 117
Ariadne, 132
Arslan Kaya, 126
Arvigo, Rosita, 171–175
Ashokan Edicts, 103
Athena, 131
Athenaeus, 137
Atole, 173
Augustus, 135, 142
Australopithecines, 33–35
Australopithecus afarensis, 34
Authentication testing, 36
Awan tribe of Balochistan, 79
Ayat, Mustafa Aga, 57
Ayubbid period, 91

B

Babylonian exile, period of, 83
Bacchus, mysteries in honor of, 131–133
"Bactrian Aphrodite," 101
Bad Deutsch-Altenburh, 147, 148
Bakchos, mysteries in honor of, 131–133
Bakongo, 191
Balochistan, Awan tribe of, 79
Bamako, 40
Bamiyan Buddhas, destruction of the, 93–95, 96
Bankoni style, 39
Banquet of the Philosophers, 140
Baringo District, 34–35
Batumi Archaeological Museum, 122
Beersheva site, 84
Begram collections, 97, 99, 100, 103
Belgae, 152
Berlin, 11
Bes, 52
Betatakin, 182
Biología Centralia America, 165
Boas, Franz, 167
Borbón Caves Anthropological Reserve, 12
Boudicca, Queen, 13–14
Bougouni, 39

Breton, Adela, 164–167
Bronze Age, 27–28, 84
Brown, Robin C., 184
Browne, Colonel Samuel, 188
Bubastis, cat cemeteries at, 63
Buddha, childhood home of the, 16–17
Buddhist culture, 105–109
Buffalo soldiers at Hembrillo Basin, 195–201
Buisson-de-Cadouin, 23
Burgess, Willis, 203–206
Burial practices, 48–49
Burton, Robert, 196

C

Cacique María, 183–184
Calusa Indians, 185
Camulodunum, 13–14
Canabae, 148
Canidud, Publius, 10–11
Cannibalism, evidence of, 21
Canyons of the Ancients, 14
Carib peoples, 12
Carlos Museum, Michael C., 57–58
Carnuntum, ruins of Roman, 147–150
Carroll, Captain Henry, 195, 197, 199
Cashels, 157, 158, 160
Caucasus Mountains, 27–28, 113
Celts, 152
Cemeteries at Abydos, 51
Cemetery U, 49
Cenotaphs, 48
Chaco Canyon, 14
Chalcolithic period fertility figurine, 24–25
Chayet, Anne, 107
Chichén Itzá, 164
Christianization, 52, 158–59
Chrysippus, bronze head of, 144
Chthonic cults, Greek, 152
Cissé, Youssouf, 40
Claudian, 142
Cleopatra VII, papyrus writings of, 10–11
Cliff Palace at Mesa Verde, 179
Coccoran, Lorelei, 11
Colchester, destruction of, 13–14
Colchi, legends of the, 112–123
Colosseum, restoration of the, 143, 144–145
Colum Cille, 160
Commagene in Syria, 149
Committee to prevent the Destruction of Antiquities on the Temple Mount (CPDATM), 89
Cordury Collins, Alana, 19
Corinth Museum heist, 16
County Antrim, 155
Cross, Frank M., 85
Crummy, Philip, 13
Cruse, General Thomas, 196
Curanderos, 172
Cussac cave, 23
Cybele, 149
Cyrus I, 78

D

Dál Riata, 155–159
Danube in Roman times, life on the middle, 147–150
Darius, King, 80
D'Auria, Sue, 64
Davis, Charles, 38
Dawson, Warren, 70
Dayan, General Moshe, 88
De re coquinaria, 135, 137
Deagan, Kathleen, 184
Dean, Jeffrey S., 179
Deir el-Bahri, mummies at, 57, 58–59
Deletaille, Émile, 40

Democratic Republic of Afghanistan, rule of, 96–97
Derveni, tomb at, 132
Dever, William G., 85
Diarra, Boubou, 40
Diodorus Siculus, 128
Dionysos, dedications to, 17
Dionysus, mysteries in honor of, 131–133
Dioscurias, 118, 120
Djenné, 40, 41
Djer, 48, 50
Doctrine of Piety, 103
Dome of the Rock, 87
Dominican Republic, 12
Domus Aurea (Golden House), 143, 144
Doña María, 184
Donnan, Christopher, 19
Dordogne region, 23
Dos Cabezas, 19
Douglas, James, 57
Dreyer, Gunter, 49, 52
Dunadd, 158
Duns, 158
Dupree, Nancy Hatch, 96–104
Dynasty I, 48, 50
Dynasty IV, 49
Dynasty VI, 53, 54

E

E. Dale Joyner Nature Preserve, 184
Early Dynastic period, 50
Early Imperial era, 140
Early Iron Age Palestine, 81–86
East Fork site, 8–9
Eggebrecht, Arne, 59
Egypt
    Abydos, tombs and temples of ancient, 47–52
    Ahmose, Dynasty XVIII king, 50–51
    Ameny, 48
    Amun, temple of God, 60
    Anatomical knowledge, 69
    Animal mummification, 63–64
    Ayat, Mustafa Aga, 57
    Bes, 52
    Bubastis, cat cemeteries at, 63
    Burial practices, 48–49
    Cemetery U, 49
    Cenotaphs, 48
    Christianization of, 52
    Climate, influence of, 48
    Deir el-Bahri, mummies at, 57, 58–59
    Dissection, prohibition of cadaver, 69
    Djer, 48, 50
    Dynasty I, 48, 50
    Dynasty IV, 49
    Dynasty VI, 53, 54
    Early Dynastic period, 50
    El-Amra settlement, 49
    Elite class, emergence of an, 49
    Falcon galleries at Saqqara, 63–64
    Forgeries of antiquities and Egyptian objects, 62–64
    Four Sons of Horus, 67
    Giza, tombs at, 49
    Heart in mummification process, retainment of, 69
    Herodotus' description of mummification, 65–66
    Hori, remains of, 58
    Horus, 63
    Hyksos, victory over, 51
    Iawttayesheret, 59
    Ibis galleries at Saqqara, 63–64
    Iww, offerings to, 54–55
    Karnak, Amun's temple at, 60
    Khentyamentiu, temple dedication to, 49–50
    Luxor, 64

Mahasna settlement, 49
Middle Kingdom, 50
Mummification (*See* Mummification)
Neferhotep, Dynasty XIII king, 50
Nekhty, grave of, 54
New Kingdom, 50–51
Niagra Falls Museum, collection at, 56–61
Nofretari, Queen, 59
Osiris, 48, 50, 51, 52
Pharonic age and civilization, dawn of, 47–52
Ramesses I, 59
Ramesses II, 51, 52
Ramesses III, 59
Rhind papyrus, 71
Saqqara galleries, 63
Self-made men, rise of, 53
Senwosret III, Dynasty XIII king, 50, 51
Serdab, discovery of the, 55
Seti-as-Osiris, worship of, 52
Seti I, 47, 51, 52, 59, 60
Settlements, 49
Taaset, mummy of, 58, 60–61
Tanakhtenttahat, coffin of Lady, 60–61
Thinis settlement, 49
Thutmosis III, 52
Toth, 63
Umm el Qa'ab, 49, 50, 52
Ushabtiu, burial with, 67
Weni the Elder, 50, 53–55
Ehrenhard, Ellen, 9–10
Eighmey, James, 66
El-Amra settlement, 49
Elagabalus, 135
Elba Island, 21
Eleusinian mysteries, 131
Elijio, Don, 171–172, 173–174
Elliava, Givi, 120
Epano Skala, 137
Erus, Justus, 33
Escharon, 152
Esquiline Wing, 144
Europe
Achaemenid Persian themes, 115
Bacchus, mysteries in honor of, 131–133
Carnuntum, ruins of Roman, 147–150
Colchi, legends of the, 112–123
Danube in Roman times, life on the middle, 147–150
Dioscurias, site of, 118
Early Imperial era, 140
Funerary custom in the age of King Midas, 126–127
Gallic rituals, 151–154
Greek composition styles, 115
Hellenization, 115
Ionian pottery, 118
Khulevi, Colchian settlement of, 117
Late Bronze Age, 113
Midas, tomb of King, 124–129
Phrygia, ancient kingdom of, 124–129
Polytheistic societies, 131–133
Republican era, 140
Roman decadence, age of, 134–138
Rome, eternal city of, 142–146
Scotland, Irish origin of, 155–161
Social and political context and symbolism, interpretation of 130-133
Third Mithridatic War, 122
Western Christendom, center of, 142–146
Wine, ancient savoring of, 139–141
Eusebios, 128

F

Falcon galleries at Saqqara, 63–64
Feasting in Roman society, 135

Finkelstein, Israel, 81–86
Flanders, World War I tunnels in, 11–12
Flatlands Reformed Dutch Church, 188
Florida Indians from Ancient Times to the Present, 184
Florida Museum of Natural History, 184
Florida's First People, 184
Fondukistan, sculptures from, 104
Food and racism, symbolism and, 203–206
Forenbaher, Staso, 17
Forgeries
  Egyptian objects and antiquities, 62–64
  West African terra cotta, 36–43
Fort Mose: Colonial America's Black Fortress of Freedom, 184
Fort Stewart, 21
Forum of Caesar, 143
Forum of Trajan, 143
Four Corners, ruins of the, 179–182
Four Sons of Horus, 67
French E-ware, 158
Fujimura, Shinichi, 7–8
Furbish, Mike, 9–10

G

Galisteo black-on-white pottery, 180
Gallic rituals, 151–154
Gallinas Springs, 180, 181
Gamsakhurdia, Zvaid, 116
Gandhara style, 100–101, 103
Gauls, 152, 153
General Harrison, 28
Geometric Art, 120–121
Georgia, 112–123
German expedition at Abusir, 10
Gezer site, 83
Ghaznavid, ornamental works of, 97, 99, 104
Ghazni, destruction of the Buddhist complex in, 93
Gila Cliff Dwellings, 14
Gila National Forest, 8–9
Gilbert, Jeremy, 22
Giza, tombs at, 49
Glebe Farm, 15
Goat hill, 182
Goliath, 81–86
Gordion, 124, 126, 128
Gournay-sur-Aronde, 152–154
Grand Canyon-Parashant, 14
Grand Staircase-Escalante, 14
Gravettian period, 23
Greco-Bactrian collection, 97
Greco-Roman religion, 131–133
Greek chthonic cults, 152
Greek composition styles, 115
Groningen, University of, 10–11
Guesero, 172
Guimiot, Phillipe, 40
Gyenus, 118, 120

H

Hadar, Ethiopia discovery, 34
Hadda, Buddhist site at, 97
Hadrian's Wall, 156
Hagar Qim, 21–22
Halpern, Baruch, 84
Haram al-Sharif (Noble Sanctuary), 87–92
Harvey, Stephen, 50–51
Haury, Emil, 182
Hawkes, Christopher, 130–131
Hazor site, 84
Healers, world of Mayan, 170–175
Heidentor, 149
Hektor, Trojan prince, 127
Hellenization, 83, 115
Hembrillo Basin, Buffalo soldiers at, 195–201

Hendrick I. Lott house, 186–191
Hera, 131, 132, 133
Herod, time of, 87
Herodotus, 65–66, 122, 127
Herod's Temple, 90
Hierakonpolis, 25–26
Hika Munshi, 79
Hindu iconography, 104
Hipponion, 132
Hirschel, Anthony, 57
H'men, 171, 172
Homo rudolfensis, 34
Horace, 139–141
Hori, remains of, 58
Horton, Mark, 21
Horus, 63
Human sacrifice, evidence of, 153
Hyksos, victory over, 51

I

Iawttayesheret, 59
Ibis galleries at Saqqara, 63–64
Ibrahim, Asma, 78
"Iceman," 25
Iceni tribesman, 13–14
Ife statues, 41–42
Igneri peoples, 12
Illyrian pottery, 17–18
Inka sacrificial children, research on, 73
Institute of France for Research and Exploration of the Sea (IFREMER), 208
Iona, 160
Ionian pottery, 118
Iron Age of the Ganges Plain, 17
Iroquois, expansion of Northern, 161
Isis, 131
Ivan IV, Czar, 20
Iww, offerings to, 54–55
Ixchel, 173
Ixchel Tropical Research Foundation, 174

J

Jamieson, Bill, 57
Japanese Archaeological Association, 8
Japanese Paleolithic sites, 7–8
Jason and the Golden Fleece, 112–123
Jequetepeque Valley, 19
Jobst, Werner, 147–148
Jornada del Muerto, 200
Jororo Indians, 185
Josiah, King, 82
Jupiter Dolichenus, 150
Jupiter Heliopolitanus, 149

K

Kachina, images of, 179–180
Kaiser, Tim, 17–18
Kakhidze, Amiran, 122
Kamata, Toshiaki, 8
Kamissoko, Samba, 38
Kamitakamori, 7–8
Kanishka, statue of Kushan king, 99, 103
Kapilavastu, 16–17
Karabenta, Seyni M., 39, 40
Karnak, Amun's temple at, 60
Karoosh-ul-Kabir, 78
Kax-bac, 172
Kayenta Anasazi, 182
Keet Seel, 182
Kelly Simpson, William, 47–52
Kenner, Charles, 198
Kenyan fossil excavation, 33–35
Kenyanthropus platyops, 33, 34
Khamam-ul-Nishiyan Dynasty, 78
Khentyamentiu, temple dedication to, 49–50

Khor-ul-Gayan, 78
Khulevi, Colchian settlement of, 117
Kimmerians, invasion by the, 128
Kollek, Teddy, 89
Kone, Issa, 39
Kotel Wall, 90
Koti Baghcha, 97
Kuhn collection, 36–43
Kvirkvelia, Guram, 114, 116
Kwaday Dän Sinchí, 25

L

Late Bronze Age, 113
Leloup, Helène, 40
Lesbos, 137
Lipe, William, 179
Little Big Horn, 195
Loch Glashan, 158
Londinium, 14
Lordkipanadze, Otar, 116, 120, 121
Lost Tribes of Israel, 179
Lott, Johannes H., 191
Lott-Divis, Catherine, 191
Lott House, Hendrick I., 186–191
Lott McNamara, Carol, 191
Lucas, Alfred, 70
Lucius Fabricius, 145–146
Ludwig-Maximilians University, 13
Lukeino Formation, 34–35
Luxor, 19–20, 64

M

MacMahon, Darcie, 184
Magdalena black on white, 181
Mahasna settlement, 49
Maiga, Mobo, 40
Malian terra cottas, 36–43
Mamluk period, 90
Mariette, Auguste, 53–55
Mastabas, 54–55
Matar, Phrygian goddess, 126, 128
Matecumbe Indians, 185
Maudslay, Alfred P., 164
Maurer, Francine, 41
Mayan murals, reproduction of, 164–167
Mayan rain forest, journey through the, 170–175
Maynard, John, 203–206
Mazar, Eilat, 89
Mecca, 88
Medea, 113, 122, 123
Medina, 88
Megiddo site, 83, 84
Menil Collection, 40–41
Mesa Verde, 179–182
Midas, tomb of King, 124–129
Middle Awash region, fossil discoveries in the, 23–24
Middle East
- Achaemenids, 97
- Afghan culture, preservation of, 96–104
- Ahab, King, 83
- Al-Aqsa Mosque, 87, 89
- Al-Marwani Mosque, 89
- Amanullah, King, 97
- Amir Abdur Rahman, 97
- Aq Kupruk, 103
- Arad site, 84
- Ashokan Edicts, 103
- Awan tribe of Balochistan, 79
- Ayubbid period, 91
- Babylonian exile, period of, 83
- "Bactrian Aphrodite," 101
- Bamiyan Buddhas, destruction of the, 93–95, 96
- Beersheva site, 84
- Begram collection, 97, 99, 100, 103
- Bronze Age, 84

Buddhist culture, 105–109
Committee to prevent the Destruction of Antiquities on the Temple Mount (CPDATM), 89
Cultural chasm between Jews and Muslims, 88–89
Cyrus I, 78
Darius, King, 80
Dayan, General Moshe, 88
Democratic Republic of Afghanistan, rule of, 96–97
Doctrine of Piety, 103
Dome of the Rock, 87
Early iron Age Palestine, 81–86
Fondukistan, sculptures from, 104
Gandhara style, 100–101, 103
Gezer site, 83
Ghaznavid, ornamental works of, 97, 99, 104
Ghazni, destruction of the Buddhist complex in, 93
Greco-Bactrian collection, 97
Hadda, Buddhist site at, 97
Haram al-Sharif (Noble Sanctuary), 87–92
Hazor site, 84
Hellenistic period, 83
Herod, time of, 87
Herod's Temple, 90
Hika Munshi, 79
Hindu iconography, 104
Josiah, King, 82
Kanishka, statue of Kushan king, 99, 103
Karoosh-ul-Kabir, 78
Khamam-ul-Nishiyan Dynasty, 78
Khor-ul-Gayan, 78
Kotel Wall, 90
Koti Baghcha, 97
Mamluk period, 90
Mecca, 88
Medina, 88
Megiddo site, 83, 84
Middle Paleolithic Tools, 103
Mohammed's ascension to heaven, site of, 88
Mousouris, Sotirios, 98–99
National Museum of Afghanistan, destruction of, 96–104
Nuristan, pre-Islamic grave effigies from, 99
Old Temple, 108
Persian Princess fraud, mummified, 77–80
Piyang, 107, 108
Sarianidi, Victor, 97
Shotorak, Buddhist schist reliefs from, 98, 104
Six-Day War, 88
"Solomon's Stables," 89
Surkh Kotal, temple at, 99, 103
Taliban regime influence, 93–95
Temple Mount, 87–92
Temple of Solomon, 90
Tepe Fullol, 102, 103
Tepe Maranjan, Buddha from, 99
Tholing, 107
Tibetan Buddhist culture, 105–109
Tillya-tepe, 97, 101, 103
Tsparang, 107
Tundal Gayan, 78
United Nations Office for the Coordination of Humanitarian Assistance to Afghanistan (UNOCHA), 98
"Wailing Wall," 90
West Bank region, 82
Western Wall, 90
Xerxes, 77, 79, 80
Middle Kingdom, 50
Middle Paleolithic Tools, 103

Milesians, settlement by, 118
Miletus, 114
Mimbres settlement discoveries, 8–9
Mingrelia, 114
Mithras, shrines of, 149
Mithridates VI, 116, 122–123
Miyagi Prefecture, 7–8
Mnajdra, 21–22
Moche burial sites, 19
Mohammed's ascension to heaven, site of, 88
Mopti, 40
Mounce, Harold, 196
Mound City, 14
Mount Vernon, 192–194
Mousouris, Sotirios, 98–99
Mummification
  Brain, removal of the, 66, 68
  Bronze and copper knives, use of, 66
  Canopic jars, 67
  Cleansing process, body, 66
  Coffin and mummy collection, 56–61
  Conservation efforts for, 59
  Dehydration process, 70–73
  Documentation and preservation of, 58
  Equipment, embalmers, 67
  Heart in mummification process, retainment of, 69
  Herodotus' description, 65–66
  Historical accounts, lack of, 65
  Internal organs, removal and storage of the, 67, 68–69
  Natron, use of, 66, 70–71
  Obsidian, volcanic glass, use of, 66
  Palm wine, use of, 66–67
  Rhind papyrus, 71
  Spices, use of, 66
  Wadi Natrun, 66
  Working-class inhabitants, of, 25–26
Muscarella, Oscar White, 79, 80
Museo Nazionale Romano, 143
Museu de Oro, 26–27
Museum of Anatolian Civilizations in Ankara, 126
Muslim Waqf, 88, 89, 90
Mystery cults in Greco-Roman religion, 131–133
Mytilene, 137

N

Na'aman, Nadav, 85
Nakovana Cave, 17–18
Namarnu, 123
National Museum of Afghanistan, destruction of, 96–104
Natsheh, Yussuf, 90, 91
Navajo National Monument, 182
Neandertals, early, 28–29
Neferhotep, Dynasty XIII king, 50
Negev, 24
Nekhty, grave of, 54
Neolithic temple complex on Malta, 21–22
Nerlich, Andreas G., 13
Nero, reign of, 135, 138
Nerva, emperor, 143
New Kingdom, 50–51
New Salem, 188
Newnan slave site, 9–10
Niagando, Baba, 37–39
Niagra Falls Museum, collection at, 56–61
Nieuwpoort, Flanders, 11–12
Nofretari, Queen, 59
Nok statues, 41
Nombre de Dios, 184
Noss, Milton "Doc," 196
Nuristan, pre-Islamic grave effigies from, 99
Nuttall, Zelia, 166

O

Ohman, Friedrich, 150
Old Temple, 108
Olmstead, Bobby, 9–10
Olympias, 132
Omar, Mullah, 92, 95
Omphalos bowls, recovery of, 126, 127–128
Order of Palestine Bulletin, The, 198
Orkneys, influence of migrating Norseman on, 161
Orpheus, 131
Orphic rites, 132
Orrorin tugenensis, 24, 35
Osiris, 48, 50, 51, 52
Ouloguem, Adama, 40
Oz, Amos, 89

P

Paleoindians, 185
Pannonia Superior, 148
Papuashvili, Rezo, 117
Patch, Diana, 47
Patroklos, funeral of, 127
Pelinna, Thessaly, 133
Pelizaeus Museum, 59
Pelotes Island, 184
Persephone, 131
Persian Princess fraud, mummified, 77–80
Petronell, 147
Petronius, 138
Pettrigrew, Thomas, 70
Pezzoli, Gigi, 41
Pharnaces, 116
Pharonic age and civilization, dawn of, 47–52
Phasis, 118, 123
Phrygia, ancient kingdom of, 124–129
Pichori, excavations at, 120
Pickford, Martin, 35
Picts, 156
Pinnacle Ruin, 178, 180, 181
Pitchvnari, site of, 121
Piyang, 107, 108
Point of Pines site, 182
Polytheistic societies, 131–133
Pomier Caves, 12
Pompeii, 137
Pompey's Pillar, 14
Ponte Fabricio, restoration of, 143, 145–146
Precolumbian rupestral works, 12
Pregnant ewe, 38
Pretty, Edith, 22
Primicia, 173
Prosthesis, first known usage of, 13
Ptolemy X Alexander, 11
Pueblo Bonito at Chaco Canyon, 179

Q

Quarrell, Michael, 9

R

Raedwald, 22
Rainforest Medicine Trail, 175
Ramesses I, 59
Ramesses II, 51, 52
Ramesses III, 59
Ramses II, 18–19
Raths, 157, 160
Reed, Jeff, 21
Reeve site, 182
Religious rituals of African slaves, 186–191
Reproductions of West African terra-cotta sculptures, 36–43
Republican era, 140
Revolution at the Table, 204
Rhind papyrus, 71
Rhodius, Apollonius, 113

Ribemont-sur-Ancre, 152–154
Ritual of the Bacabs, 173
Rituals of African slaves, religious, 186–191
Rizzo, Silvana, 143
Roadmap site, 180, 181
Roman decadence, age of, 134–138
Romanova, Anastasia, 20
Rome, eternal city of, 142–146
Rosenbaum, Mike, 12
Rosenthal, Evan, 67
Round Temple in the Forum Boarium, restoration of, 143, 146
Russell Cave, 14

S

Salima, Ikram, 64
Salzer, Matthew, 179
San Cristobal, Dominican Republic, 12
San Pedro de Mocama, 184
Saqqara galleries, 63
Sargon II, Assyrian king, 128
Sarianidi, Victor, 97
Sastun, 173, 174
Satyricon, 135
Savannah, Georgia, 21
Sawyer, Gerald, 188
Schonburgk, Sir Robert, 12
Scotland, Irish origin of, 155–161
Scott, Douglas, 197, 198
Seligman, Jon, 90–91
Semele, 131
Seminole Indians, 185
Seneca, 138
Senut, Brigitte, 35
Senwosret III, Dynasty XIII king, 50, 51
Serdab, discovery of the, 55
Seti-as-Osiris, worship of, 52
Seti I, 47, 51, 52, 59, 60
Sévaré, 40
Shakespeare, John, 15
Shakespeare Birthplace Trust, 15–16
Shotorak, Buddhist schist reliefs from, 98, 104
Shropshire, Greg, 171
Sierra Madre Mountains, 171
Silva, Michael, 66
Sipán, 19
Six-Day War, 88
Slave gravesites, 9–10
Slaves, African religious rituals of, 186–191
Sobadera, 172
Social and political context and symbolism, interpretation of 130-133
"Solomon's Stables," 89
Sonia and Marco Nadler Institute of Archaeology, 81
Soshinfudozaka, Paleolithic site of, 7–8
Souterrain ware, 158
Souterrains, 157
Spanish colonial Florida settlements, historical documentation of, 183–185
Spencer, Maria, 203–206
Stewart, Andrew, 19
Stoneware, Paleolithic period, 7–8
Stratford-upon-Avon, 15
Surami Mountains, 114
Surkh Kotal, temple at, 99, 103
Sutton Hoo, 22
Syene, 11

T

Taaset, mummy of, 58, 60–61
Table Talk, 140
Taíno cave, 12
Taliban regime influence, 93–95
Tanakhtenttahat, coffin of Lady, 60–61
Tbilisi, 114, 116, 123

Tel Dor, Israel, 18–19
Temple Mount, 87–92
Temple of Diana, 150
Temple of Hercules Olivarius, 146
Temple of Peace, 143, 144
Temple of Solomon, 90
Temple of the Tooth, 20
Temple of Vesta, 146
Tepe Fullol, 102, 103
Tepe Maranjan, Buddha from, 99
Tequesta Indians, 185
Terra Nova Medicinal Reserve, 171–175, 175
The Bible Unearthed: Archaeology's New Vision of Ancient Israel and the Origin of its Sacred Texts, 83, 85
Thebes, 13
Theodosius II, 11
Thermoluminescence tests (TL tests), 36, 38–39, 42–43
Thinis settlement, 49
Third Mithridatic War, 122
Tholing, 107
Thracian funerary ritual, 127
Thurii, tomb at, 133
Thutmosis III, 52
Tiberius, 148
Tibetan Buddhist culture, 105–109
Tigellinus, 135
Tilaurakot, excavations at, 16–17
Tillya-tepe, 97, 101, 103
Timucua Indians, 184, 185
Titanic, exploration of the, 207–211, 212–215
Titus, emperor, 144
Tocobaga Indians, 185
Tohoku Paleolithic Institute, 7–8
Tokyo National Museum, 8
Toth, 63
Traditional Healers Foundation, 175
Trajan, emperor, 143, 148
Traore, Denba, 38
Traore, Mamadou, 37–39
Tres Castillos, 201
Triclinia, 136, 137
Trimalchio's Feast, 135–137, 137
Tsikhisdziri, 122
Tsparang, 107
Tucci, Giuseppe, 108
Tugen Hills fossils, 34–35
Tumulus MM, 125–129
Tundal Gayan, 78
Turner, Christy, 179

U

Umm el Qa'ab, 49, 50, 52
United Nations Office for the Coordination of Humanitarian Assistance to Afghanistan (UNOCHA), 98
Ushabtiu, burial with, 67
Ussishkin, David, 84
Uzita Indians, 185

V

Van Minnen, Peter, 10–11
Vani, 114, 115, 116, 120, 121, 122
Vermillion Cliffs, 14
Verulamium, 14
Vespasian, emperor, 144144
Via dei Fori Imperiali, 143
Via dell'Impero, 143
Victorio Peak, 196
Villa of the Mysteries at Pompeii, 133
Vitali, Roberto, 107

W

Wade, Ronn, 68
"Wailing Wall," 90
Wainwright, Angus, 22
Wakeman, Jim, 197
Washington, George, 192–194
Webb, Steve, 9–10
Wegner, Josef, 50
Wegner, Mary Ann Pouls, 52
Weni the Elder, 50, 53–55
West Bank region, 82
Western Christendom, center of, 142–146
Western Wall, 90
Whiskey distilleries, birthplace of, 192–194
White, Esther, 193
Wilson, Jean, 16
Windover, 185
Wine, ancient savoring of, 139–141
Winlock, Herbert, 67
Wood, Tom, 67
Woodson, Kyle, 182
World Atlatl Association (WAA), 168–169

X

Xenophon, 137
Xerxes, 77, 79, 80

Y

Young, Rodney S., 125

Z

Zeus, 131, 133
Zugdidi, 119